Religious Right: The Greatest Threat to Democracy

Religious Right

The Biggest Threat to Democracy

By A.F. Alexander

**Blazing Sword
Publishing Ltd.**

Colorado Springs, CO

For information, address Blazing Sword Publishing Ltd.

PO Box 8088, Colorado Springs CO 80933

Cover artwork "Miss Liberty Decayed" by Rainer Kalwitz,
www.kalwitz.kunstprodukt.com   www.facebook.com/rainer.kalwitz.

Cover Design by Blazing Sword Publishing Ltd.

Many sources have been quoted and the author
maintained use of the Fair Use standard.

For more information or to book an event,
please refer to the author website at religiousright101.com.

Library of Congress: Pending

ISBN-10: 0615515630

ISBN-13: 978-0-615-51563-2

1 – Religion

2 – Current Events

3 – Politics, United States

Acknowledgements

Writing this book was a long process, and I was often writing or researching rather than attending a social gathering. I thank my spouse and friends for their patience, and for believing in this book's importance.

I particularly appreciate the interviews with Dr. C.J. Pascoe, and with former Quiverfull member, Vyckie Garrison. I can't express how thankful I am for your contributions. I am grateful to my test readers, and my editor, K.C. Arceneaux, for their diligence. A big thank you goes to Rainer Kalwitz, for his stunning artwork that graces the front cover and first page.

I thank all those who believe in liberty, justice, and freedom

for all citizens, without exceptions or caveats.

Table of Contents

Section 5: The Family Mountain

Section 6: The Past and the Future

Introduction

The threat from the Religious Right is ominous, and requires immediate attention before their ideologies gain more power and control. It is not too late. Within this book you will gain the tools to understand the threat to your life, liberty, family, neighborhood, and country. The multi-pronged agenda of the Religious Right is carefully explained, and their tactics revealed. You will be given various ways to make a difference in your home, school, neighborhood, state, and country. It is time to turn off the celebrity news and find out how you can preserve this great democracy, and strengthen it for the next generation.

Who am I to write a book on the Religious Right? I was a member of the Religious Right, graduated from a church-sponsored Bible institute, sat in Religious Right pews, taught Sunday school to their children, and was a church secretary, and even wrote for the church's monthly publication, and became its editor. Even in my college years, I was an early Religious Right follower, and was fully integrated into its culture. Because of this unique rank-and-file perspective, I delve into the rationale behind the movement's agenda as only an insider can understand it. This allows me to explain, authentically, their worldview and tactics. I relate what this means to the larger picture of our country, and its future -- from our First Amendment struggles, to the public-square arguments, and even the historical record of the conflict between church and state, from the perspectives of both.

When I shared with a Buddhist acquaintance that I was writing this book, I was asked if I was writing it with love. I vow that this is the case, through a great love for democracy and its continued vitality in this country that I dearly love. If you love democracy and want to participate in making this country the best it can be, with "justice and liberty for all," please keep reading.

About This Book

The book is divided into six sections. Section One, "The Critical Issue," presents an overview of the importance of the separation of church and state.

Section Two, "Who They are and How We Got Them," comprises a history of the rise of the Religious Right from their origins, to their joining with the Republican Party; there is information about Dominionists and Reconstructionists, and the Religious Right's tactics are detailed. Key players in this ongoing threat are named. Section Three is "The Resulting Worldview," including discussion of the importance of End Times to the Religious Right, higher law ethics, and the religious caste system. Section Four is entitled "The War is On," and presents a detailed discussion of six of the Seven Mountains of Influence strategy for achieving Christian dominion. The seventh Mountain, that of the family, is discussed in Section Five, "The Family Mountain." Included in that section is information about the Religious Right and the role of women, abortion, birth control, the Quiverfull movement, attitudes about gays and gay marriage, and the war for children's minds and beliefs. Section Six, "The Past and the Future," presents ideas about the church in history, and the penalties for a lack of separation of church and state. Also in this section are positive suggestions about how to become active in preserving that vital church and state separation in the U.S. government, including an array of resources and useful techniques for fighting back. The final chapter is a summation of the concepts in this book.

I provide many quotes throughout the book. Rather than a works-cited page, footnotes, or endnotes, each work is cited within the text, because it's often useful to see the source in proximity to the quote. I have followed a simplified MLA 7th Edition format. The citations do not provide page numbers. A bibliography is provided at the end of the book, with books (but not articles), listed in MLA format.

I hope you take from this book a greater understanding of the risks of losing the separation of church and state, the history of the Religious Right in this country, and the methods they are using. It is not enough to watch this unfold in a passive way, and so the book includes positive steps one can take to counteract this growing threat to democracy.

Section 1 The Critical Issue

In this section:

Religious liberty is guaranteed in the very first sixteen words of the Bill of Rights. The rest of this book hinges on these words, their interpretation, and their intention in our national Constitution. We begin with this crucial aspect.

Religious Right: The Greatest Threat to Democracy

Chapter 1
Separation of Church and State

<u>What to Expect From this Chapter</u>

➤ Thoughts on the simple guarantee of religious liberty for all.

➤ Why it was important at our nation's founding, and is still critical today.

➤ Why a battle over the separation of church and state is being fought today and the arguments used against it.

➤ How the separation of church and state impacts your rights.

What does the separation of church and state really mean and why is it important? You may have heard of it and dismissed it or felt such matters were for others to sort out. The time has come for every household to understand what the phrase means and how important it is to the very fabric of Democracy upon which our nation was built.

"Some people are fiercely protective of their own beliefs and don't want to support any other religions, directly or indirectly. Like Thomas Jefferson, they contend that it is 'sinful and tyrannical' for the government to force citizens to give material support or public acknowledgment of religions in which they disbelieve. Accordingly, these people demand that they never be taxed to support any church or church-related institution, such as parochial schools, or be asked to take part in religious events against their will.

Others are motivated by self-interest. If the government can sponsor my religion today, they argue, it can just as easily denounce it tomorrow and sponsor someone else's. It's better, they say, to keep the government neutral toward religion, thus placing every faith on the same footing...

It's clear that Americans support separation of church and state for a variety of reasons. Religious Right groups try to say only atheists support church-state separation or that support for separation is always motivated by an anti-religious bias. They're wrong." Robert Boston and Barry Lynn, *Why the Religious Right is*

Wrong about Separation of Church and State, Prometheus Books, 1993.

You can see from the preceding quote that the separation of church and state concept is important to many Americans. Actually, it is becoming an increasingly controversial topic and spawns lawsuits and newspaper headlines daily.

It is Constitutional

Where do we get the concept of a separation of church and state, religion and politics? We must start with the first amendment to the United States Constitution, which says:

> *"Congress shall make no law respecting an establishment of religion, or prohibiting the free exercise thereof; or abridging the freedom of speech, or of the press; or the right of the people peaceably to assemble, and to petition the Government for a redress of grievances."*

The first ten amendments to the U.S. Constitution are called the Bill of Rights. The first sixteen words of the First Amendment are commonly referred to as the Establishment Clause, and very carefully and specifically assert that there is to be no establishment of religion and no restricting of religion. "No law respecting an establishment of religion" can be understood as any preference of one religion over another, no religion over religion, or religion over no religion. This is very clear. That is in the Bill of Rights, that it is every citizen's *right* for the government to remain impartial in matters of religion.

In this First Amendment to our Constitution, our founders clearly believed faith was a personal issue and wanted to ensure citizens the right to believe spiritually as they chose, harrasement – free. Thus to show favoritism toward one spiritual belief over another that operates within the laws of the country, is against our founding document, and our rights as citizens.

Why is this amendment in our Constitution? Because the pilgrims, or Separatists, who came and settled the New England area were leaving England because they didn't agree with the national church of England. They experienced some level of persecution because their type of Christianity was not accepted by England's national Church and its prescribed beliefs. Also, there is the fact that several of our Founding Fathers were Diests by some accounts, and not considered Christians. They saw this country as a melting pot where varied people of different backgrounds and beliefs could live in freedom. The ability to hold whatever spiritual tradition that resonates with an individual, without there being a government sanctioned belief structure setting a preference, was important because many of our citizens had felt the sting of sanctioned prejudice.

Perhaps it is clearer to refer to the intent of the First Amendment and the Establishment clause by saying the government is not to show any preferential treatment in matters of faith. Preferential treatment, for example, would be providing taxpayer dollars in the form of federal funding to any organization, charity, school etc., that promotes Christianity (or another faith) solely and exclusively and thereby giving approval to a preferred (and thus federally endorsed) religion over others.

<u>Taxes verses donations supporting religion</u>

This idea of the taxpayer's money being funneled to support only one belief system is important. What if you are dutifully paying your taxes as a good citizen and you are not a follower of the Christian faith, yet your money is going to fund Christian churches or organizations? Is that fair? Is that a setting up of a national religion? Many scream foul, that it most certainly is a setting up of a nationally endorsed religion.

To avoid any preferential treatment toward any particular belief system and yet allow all to flourish our government allows all churches and spiritual organizations to conduct themselves without being taxed. Followers can donate or tithe however much money they choose to a church or spiritual organization of their choice. Donated money and a church's purchases (even real-estate) are all tax-free. Thus, people are free to exercise their beliefs and decide for themselves where their money goes. It is a simple solution to allow spiritual freedom for every citizen. This is a Democratic system of the people, by the people, and for the people. The system is rather ingenious in its simplicity, let the people decide what works for them spiritually, rather than having the government as a middle man with tax money in matters of spirituality, let everyone be free to believe what they will and give their money to which ever religious system they want, or not. This is true religious liberty for all.

The other side to that coin is if an organization <u>does</u> receive federal funds, then they are expected to leave spiritual judgments toward individuals or groups aside. This keeps the Federal Government from funding violations to citizen's rights when the citizens gave their money via taxes. The following news item found in the popular *Parade* magazine gives an example of this principle in action.

> *"The Supreme Court will soon hear arguments to determine whether official student organizations at public universities can exclude students based on their religious views.*
>
> *The Christian Legal Society (CLS) is a national association of lawyers, judges, law professors, and law students with chapters at universities across the country. In 2004, CLS members at the University of California Hastings College of the Law requested recognition as an official student organization, <u>hoping to secure benefits including financial support</u> and meeting space. The University refused, saying CLS violated its nondiscrimination policies by denying membership to practicing homosexuals and anyone who refuses to sign the group's 'statement of faith.'*
>
> *...Choper [Jesse Choper, a law professor at UC Berkeley] notes, 'even if you have a First Amendment right to do something, it does not entitle you to funding to exercise your right.'"* "Can Campus Religious Groups Exclude NonBelievers," *Parade Magazine*, February 28, 2010.

Politics from the pulpit

Yet another side to this would be that a church or spiritual organization is to be about the business of spiritually caring for its people and conducting its own affairs. But what happens when a church decides to have a sermon about the candidates in the upcoming election, rather than on the attendees' spiritual welfare and development? They have moved into the realm of a political organization, which has strict rules and regulations, that churches don't. Many believe this is not just morally but ethically wrong, so much so that we now have watchdog groups looking for such violations.

Again, we come back to the issue of taxes for a moment. Churches are tax free, but to start promoting political candidates is actually a violation of IRS statutes, specifically Section 501(c)(3) of the IRS Code. Interestingly, churches have some capability within the IRS regulations to speak about politics, up to a point. The line in the sand is that they can't endorse one specific candidate over another. Many churches have been reported to the IRS to have their tax exemption revoked for their political endorsements from the pulpit, since that denotes that they have moved into a completely different tax classification, a political organization that has different rules. This is more than just a matter of classification or labeling, but treating an organization according to what they really are and what their purpose is. This is a drama that many don't realize is taking place.

The Religious Right proclaims they are being muzzled, and it is their rights that are in jeopardy in spite of their freedom of speech on politics, within certain boundaries. Here is Tony Perkins of the Religious Right's Family Research Council on the subject:

> *"What liberals who misread America's original document are really saying is that the federal government should not only silence churches but also exclude their members from any influence on government. In the name of tolerance of others, they would be intolerant to Christians."* Tony Perkins, *Personal Faith, Public Policy*, Frontline, 2008.

It is amazing how a system designed to encourage religious freedom for everybody is now branded as silencing churches and being intolerant. The Constitution provides protection of the rights of all citizens, and as you shall see as we progress in the book, the rights of all citizens are not the Religious Right's true concern at all.

Tax free status of churches

The tax issue may seem like a small issue, but let's take a look at how significant it is. The following quote brings to light the tax exemption figures for one city, only.

"...*According to the 2009 county assessor's records, these entities hold tax-exempt properties with a market value of $736,383,836. If taxed, these properties would provide the city with an additional $15,061,235 in actual revenue.*

...Over half of the city's General Fund budget comes from sales tax revenue. Virtually all, if not all, of the religious exempt organizations qualify for a sales tax exemption. Any purchase made with organizational funds is exempt from sales tax, to include the materials used in the construction of churches, offices, etc., as well as any furnishings, equipment, ornamentation and automobiles, even the bullet-proof vehicle in which one local prominent religious leader is chauffeured.

What happens when so many are exempt from paying the taxes that provide for our infrastructure, public works, schools, libraries, etc.? Those who pay taxes make up the difference in this much-needed revenue through higher taxes, increased mill levies and reductions in vital services as well as those services which contribute to quality of life. Even their own supporters and parishioners are burdened by this inequity in our tax system.

...According to the latest financial statements available through the Colorado secretary of state's office Web site on 113 charitable organizations (45 of which operate out of private residences, 68 operating out of commercial properties either owned or leased) received contributions from supporters in the amount of $861,491,874, had total revenues of $1,049,442,279 to include $3,212,858 in federal grants. Out of the total revenue, $91,860,675 went to administrative costs, $68,074,578 for fundraising and $895,056 was spent on the services of professional fundraisers. The ending fund balances of these organizations totaled $841,051,247.

The sales tax exemption applies here as well, even for the exempts operating *out of private residences though they do pay property tax. In addition, there are financial incentives being offered for these businesses to come to Colorado Springs. Focus on the Family received a $4 million land grant from the El Pomar Foundation to locate their headquarters here."* Pamela Mason, "Religious extortion of our city" *The Gazette*, [Colorado Springs, CO] July 3, 2009.

The dollar amounts in the above newspaper quote were only for one city. Think how much the figures add up to for all 50 states and you start to see why this is a big issue. All citizens of this country have to pay their taxes according to the IRS rules and tax codes, but now we see the Religious Right feeling that they don't have to follow the IRS rules they operate under, and greatly benefit from in their tax-exempt status when it comes to politics.

Spiritual blackmail

IRS and taxes aside, the Religious Right has a captive audience to preach spiritual concepts to and provide encouragement to, in their personal struggles. They choose instead to direct congregants to candidates they feel are more worthy of receiving their collective vote. What is the personal guilt factor if you don't vote that way? Are you actually going against God's divine wishes if you should vote other than the pastor directed from the pulpit? Some pastors have reportedly stated a person can't be a good Christian if they vote contrary to the pastor's thinking. This is a spiritual blackmail of sorts.

> *"During the 2004 election season, he [Pastor Kalnins, the senior pastor of Wasilla Assembly of God since 1999] praised President Bush's performance during a debate with Sen. John Kerry, then offered a not-so-subtle message about his personal candidate preferences. "I'm not going tell you who to vote for, but if you vote for this particular person, I question your salvation. I'm sorry." ...But Pastor Kalnins has also preached that critics of President Bush will be banished to hell;*
>
> *... Months after hinting at possible damnation for Kerry supporters, Kalnins*

bristled at the treatment President Bush was receiving over the federal government's handling of Hurricane Katrina. 'I hate criticisms towards the President," he said, 'because it's like criticisms towards the pastor -- it's almost like, it's not going to get you anywhere, you know, except for hell. That's what it'll get you.' " Nico Pitney and Sam Stein, "Palin's Church May Have Shaped Controversial Worldview," *The Huffington Post*, September 2, 2008.

It is spiritual blackmail no matter how you spin it. What is perhaps the most disturbing is that the people in the pews often don't see it that way. Far too many people don't speak up against such spiritual manipulation and extortion.

"Just a year earlier, a pastor at East Waynesville [North Carolina] Baptist Church had expelled nine members of his congregation for committing the sin of voting for [John] Kerry." Ari Berman, *Herding Donkeys*, Farrar, Straus, and Giroux, 2010.

Yes indeed, spiritual blackmail. In Reed Cowan's documentary *8 The Mormon Propo$ition: Equality for Some*, the massive amounts of money spent in California's Proposition 8 vote is traced back to the Mormon church in Utah, not even California, where the law would go into effect. What is even more disturbing is how they raised that money. The documentary details how the church leadership visited Mormon families and told those families how much they were to donate to the cause based on their finances. Their very spiritual good standing was held over their heads, as a spiritual coercion.

Individual religious liberty

At issue within the separation of church and state is the constitutional concept of religious liberty, which is a matter of individual rights. This concept of walking your spiritual path without interfering with another's walk is upheld with the separation of church and state firmly in place. The intention of the Bill of Rights is largely concerned with protecting individual rights, not organizations. At this point, it might be beneficial to look to President John Fitzgerald Kennedy during the presidential race of

1960, since he faced religious scorn because he was a Catholic. Some felt that the Pope might influence Kennedy's presidency, and thus would compromise his ability to lead the country.

America's collective memory seems amazingly short too often. Today we have arguments over candidates being Christian enough seen in the hysteria over President Obama, to the suspicion of Mitt Romney for his Mormon faith. Yet, according to the Religious Right, we are to allow an extremist Christian movement determine the president, and every aspect of life, when in the 1960s, the nation fretted over voting a man to the presidency who might take direction from a spiritual leader. Let's look at just how far we have digressed by taking a little trip back to 1960 and learning from the man who would become one of the most well known and loved presidents in our history.

"...I believe in an America where the separation of church and state is absolute. Where no Catholic prelate would tell the President, should he be Catholic, how to act, and no Protestant minister would tell his parishioners for whom to vote; where no church or church school is granted any public funds or political preference, and where no man is denied public office merely because his religion differs from the President who might appoint him, or the people who might elect him.

I believe in an America that is officially neither Catholic, Protestant nor Jewish – where no public official either requests or accepts instructions from the Pope, The National Council of Churches or any other ecclesiastical source; where no religious body seeks to impose its will directly or indirectly upon the general populace or the public acts of its officials, and where religious liberty is so indivisible that an act against one church is treated as an act against all.

For while this year it may be a Catholic against whom the finger of suspicion is pointed, in other years it has been -- and may someday be again -- a Jew, or a Quaker, or a Unitarian, or a Baptist. It was Virginia's harassment of Baptist preachers, for example, that led to Jefferson's statute of religious freedom. Today, I may be the victim, but tomorrow it may be you -- until the whole fabric of our harmonious society is ripped apart at a time of great national peril....

And in fact this is the kind of America for which our forefathers did die when they fled here to escape religious test oaths that denied office to members of less favored churches -- when they fought for the Constitution, the Bill of Rights, the Virginia Statute of Religious Freedom, and when they fought at the shrine I visited today, the Alamo...." Senator John F Kennedy, "Address to the Greater Houston Ministerial Association" Rice Hotel, Houston TX, September 12 1960. http://www.jfklibrary.org

John Fitzgerald Kennedy was facing tremendous opposition because he was Catholic, not a Protestant. He served as a commander in World War II., for which he was awarded the Navy and Marine Corps Medal citing extremely courageous conduct. He was elected to the U.S. House of Representatives for six years, then was elected to the U.S. Senate for seven years. His record and capability as a leader was less of an issue than his personal faith during the election. Notice his references to history and why the separation of church and state was important to the founders. "It was Virginia's harassment of Baptist preachers, for example, that led to Jefferson's statute of religious freedom. Today, I may be the victim, but tomorrow it may be you -- until the whole fabric of our harmonious society is ripped apart at a time of great national peril." Could those be prophetic words from 1960 that seem to foreshadow our struggle today?

Christians need to understand that the separation of church and state protects them as much as it does others. However, that is not what you will hear from the Religious Right today. It is noteworthy how John F. Kennedy made it clear that such infringing on the religious liberty of others rips apart our "harmonious" society. That accurately describes what we have seen in the last thirty years at the hands of the Religious Right, the fabric of our society progressively ripped to shreds. It is equally important to remember the right to religious liberty in the First Amendment is to guarantee an individual's religious rights. The Religious Right attempts to twist it to be for a church, or religious organization's benefit. There is a big difference between the two.

A one way barrier?

The Religious Right loudly proclaims that the Establishment clause of our constitution was meant to stop the government from interfering in the church's affairs, but not the other way around. The Right insists that the first amendment and the Establishment clause were never intended to stop Christianity from interfering in government's business. The very concept of our democracy is "of the people, by the people and for the people," not the church leaders. So what would be an example of Religious Right interfering, or even coercing our government?

> "...the US Catholics Conference on Bishops circulated a memo...and "supporting" documents to all bishops urging them to use this Sunday's mass as a lobbying event designed to defeat health care reform if the bishops don't get what they want on abortion. What do they want? They want to scuttle the well crafted compromise moderate pro-lifers and all prochoice groups have reluctantly supported and insist that health care reform efforts be used to cut off all sources of funding for abortions for all women -- whether they are on Medicaid or currently have coverage for abortion _in their private insurance plans._" Frances Kissling, "Catholic Bishops to Use Mass to Lobby Against Health Care?" _Religion Dispatches_, October 30, 2009.

The Religious Right never compromises; it is to be their way, only. They want to take the opportunity and use it to go beyond what the bill is addressing, to do their bidding and their bidding only, no matter what scores of other American citizens may feel or want. Democracy is lost in this attitude.

Origin of "Wall of Separation"

Let's hear from James Dobson and his take on the separation of church and state, televised on CNN's Larry King Live.

Larry King: "You don't believe in separation of church and state?"

James Dobson: "Not the way you mean it. The separation of church and state is not in the Constitution. No, it's not. That is not in the Constitution. That was..."

Larry King: "It's in the Bill of Rights."

James Dobson: "It's not in the Bill of Rights. It's not anywhere in a foundational document. The only place where the so-called 'wall of separation' was mentioned was in a letter written by Jefferson to a friend. That's the only place. It has been picked up and made to be something it was never intended to be. What it has become is that the government is protected from the church, instead of the other way around, which is that church was designed to be protected from the government."* James Dobson Interview, "Larry King Live" *CNN*, November 22, 2006.

What James Dobson is referring to in the preceding quote is a letter that Thomas Jefferson wrote that used the actual terms separation of church and state. It can't be stressed enough that Thomas Jefferson was the author of the Declaration of Independence and an influential Founding Father, so his explanation of the Establishment clause sheds light on the real intention of this amendment to the Constitution. The infamous letter that Thomas Jefferson wrote was to the Danbury Baptists, no less.

Let's put the "wall of separation between church and state" statement in its full context. The Danbury Baptist Association from Connecticut was a minority denomination. They wrote to the new president, Thomas Jefferson expressing their concern that their state constitution didn't have enough protection for religious liberty to ensure their freedom. Since it was common in that day and age to have persecution of less widely accepted expressions of faith, even within Christianity, it is no wonder this small Christian denomination was concerned. Harassment would often extend to followers, and included boycotts of their businesses, and bullying of their children.

Three months later, on January 1, 1802, President Jefferson replied to the Danbury

Baptists in an attempt to reassure them of their religious liberty in spite of their minority status. "I contemplate with sovereign reverence that act of the whole American people which declared that their legislature should 'make no law respecting an establishment of religion, or prohibiting the free exercise thereof,' thus building a wall of separation between Church and State." It is that term "wall of separation between Church and State" coined by Jefferson in this letter that the Religious Right despise and loathe.

This letter, by the author of the Declaration of Independence and a highly esteemed Founding Father, was meant to define what the First Amendment and the Establishment clause intended, and how it guaranteed religious liberty for all citizens. The very concrete phrase, wall of separation between church and state, makes it clear, and final. A wall of separation impacts both sides from influencing the other. The term "wall of separation" is specific in its enforcement on both sides, not a one-way passage. Yet, the Religious Right continue to put a spin on this by claiming no such thing was ever intended. Somehow that "wall" was only one sided? Perhaps it had a one-way door that Jefferson failed to mention?

Because Thomas Jefferson made it absolutely clear in his letter to the Danbury Baptists what the intention of the First Amendment truly was, he has become the target of the Religious Right. If there were a Most Valuable Player award for laying the foundation for this country, it would most likely go to Thomas Jefferson.

The book *The Myth of Christian America,* by Mark Weldon Whitten, explains the Religious Right's spin on the First Amendment Establishment clause. They teach the position that it was only for Christian expressions of faith that our Founding Fathers intended religious liberty, not all religions inclusively. Whitten goes on to poke holes in the claims that the religious liberty our Founding Fathers were protecting was only Christian liberty, and all other beliefs don't get protection.

> *"But what constitutes a 'Christian' church or denomination? A Christian religious group extant* [existing] *in the 1780s and recognized to be such by the*

Founding Fathers and their original intent? If not, what would be the contemporary criteria for a Christian church or denomination? Who would decide upon and apply the criteria? The legislatures and courts influenced by the Religious Right?...

What about liberal Christian churches who are viewed as heretical by fundamentalist Christianity? Even the religious liberty of professed Christian churches might be threatened by a narrow, nonpreferentialist interpretation of the First Amendment....

One will do well in these matters to heed the warning of the 'Father of the U.S. Constitution,' James Madison:

> *Who does not see that the same authority which can establish Christianity, in exclusion of all other religions, may establish with the same ease any particular sect of Christians, in exclusion of all other sects? That the same authority which can force a citizen to contribute three pence only of his property for the support of any one establishment, may force him to conform to any establishment in all cases whatsoever?'...*

Indeed it would be a different America than that envisioned by the saints and patriots who gave their lives for a nation that guarantees 'liberty and justice for all.' Quite honestly, such a view is profoundly and dangerously subversive. Richard Taylor was right on target when he wrote,

> *...If anyone were to try and replace the Constitution by, say, the Koran, then no one would doubt that this would be an act of subversion.... Similarly, for anyone to subordinate the principles embodied in the Constitution for those of the Bible, or to those of one of the various churches or creeds claiming scripture as its source, is political subversion."* Mark Wheldon Whitten, *The Myth of Christian America*, Smyth & Helwys Publishing, 1999.

This separation of church and state extends to many further issues that we see splashed in the headlines regularly. It is this very separation of church and state that is at stake when a federally funded high school has its graduation ceremony in a church. It is a matter of your mandatory tax dollars showing a preference for one spiritual belief over another. The same is true when a nativity scene is displayed on government property (tax dollars showing a preference towards one specific spiritual expression), or a cross on state-funded license plates, or prayers at the beginning of a political session, and our military forces proselytizing. It is the same issue when "In God We Trust" is on our federally minted money, or "one nation under God" in the pledge of allegiance that is said in federally funded schools. This is a fine line the Religious Right attempting to erase, rather than respect. "...he who is unrighteous in a very little thing is unrighteous also in much." Luke 16:10.

How about a National Day of Prayer? Our president, joined by state and local officials, annually issues a proclamation asking citizens to pray, a day that has been designated as a day of prayer when there are multitudes of agnostics, atheists, or faiths that don't petition their deity in that fashion. The National Day of Prayer is seen as violating the First Amendment because the government is endorsing religion over no religion, and promoting a specific religious act (prayer).

<u>Bible warnings</u>

The Bible seems to recognize just how dangerous unity of church and state is. Let's revisit the final hours of Jesus as the Bible relates those events. Mark Chapter 15 tells how the chief priests with the elders and scribes and the whole council, after Judas is paid by the religious leaders to betray Jesus, bound Jesus and delivered him to the governmental Roman authority. Pilate asked the people for his annual releasing of a prisoner if he should release Jesus because *"he was aware that the chief priests had delivered Him up because of envy. But the chief priests stirred up the multitude to ask him to release Barabbas for them instead."* Mark 15:10-11. After this, Pilate persisted, but the manipulated crowd then chanted to crucify Jesus. This record in the gospel of Mark makes it clear it was the religious leaders, influencing the government and manipulating the people, that crucified Jesus. I contend that we see the same factors in play today, with not just influencing, but hijacking the government, and widespread manipulation of the people. We have a Bible record showing how the mixing of religion and politics is disastrous at best, and evil at worst.

The Bible predicts in the final days on this earth that the Anti-Christ will be the political leader aided by a religious leader – the False Prophet to be the dynamic evil duo. It would appear that the ultimate power combination of religion and politics is recognized in the Bible again as extremely dangerous. Christ seems to have had a working concept of the separation of church and state. "And Jesus said to them, 'Render to Caesar the things that are Caesar's, and to God the things that are God's.' And they were amazed at Him." Mark 12:17. Perhaps such Bible examples will help Christians to see religious leaders with political power as perhaps more corrupting than the love of money, or at the least, equal with it.

Increasingly, it seems old beliefs get a modern make-over and resurface. Even two hundred thirty years ago, there existed in America variations on what seemed to be a Christian theme. Our Founding Fathers were a diverse group. The Deists among them were not Christians (i.e. born again and believed Jesus was the savior or Son of God.) Yes, we seem to have a greater variety than ever before of spiritual paths available, and this seems to threaten the Religious Right, as if there is a competition and they absolutely must have the highest number of followers. One way to stack the deck in this competition is to marginalize all other belief systems.

Separation of church and state is the crux of the matter, and the Religious Right are zealously and feverishly working towards tearing down that wall of separation as if it were the Berlin wall. As long as separation of church and state is kept intact, the Religious Right cannot have dominion over all aspects of American politics and the judicial branch of government. In later chapters you will read about the efforts to rewrite our nation's history to legitimatize this wall breach. But it is time to look at where the Religious Right came from, and who they are.

Take With You From This Chapter

➢ Separation of church and state and the Establishment Clause are vital to true religious liberty and freedom for all.

➢ Religious prejudice in politics has become more public since President Kennedy ran for president.

➢ There are many warnings concerning the dangers of mixing religion, and politics, even from the Bible itself.

Section 2: Who are they & how we got them

In this section:

The conditions that slowly created what we call the Religious Right are documented. We explore their early issues, tactics and the driving forces that have mandated their involvement in government and all of U.S. culture. Exactly who are main power players and the organizations that influence politics and culture?

Chapter 2
Origins and Initial Tactics

<u>What to Expect From this Chapter</u>

➤ Why fundamentalists, who otherwise felt politics were a corrupting force, are compelled to take an active role in politics.

➤ What is the one political issue that provided the initial fire to the movement?

➤ Milestones in the timeline of the early movement.

➤ The tactics of this early rag-tag movement.

The definition of the Religious Right that this book ascribes to is that of a radical Christian movement that strives for control over every aspect of life in America. Their mantra is "absolute truth." This radical, even extremist, movement is comprised of followers, from Catholics to Baptists, Mormons to Presbyterians, and others. Many people mistakenly feel that to criticize the Religious Right is equal to criticizing a person's faith, when in fact it is exposing a political ideology that has no regard for dissenters' rights. The Religious Right believes in a politicized faith in order to legislate their specific concept of a Christian nation. Often the only face to this movement is the leadership that has surfaced over time due to far reaching television, radio shows, and political non-profit groups (James Dobson, Pat Robertson, D. James Kennedy, and Tony Perkins etc.) The phrase "Religious Right" is not always the term used to identify the movement or its adherents, and even the leadership of this radical movement has not settled on a title that best describes them.

"Many Christian Right leaders object to the term 'Christian Right' which they believe depicts a narrow movement. Some prefer the term 'Religious Right,' which would encompass all 'people of faith,' including conservative Jews and possibly Muslims. Yet despite the visible presence of orthodox Jews at Christian Coalition conventions, the movement remains concentrated primarily among white evangelical Christians (Green, 1995). Others object to both 'Christian Right' and

*'religious Right' on the grounds that labeling the movement as part of the 'Right'
implies that it is outside the political mainstream. Ralph Reed, formerly of the
Christian Coalition, prefers the term 'Christian conservative,' but many
conservative Christians oppose the Christian Coalition and similar
organizations. Other Christian Right leaders insist that theirs is truly a 'pro-
family' movement, although the agenda of the Christian Right includes many'
issues unrelated to the health of American families....*

*Robert Zwier argued that 'the primary audience, or constituency, for these
groups was the approximately 50 million evangelicals in the country, and in
particular the fundamentalist wing of that community. The aim from the
beginning was to mobilize a group of people who had traditionally avoided
politics because they saw it as dirty, corrupt business...by convincing people that
political involvement was a God-given responsibility.' (Zwier, 1984, pp.9-10)"*
Clyde Wilcox and Carin Robinson, *Onward Christian Soldiers: The Religious
Right in American Politics,* Westview Press, 2006.

It is interesting to note that even what the movement wanted to be called was
steeped in marketing appeal and is not clear-cut. The quotes in the following chapters
may refer to this movement using different names, but they are about the same
Religious Right and its leadership.

Regardless what you call them, people either agree with them heartily, or
passionately dislike everything about them. A few dismiss the movement as being
irrelevant and don't take it seriously, perhaps considering the statements that surface
in the media as too ludicrous to be believed. That is a very dangerous position to take.
Agree with them or despise them, but to reject them as unworthy of careful monitoring
is lazy and extremely risky. The Religious Right isn't going away if you simply ignore
them; in fact ignoring furthers their efforts.

Timeline

As a result of the Scopes "Monkey" Trials in 1927, Fundamentalists seemed to retreat from the spotlight due to the humiliating way they were portrayed as hicks.

"More than fifty years earlier, Bible-believing Christians had trekked into the political wilderness following the infamous Scopes Monkey Trial held in Dayton, Tennessee, over the summer of 1925. Although Christian statesman William Jennings Bryan had successfully argued the case in court, biblical fundamentalists, who opposed the teaching of evolution, lost the bigger battle in the court of public opinion. They were not prepared to stand in the face of the relentless assaults by the media and academic elites who attacked their values as outdated and portrayed them as 'uneducated, unthinking and reactionary.'" Tony Perkins and Harry Jackson Jr. *Personal Faith Public Policy,* Frontline, 2008.

In 1935, Abraham Vereide founded an anti new-deal group that developed into "The Fellowship," or "The Family," as it is commonly known. This organization claims to have a benign mission to politicians and influential businessmen via Bible studies and prayer meetings. But their actual mission is best described as bringing about their vision of a Godly government. They have been instrumental in several Democrats voting like far right Republicans, such as Bart Stupak, Joe Pitts, Ike Skelton, Mike Mcintyre, John Tanner, Lincoln Davis, Dan Boren, and Heath Shuler, who all live at the Family's C Street facility. The Family also founded the annual National Prayer Breakfast in 1953. The event is attended by roughly three to four thousand participants and includes international attendees as well. Until very recently the internal workings of the group were held in highest secrecy.

"In 1985, President Ronald Reagan said about the Fellowship, 'I wish I could say more about it, but it's working precisely because it is private.'" Jeff Sharlet, *The Family,* Harper Perennial, 2008, p.19.

Jeff Sharlet exposed this group in the books *The Family: The Secret Fundamentalism at the Heart of American Power* and the follow up book *C Street: The Fundamentalist Threat to American Democracy.*

"Vereide organized the first annual National Prayer Breakfast in 1953.

*President Eisenhower attended that year, as has every U.S. President since. Vereide died in **1969** and passed the reins to Douglas Coe. Coe, who avoids the limelight, has been closer to more U.S. presidents than any other religious leader, including Billy Graham. Indeed, he has been called a 'stealth Billy Graham.'*

Of the leaders that I interviewed, one in three mentioned Coe or the Fellowship as an important influence. Indeed, there is no other organization like the Fellowship, especially among religious groups, in terms of its access or clout among the country's leadership.

Several people I interviewed referred to the Fellowship as an 'underground State Department.'" D. Michael Lindsay, *Faith in the Halls of Power: How Evangelicals Joined the American Elite*, Oxford University Press, 2007.

In April 1942, a group of 147 people formed The National Association of Evangelicals. They provide a unified voice for their membership in political issues. NAE were reportedly included in weekly phone sessions with George W Bush during his presidency.

Simultaneously to the formation of the NAE, yet apparently unrelated, the popular evangelist Billy Graham began to break down the wall of separation between the church and state by becoming a regular visitor with presidents. Beginning in the 1950s, Graham reportedly had personal audiences with every president, from Harry Truman to George W Bush, and was known to urge presidents to action on a few issues. Graham was a supporter of Nixon in his presidential candidacy bid and was an advisor to Nixon's administration. Nixon went so far as to offer Graham an ambassadorship to Israel, that was turned down. This seemingly innocent mingling of church and state nevertheless created a predisposed mindset that broke down the separation of church and state in the public's psyche. The common occurrence made formation of the Religious Right practically inevitable.

Two very significant events took place in the early 1970s that we will briefly mention here. Rousas J. Rushdoony, after successfully attacking public schooling, was followed up by paving the way for home schooling. Then, he wrote about an alternate American history in which a Calvinist Christianity is the prime influence on the revolution and founding of the nation. He published in 1973 his nearly two thousand–page book, *The Institutes of Biblical Law*. This book went on to spawn an entire movement determined to take dominion over every aspect of American life. Secondly, in 1975, Loren Cunningham, founder of Youth With a Mission (YWAM) and Bill Bright, founder of Campus Crusade for Christ, developed a systematic approach to social transformation of the United States, called the Seven Mountains Mandate or Strategy. They devised the blueprint for taking dominion of seven strategic areas of American life. These will be covered in more detail later in the book.

"Evangelical leaders have gained access to powerful social institutions – the U.S. Military, large corporations, and many others – and because their religious identities are so important to them, they have brought their faith to bear on their leadership, <u>changing the very institutions they lead in the process</u>...Evangelicals have spent the last thirty years building and strengthening an array of organizations <u>focused on transforming the cultural mainstream</u>...it has allowed evangelicals from different sectors of society to join together and influence major institutions like Congress and the White House...And evangelicals in government have enlisted the help of fellow believers in other areas like Hollywood and Wall Street <u>to bring about their vision for a moral society</u>...

Evangelicals have been particularly active in higher education...promising evangelical students have been given an upper hand in gaining admission to major universities...They have founded institutions and supportive networks within the heart of mainstream culture – Hollywood and Manhattan...In the world of business, evangelical executives have focused their energies on building corporate cultures amenable to people of faith. Executives now feel more comfortable incorporating prayer in to business activities, such as offering an invocation before a board meeting...They want young people with faith-shaped vocations not just at First Baptist Church but also at Goldman Sachs, the State Department, and the University of Chicago...Evangelicals populate elite centers like New York and Los Angeles now more than ever. They can be found at the top of nearly every social institution in America, and their influence can be seen in public policy, commerce, and the media." D. Michael Lindsay, *Faith In The Halls of Power: How Evangelicals Joined the American Elite*, Oxford University Press, 2008.

On the surface, the Religious Right being found across America in widely varying careers and top positions seems ordinary. It is only when you understand the magnitude of the Religious Right's infiltration of most every powerful or influential organization with the express goal of utilizing those positions towards entrenching and politicizing their faith excluding anyone outside their dogmatic views, that you realize that a widespread and careful conquest is taking place.

The next major event in the pre-history of the Religious Right arrived when the Equal Rights Amendment appeared close to being ratified, when it initially passed the House and Senate. The Equal Rights Amendment had a seven-year deadline to get 38 states to ratify it, that was extended from 1979 into 1982. In 1972, it obtained ratification in 22 states right away. This outraged evangelicals and fundamentalists. In particular, the Fundamentalist women, who formed activist groups to defeat the ERA. This outrage unified a wide range of Christians around a political issue that formed the corner-stones of the modern Religious Right, and even defined early-on tactics that are still used today.

"...they feared that entrenching feminist values in the Constitution would mean the end of their Bible-based way of life. Their fundamentalist understanding of the Bible was that women were to be responsible for home and family and to be submissive to their husbands... What they didn't know was that they were also laying the foundation for what came to be called the Christian Right." Ruth Murray Brown, *For A Christian America,* Prometheus Books,

August 2002.

The outraged response to the Equal Rights Amendment began what evolved into the Religious Right. It seems benign to state that women have equal rights, and to stand behind that concept with an amendment to our Constitution. But the mere idea of including women's equality in our founding documents was met with absolute outrage by the radical Christians of the time.

It is significant to note that what unified differing church groups, from Catholics to Baptists, and spawned the loosely organized movement that became the political power broker of today, was the horror that an Equal Rights Amendment might become part of our nation's Constitution. That revulsion that some citizens dared to think of declaring women equal and put it in the founding documents set in motion an us-verses-them mindset and posture.

Here is the exact text of the entire Equal Rights Amendment that created such outrage:

> ***Section 1.*** *Equality of rights under the law shall not be denied or abridged by the United States or by any State on account of sex.*
>
> ***Section 2.*** *The Congress shall have the power to enforce, by appropriate legislation, the provisions of this article.*
>
> ***Section 3.*** *This amendment shall take effect two years after the date of ratification.*

Seven years to get 38 states to accept it might seem like plenty of time, but it gave the radical Christian element plenty of time, to form, organize, and determine the most effective tactics on a shoestring budget. Since this early movement was only loosely organized and no slick fund-raising efforts were taking place, they needed very low-budget yet highly effective methods of mobilizing church members everywhere. The anti-ERA activist tactics were purposely designed to appall people into action (often exaggerating consequences of ERA passage), and they worked better than anyone imagined. Ruth Murray Brown highlights one such highly successful tool, The Pink

Sheet, in her book *For A Christian America.*

The Pink Sheet, so named because it was printed on pink paper, proved to be a simple yet powerful tool that relied heavily on conjecture as to how the amendment might impact various areas of life; the most disturbing imaginings were chosen. Note this one: "It will invalidate all laws which require the husband to support his family and will make the wife equally responsible for support." Ruth Murray Brown *For A Christian American*, Prometheus Books, August 2002. When were there ever any laws saying a man was required to support his family? Witness the beginning of scare tactics, exaggeration, Olympian stretching-of-the-truth, and fabrications, that worked so well against the ERA that such tactics continue to be used extensively by the Religious Right today.

The Pink Sheet isn't much different than the action alerts and fund-raising mailings sent out currently by the Religious Right organizations to supporters. They are no longer on pink paper, and are more sophisticated, the same tactics are being used.

The radical Christian element of the 1970s felt that an Equal Rights Amendment would infringe on their rights somehow. They felt that securing rights for a segment of society would legislate a position that was contrary to their Bible-based views, so their views must have prime consideration.

> *"From their point of view, [ERA would] allow the government to interfere in God's plan for the family. Not only was the government attacking fundamentalist religion, it was trying to establish in its place the "religion" of secular humanism...[which] gives higher priority to human wants and needs than to God's word as revealed in the Bible. Feminists were accused of seeking their own selfish ends rather than accepting their role in "God's plan."* Ruth Murray Brown *For A Christian America,* Prometheus Books, August 2002.

This is very important to understanding their worldview, and it serves as a useful tactic on their part. Optimistically, it would appear they are unable to conceive that they may be considered the ones dictating or controlling. More realistically, they feel they have divine knowledge of the real issues and need to take a strong hand. In other words, they know what is best for the estimated 305+ million people in the United States today – and you.

In 1976, Jerry Falwell started his *I Love America* rallies across America that positioned him to found the Moral Majority in 1979. Falwell cited moral decline in America as his reasons for breaking with traditional Baptist policy of not touching dirty, filthy, corrupting politics.

> *"At the rebirth of the conservative Christian civic involvement in 1979* [referring to the forming of the Moral Majority], *the new leaders were determined not to repeat the 'sins' of the fathers. They would not shy away from controversy, nor would they yield to criticism; they would work with others to restore the moral foundations of the nation. In a short time the new movement would become highly influential in American politics. Its commitment to nonnegotiable, explicitly moral and biblical values caused it to be revered and ridiculed, embraced and eschewed, loved and loathed. But there was one thing few politicians could afford to do: ignore it."* Tony Perkins and Harry Jackson Jr., *Personal Faith Public Policy*, Frontline, 2008.

1977 was the auspicious year that James Dobson founded Focus on the Family. In 1981, Dr. Dobson jumped headlong into the political fray by organizing the Family Research Council.

But, the 1983 Supreme Court decision in Bob Jones University versus United States was truly the game changer. The battle began in 1970 when the IRS notified Bob Jones University that its discrimination against interracial married or dating students, or those who supported interracial couples, had put its IRS tax-exempt status in jeopardy.

This resulted in thirteen years of legal battles, culminating in the Supreme Court decision that the IRS could revoke tax-exempt status without the approval of Congress if an organization operated contrary to established U.S. policies. This was an outrage, and essentially poured gasoline onto the modest fire, creating a roaring passionate blaze.

"... he [Paul Weyrich] *said animatedly, that the Religious Right did not come together in response to the Roe decision. No Weyrich insisted, what got us going as a political movement was the attempt on the part of the Internal Revenue Service (IRS) to rescind the tax-exempt status of Bob Jones University because of its racially discriminatory policies.*

'What caused the movement to surface,' Weyrich reiterated, 'was the federal government's moves against Christian schools.' The IRS threat against segregated schools, he said, 'enraged the Christian community.' " Randall Balmer, *Thy Kingdom Come, An Evangelical's Lament: How the Religious Right Distorts the Faith and Threatens America,* Basic Books, 2006.

Then in 1988, Pat Robertson, of "The 700 Club" fame, formed the Christian Coalition from the network he began during his failed presidential attempt. The Christian Coalition reportedly reached its peak of power from 1989 to 1997.

In this section we have traced the very early conditions and events that constituted the beginnings of the Religious Right movement, from Billy Graham's subtle, and perhaps unintentional, chips in the wall of separation of church and state, to religion's very passionate entry into political activism. The Religious Right as we know it essentially was started and organized due to the Equal Rights Amendment. It began as a grass-roots effort and used many tactics to instill fear and outrage; whether they were completely true or not was totally unimportant so long as the end result was met. The Pink Sheet tactics and the long seven years of fighting ratification of the ERA paid off. The ERA was never passed.

The gestation of the Religious Right began with a gigantic political victory. It appears that victory served to whet this rag-tag group's appetite and encourage them to push for more political power.   The National Association of Evangelicals in 1983 had Ronald Reagan deliver his now famous Evil Empire speech at their conference in Orlando. That was the wake-up call to all Americans, but one that largely went unnoticed.

Take With You From This Chapter

➤ The forming of the present Religious Right had several decades of building the foundation with resentment from the Scopes Trial, Abraham Vereide founding The Fellowship (aka the Family), and the National Association of Evangelicals.

➤ The seventies brought the ingredients together with the Equal Rights Amendment, Rousas J. Rushdoony's book; the seven mandates were defined; Focus on the Family was founded, and the Moral Majority formed.

➤ Bob Jones University discrimination lawsuit that revoked their tax-exempt status has been noted as the fuel that set the movement on fire.

➤ The fight against ERA shows how the Religious Right is single-minded in requiring laws in alignment with their worldview, or they perceive they are being persecuted, rather than the rights of individuals being protected.

➤ The initial tactics were exaggeration to shock and anger people to predefined action, and it worked very well.

Chapter 3
Joining With The GOP

<u>What to Expect From this Chapter</u>

➢ Documenting the Republican Party and the Religious Right joining ranks.

➢ Francis Schaeffer helps pave the way and Ronald Reagan ushers the Religious Right into politics and power.

➢ Current examples of their continued solidarity.

The desire for consistent, organized and potent political power became a burning desire for the loosely organized Religious Right. The dilemma was how to achieve that when a new political party wouldn't be met with enthusiasm in the entrenched two-party system. Although the Constitution Party, founded in 1999, is Religious Right (Christian Reconstructionist, to be specific) it has never realized the power and position they lust for. One might think they stumbled upon a mutual vision with the Republican Party, but the reality is likely far different. A mix of radical Christians purposefully choosing politics for a vocation and the strategic wooing of existing politicians resulted in the convenient marriage of the Republican Party and the growing Religious Right. Some of their courtship and union you may be familiar with, but likely not the entire story.

<u>Francis Schaeffer's contributions</u>

In the 1970s, a religious community in Huemoz Switzerland, L'Abri, founded by Dr. Francis Schaeffer began the process of quietly politicizing faith; this happened unintentionally at first. L'Abri loosely contained elements of a retreat, a commune, and a seminary all wrapped into one as son Frank characterizes it in his book *Crazy For God: How I Grew Up One of the Elect, Helped Found the Religious Right, and Lived to Take All (or Almost All) of it Back*. L'Abri was unique and drew people to it like moths to a light bulb. It was at L'Abri that influential political figures and their families continued to break down the wall of separation between Church and State further and give the characteristic of an intellectual fundamentalism to the still coagulating Religious Right.

> *"At the moment, the Schaeffers were evangelical royalty. When I was growing up in L'Abri, my parents' religious community in Switzerland, it was not unusual to find myself seated across the dining room table from Billy Graham's daughter or President Ford's son, even Timothy Leary. The English actress Glynis Johns used to come for Sunday high tea. I figured it was normal. They were just a few of the thousands who made it through our doors. Only later did I realize that L'Abri attracted a weirdly eclectic group of people who otherwise would not have been caught dead in the same room....*
>
> *When Gerald Ford died in January 2007, I recalled that on the day he had assumed the presidency, his daughter-in-law Gayle was babysitting my daughter Jessica as her job in the work-study program at L'Abri, where Mike Ford, the president's son, was a student.*
>
> *Mom and Dad* [Francis and Edith Schaeffer] *met with Presidents Ford, Reagan, and Bush Sr. and stayed in the White House several times."* Frank Schaeffer, *Crazy For God: How I Grew Up One of the Elect, Helped Found the Religious Right, and Lived to Take All (or Almost All) of it Back*, Carroll & Graf, 2007.

Francis Schaeffer, wife Edith, and son Frank were the catalyst that turned abortion into a political wedge issue that has been likened to the next Civil War brewing for America...and in the wake of Dr. Tiller's murder it seems closer than ever. Francis wrote the books that became films *How Should We Then Live* and *Whatever Happened to the Human Race*. Those two books and subsequent films changed abortion from being a Catholic issue to a Christian line in the sand, and eventually a Republican agenda item that has led to a divisive and volatile maelstrom. Thus began a further coalescing of the radical Christian elements into the Religious Right.

But also of significance is Francis Schaeffer's book *The Christian Manifesto,* which clearly stands out as the first shot in the war between anything remotely humanistic and the faithful Christian. This book drew the lines of battle in its declaration of war and essentially stated that every good Christian should be "in it [war against humanism] to win it" with no mercy shown the enemy. Humanism is seen as the placing of the individual's own will, desire, or logical reasoning above God's, and therefore believing Satan's lies. Humanism is viewed today as analytical thought, science, human rights, feminism and gay rights. Thus, all these are at war with God.

Ronald Reagan rolls out the red carpet

Politics and organized religion had been flirting with one another in public view for a number of years whether at the White House and Oval Office with Billy Graham or tucked away in Switzerland learning at the feet of Dr. Francis Schaeffer. As this had been happening, more and more radical Christians felt they had to enter politics to safeguard their interests. Washington DC's red carpet was inevitably rolled out to the emerging founding fathers of the Religious Right by the Republican party in the form of Ronald Reagan.

"Reagan is credited with bringing the Religious Right fully into the GOP [Republican Party] fold. "I will remember Mr. Reagan primarily for his relationship with the evangelical Christian community in our nation," Moral Majority founder Jerry Falwell recalled in 2002, in a column on the Web site WorldNetDaily.com. Baptist Falwell said of the president's 1980 election: "We had long been shut out of the White House when Mr. Reagan took office."

Falwell noted that Reagan introduced ideas to the Republican platform that were important to conservative evangelicals--such as opposition to abortion and homosexuality, and unwavering support for Israel. Evangelicals helped elect Reagan." Robert Marus, "Reagan Political Years Paralleled Right's Rise Christian Century," *The Christian Century,* June 29 2004.

Former President Ronald Reagan gleefully courted and ushered the Religious Right into the White House and gave certain Christian leaders unprecedented access to the leader of the free world. Since Reagan, the Religious Right has continued to establish more footholds into the Republican Party (aka GOP). They continue to shape the Republican Party into what they want it to be.

> *"He [Reagan] went on: 'I'll confess that'* – *and here his voice faltered momentarily* – *'I've been a little afraid to suggest what I'm going to suggest.' A long pause ensued, followed by this: 'I'm more afraid not to. Can we begin our crusade joined together in a moment of silent prayer?' The entire hall went silent, and heads bowed. Reagan then concluded: 'God Bless America.'"* David Domke and Kevin Coe, *The God Strategy: how Religion Became a Political Weapon in America*, Oxford University Press, 2010.

~ ~ ~ ~ ~ ~

> *"The signature closing line commonly used in speeches 'God bless America' is a Ronald Reagan legacy and had only been used one time prior to Reagan in a major Presidential address which was Richard Nixon closing an address during the Watergate situation. By the end of Reagan's presidency he is using it to close every major speech and George H.W. Bush did the same, Clinton did the same, George W and Obama the same."* Kevin Coe, "Tucson Festival of Books: Politics Panel," BookTV, CSPAN2 Sunday May 29 2011.

Despite Nancy's belief in horoscopes and ESP, the Religious Right gladly supported Reagan and practically enshrined his presidency in memorial, in exchange for that coveted political power.

Continued Religious Right and Republican marriage

Yes, Ronald Reagan is the man who brought the Religious Right into the White House, and politicians ever since have been conceding to that voter block to varying degrees. As a testament to how married the Republican Party and the Religious Right are, we see Liberty University that was founded by "the moral majority" leader Jerry Falwell, disavow a student club of Democrats.

> *"In a May 15 e-mail to the student group, Liberty Vice President for Student*

Affairs Mark Hine said the club must end its affiliation with University. The group can no longer use Liberty's name, logo, or seal for its publications, Web sites, Facebook page, Twitter account or anything else.

'The Democratic Party platform is contrary to the mission of LU and to Christian doctrine (supports abortion, federal funding of abortion, advocates repeal of the federal Defense of Marriage Act, promotes the 'LGBT' agenda, Hate Crimes, which include sexual orientation and gender identity, socialism, etc),' Hine wrote in the e-mail to the LU College Democrats.

Liberty, which was founded by the late Christian evangelist Rev. Jerry Falwell, has had a College Republicans club for years. The College Democrats formed late last year and supported Barack Obama in the presidential election." Stephanie Condon, "Liberty University Revokes Recognition of Democratic Club", <u>CBS News Online</u>, May 22, 2009.

The preceding quote shows the Religious Right, in the person of Liberty Vice President for Student Affairs Mark Hine, speak for all Christians as to what real Christians believe and that Democrats do not fall in alignment. Yet there are Christian students who disagree with him and formed a Democratic student group, which evidence in their very existence that what he says is not true. The email is insulting when you see that the students have just been told that they are either 1) mislead 2) deficient examples of Christians or 3) not true Christians at all.

In the heated bar-room-brawling atmosphere of the August 2009 town hall meetings, did the Religious Right stay above the ruckus (WWJD?). The Family Research Council Action organization (FRCAction), the political action branch of Tony Perkins's Family Research Council, jumped into the increasing battle lines alongside the Republican Party with their very own webcast town hall. The webcast was live on September 10, 2009 at 8:30 ET at www.frcaction.org/webcast but was not available for long after that.

This town hall webcast further stirred the pot over health care reform and used the power of the internet to ensure the Religious Right adherents knew where good

Christians should stand on this political issue. The Religious Right webcast town hall meeting had Republican participants Senator Jim DeMint of South Carolina, Republican House leader John Boehner of Ohio and Representative Chris Smith of New Jersey presenting with Religious Right persons the Republican/Religious Right vehement stand against Health Care reform. The webcast completely mingled Republican rhetoric and extremist Religious Right posturing beyond any distinguishing one from the other.

It seems ridiculous to be in the Republican Party for the last twenty years and not realize the steady take-over, or is it surrender, of the Republican (GOP) party to the Religious Right. Perhaps they never grasped the depths of the take over until far too late.

> *"Some elite Republicans are shocked, shocked, to discover the ugliness lurking in their party. Figures from Peggy Noonan to Colin Powell cannot believe it! The party of the shining city on the hill is turning vulgar! The feigned surprise is laughable. After all, the only card left in the Republican deck is straight out of the religious right's 30 year-old battle plan, which the GOP has warmly embraced since Reagan. Since the mid-1970s, the Republican Party has validated the religious right's mythology of America's Christian nationhood, cowed to its authoritarian litmus tests, and made demagoguery not only fashionable but heroic."* Sarah Posner "The FundamentaList #55," *The American Prospect,* October 2008.

"Made demagoguery not only fashionable but heroic" as Sarah Posner, author of *God's Profits: Faith, Fraud, and the Republican Crusade for Values Voters,* sums up the love affair between the Republican party and the Religious Right where all is fair in extremist religion driven politics.

We see another example of the Religious Right's contributions to the Republican Party in the interns from Patrick Henry College, the Religious Right's political training ground for its youth. The College has a bus that goes to the White house every morning since the majority of students are interning with Republican politicians. How much influence has the Religious Right really managed to pull together in their venture into politics? This next quote sheds some light on why the Religious Right was the most fervent and staunch supporter of George W Bush's flawed presidency, why Obama is seen as such an affront, and was even labeled the anti-Christ during the 2008 campaign.

> *"When it comes to actual policy decisions, the most powerful evangelical voices come from within an administration and explains, in part, why the Carter administration had a much less evangelical tenor than that of George W. Bush.*
>
> *Bush has surrounded himself with more evangelicals than any other U.S. president in the last fifty years. Even among the nonevangelicals, there is a general affinity for religious faith; for example, former White House chief of staff Andrew Card is married to a mainline Methodist minister. And many who have been the president's top advisors are evangelicals ... Additionally, I found dozens of appointees at slightly lower levels who share the president's style of evangelical faith. And whereas in previous administrations six to ten White House staffers would regularly attend Bible study, today's White House Christian Fellowship is attended by fifteen to a hundred people. Similar Bible study groups honeycomb the administration. Frum wrote that this was a 'White House where attendance at Bible study was, if not compulsory, not quite uncompulsory, either,' a fact he says 'was disconcerting to a non-Christian like me.' ... Still, the Bush White House has consulted with evangelical leaders more regularly and forged closer relations with the evangelical movement than any other administration in recent history."* D. Michael Lindsay, *Faith in the Halls of Power: How Evangelicals Joined the American Elite*, Oxford University Press, 2007.

This explains much of the widening chasm between the two political parties. The Republicans have been so consumed by the Religious Right that there are no compromises and politics has become as black and white as the Old Testament is rigid.

For the Bush administration was just the beginning and they anticipated even more Religious Right brethren in the White House in ever increasing numbers and positions of power. Barack Obama was a slap in the face since he had shown early a tendency to listen to academic and scholarly advisors. The Religious Right viewed him as humanism taking the seat of power away from them. Suddenly it was a huge strike against you in politics to have a higher education or to turn to such experts.

Out of the ashes of the Scopes Trial, we have seen the birth of the Religious Right. We have briefly reviewed how they gained access into politics quickly, and somewhat easily. With Ronald Reagan's ushering the Republican's new bride into the White House, The Republican party seemed eager to disregard the First Amendment of the US Constitution and give preferential access to the Religious Right. One can almost hear the vows of 'till death do us part."

Take With You From This Chapter

➢ Ronald Reagan is given the dubious honor of rolling out the red carpet for the Religious Right's direct access to the Oval Office. This surpasses Billy Graham and Dr. Francis Schaeffer's influence and seals the marriage.

➢ The Religious Right and the Republican party are henceforth joined and nearly inseparable in message and purpose.

Chapter 4
Moving On Up – to the Courts

<u>What to Expect From this Chapter</u>

➤ The Religious Right hates the decisions of the Warren Supreme Court and strategically moves to take courts over and raise an army of lawyers.

➤ The Religious Right founds their own legal centers to further their agendas complete with large budgets and staff of lawyers.

➤ Evidence of infiltration of Religious Right into the Supreme Court.

> *"Judges are granted great latitude to intervene in personal family issues. The kingdom would be best served if judgeships were filled by sons and daughters of God who understand the King's ways. Only Holy Spirit–filled judges can have the proper instinct for how much mercy or justice to dispense. We need judges who know that God really considers them pastors and are willing to bring His light in this way. ...*
>
> *To fully dethrone Baal and take this mountain, we will have to bring His influence to the Supreme Court. The emerging Elijah Revolution will begin to bring God's order to the top of this mountain."* Johnny Enlow, *The Seven Mountain Prophecy: Unveiling the Coming Elijah Revolution*, Creation House, 2008.

We have seen the beginnings of the Religious Right and followed its entry into the White House like never before thanks to Ronald Reagan. We will now look at the Extremist Christian Right's march on the courts, particularly the Supreme Court, to legislate their views as law. Such focus on the legal system is not a new idea. Making extremist ideals law so those views are accepted by the populace as normal and correct has occurred all through history.

<u>Supreme Court rulings set the stage</u>

In the 2007 book *The Jesus Machine*, Dan Gilgoff sets forth that the Religious Right in the late 1980s and 1990s got angry with the court system: *"As the movement grew, it began tracing the decline of religion's role in public life to earlier Supreme Court decisions, like the 1960s-era Supreme Court rulings that struck down the mandatory school prayer and devotional Bible readings in government funded public school classrooms. In the 1980s, Supreme Court rulings banning public prayer at graduation ceremonies and stopping the mandatory posting of the Ten Commandments in public schools reinforced the Christian Right's view of the nation's high court as an unaccountable oligarchy* [a political system governed by a few people]." The Religious Right moved to develop their own army of lawyers, and influence who would get elected to the Supreme Court.

Chief Justice Earl Warren, the 1948 Republican Vice Presidential nominee, led the court from 1953 through 1969. The impact of the Warren Court is still felt every day by citizens whether they know it or not. The Warren court ended segregation of schools and public-school-sponsored prayer, and ruled for "one–man–one vote" standards of district apportionment that is surprisingly controversial, and established our Miranda rights. The Warren court was hated for ending school segregation and prayer in school, which eventually led to rulings against officially led prayer at school sports games and graduations. Then the Chief Justice Warren Burger led Supreme Court ruled on the infamous Roe vs. Wade case. Associate Justice Harry Blackmun, a lifelong Republican, authored The Roe vs. Wade official opinion that is used to divide the nation today. The courts had a mix of conservative and liberal justices, but they did not rule the way the Religious Right insisted those issues should clearly have been decided. I make note of these justices being Republican only to highlight how the party has changed since the Religious Right has hijacked the party.

"Now that the Republican Party and the Christian Right have become one seamless political machine, they are taking no prisoners. With a Bible in one hand and a voter guide in the other, the political Right is firmly in control of two branches of government and has its sights set on the third, the judiciary, the last

bastion of reason and respect for the separation of church and state. Even though the life appointment process was intended to make the courts the most apolitical entity left in the Republic, judges often make rulings that frustrate the Christian Right because they are not based on 'biblical law.' For this reason, judges are considered the 'new enemy.' They are all that stand in the way of an American Theocracy." Robin Meyers, *Why the Christian Right is Wrong: A Minister's Manifesto for Taking Back Your Faith, Your Flag, Your Future*, Jossey-Bass, 2006.

The Conservative Christians were upset over such rulings but, as we noted earlier, the 1970 Supreme Court ruling against Bob Jones University, due to its segregation and discriminatory practices, was the fire that set off the powder keg of stored anger against the courts. The courts, particularly the United States Supreme Court, became the consistent thorn in the radical right's side, with its centrist rulings and defense of separation of church and state.

Religious Right army of lawyers

Thus, the Religious Right started launching public interest and nonprofit law firms to carry out their agenda in the courts. The first was started by Pat Robertson named the American Center for Law and Justice (ACLJ) in 1990 – which Mr. Gilgoff reports has a budget of around thirty million dollars. The ACLJ even derives its name in opposition to the ACLU (American Civil Liberties Union) and is to do battle against the humanist influence in the legal system. In 1997, the ACLJ branched out and opened the European Center for Law and Justice in Strasbourg. Other legal organizations followed, such as the Alliance Defense Fund begun by James Dobson which according to Mr. Gilgoff:

"ADF [Alliance Defense Fund]...helped fund the Terri Schiavo litigation for Schiavo's parents and successfully fought to revoke the nearly four thousand marriage licenses granted by San Francisco mayor Gavin Newsom to same sex couples in 2004...the firm has a seventeen-million dollar budget and a hundred-

*person staff, including twenty in-house lawyers...trained a national attorney network of 850, with each lawyer pledging 450 pro bono [free] hours over three years. When Phil Burress needed a **team of lawyers** to draft an amendment to Ohio's constitution banning gay marriage and to protect it from dozens of legal challenges in 2004, it was ADF that stepped in to help."* Dan Gilgoff, *The Jesus Machine*, St. Martin's Press, 2007.

That is a strong legal organization with a one hundred person staff, twenty in house lawyers and a pool of eight hundred and fifty lawyers to pull from. That is a judicial force no matter how you look at it, and it is only one of the several established. Even the Christian Left or moderates, those Christians who don't agree with the radical right view, don't get this sort of massive weight to throw around. This allows them to draft legislation and introduce it to state elections simultaneously with few organizations capable of combating such a force. The Religious Right is truly powerful and is tapping massive amounts of money and legal man-power. Most of the court motions and battles are going on issue by issue and may not get national attention.

Eyes on the prize: The Supreme Court

Raising multitudes of lawyers to draft, defend and push the Religious Right's agendas through the courts is just one part of their judicial attack. Once they fostered hard hitting lawyers it was time to contemplate taking over the highest court in the land for their own personal use.

"The goal of the Christian Right, already closer to realization than most suspect, is not only a Supreme Court markedly more hostile to rights that Americans have taken for granted for more than a generation, but a return to a time when state legislatures and courts could create a patchwork quilt of personal liberties and individual freedoms...

"Since the 1970s, in the wake of Francis Schaeffer's call to arms, the Religious Right has viewed the composition of the Supreme Court as a political problem, and Christian conservatives have aggressively used the tools of politics to try to

solve that problem. If Americans who value such fundamental principles as separation of church and state and personal privacy do not do the same, they may be stunned by the rapidity with which those values are severely diminished or eliminated altogether.

More than anything else, the relative success of the Religious Right in reshaping the Supreme Court – has stemmed from the fact that all too many people take the decisions of the Warren Court for granted. More than any other single interest group, the Christian Right has educated its supporters on the connection between political success and judicial change, and it has consistently and aggressively worked for the appointment of federal judges and Supreme Court justices who share its philosophical opposition to the Warren Court's rulings. The time has come for the nation's political left to remind voters that so many of the rights and privileges that people enjoy today were established more than a generation ago by a Supreme Court that viewed the Constitution as a tool for expanding and defending human dignity and independence.

If that education does not take place, much of what the remarkable Warren Court accomplished will be weakened or wiped out by a social and political movement that ***more than anything else wants to baptize the United States as a Christian nation and use the Bible as its primary source of legal authority. In the end, the goal of the Religious Right is nothing less than to bring this country to its knees.****"* Frederick S. Lane, *The Court and the Cross: the Religious Right's Crusade to Reshape the Supreme Court*, Beacon Press, 2009. (emphasis added.)

Supreme Court Justice appointments

Many have been aware of the struggle over Supreme Court justice nominations, but this is why the process has become so political and a media circus event. The rant against "activist" judges is becoming more and more prominent. This is just the tactic they use when they are angry that rulings aren't favorable to their worldview. The concept of the highest court in our country being representative of the diversity of the citizens is lost on the Right. They want justices nominated and confirmed who have been fostered and nurtured by them, whose allegiance is with the radical Right and their views. But they also want to remake the judicial system itself.

U.S. Supreme Court Justices who are Religious Right leaning

In a relatively short time, the Supreme Court has been taken over and most people aren't aware of the danger, nor the ultimate intention behind this strategic assault.

"Why, though, does the conservative rhetoric against judicial activism survive, even at a time when most activism by the Supreme Court is in a conservative direction?

All justices, liberals and conservatives, have to make value choices about the meaning of the Constitution and how it applies in particular cases. Throughout this book, I have tried to show that for the last several decades conservatives have dramatically changed constitutional law to further their ideological agenda. A key step in reclaiming the Constitution is to understand that the conservative rhetoric about judicial restraint and a neutral methodology is an emperor without clothes.

Conservatives, both on and off the Court, have claimed for a generation that they are following the Constitution's original meaning and not making value choices. There are many flaws in this claim. It is clear that conservatives often abandon the original-meaning approach when it does not serve their ideological purposes." Erwin Chemerinsky, *Conservative Assault on the Constitution*, Simon and Schuster, 2010.

The consistent use of the term "activist judges" is outrageous and hypocritical when you consider that conservative judges have *"dramatically changed constitutional law to further their ideological agenda."* Even more disturbing is the thought that there are Supreme Court justices aiding such alterations, justices who are promoting Religious Right concepts from their position. The following shows Supreme Court Justice

Clarence Thomas giving a skewed view of the separation of church and state.

> *"He repeatedly has argued that the Establishment Clause does not apply to state and local governments. His view, expressed in many opinions, is that the Establishment Clause was meant to prevent the federal government from establishing church that would have competed with state churches that existed at the time the First Amendment was adopted. This view, of course, would mean a dramatic change in the law since state and local governments would be unconstrained by the Establishment Clause. Utah could declare itself to be a Mormon state; Georgia could officially be a Baptist state; Connecticut could deem itself to be a Catholic state. State and local governments never could be found to violate the Establishment clause no matter what they did."* Erwin Chemerinsky, *Conservative Assault of the Constitution*, Simon and Schuster, 2010.

A common hallmark of the Religious Right is their view against the wall of separation of church and state. Justice Thomas is saying that what the First Amendment really meant was each state could declare an official religion (one that presumably could receive state tax funds) but that the Federal government could not declare a national religion and thus compete with any state's religion in favor or money. This is opposed to Thomas Jefferson's explanation of the true meaning of the First Amendment. Justice Thomas' view corresponds with the desires of the Religious Right, specifically the Christian Reconstructionists. Surely the other Supreme Court Justices uphold the separation of church and state and Justice Thomas is the odd man-out.

> *"… the Supreme Court for decades espoused the view that the Establishment Clause was meant to separate church and state. Yet, when I stood before the justices in March 2005 to argue Thomas Van Orden's challenge to the Texas Ten Commandments monument, there were only three justices – Stevens, Souter, and Ginsburg – who espoused the view of Thomas Jefferson that there should be a wall that separates church and state.*

Four justices – Rehnquist, Scalia, Kennedy, and Thomas – repeatedly had said they rejected the notion of a separation of church and state.

But how did it come to be that the Court had gone from having nine justices who believed in the strict separation of church and state to just three? The answer reflects a major change in the political landscape." Erwin Chemerinsky, *Conservative Assault of the Constitution*, Simon and Schuster, 2010.

Laws to be based on the Bible?

To be clear, the Religious Right emphasizes how the laws of this country should be based squarely on the Bible, including the Old Testament and the Ten Commandments. But the Religious Right's schemes are yet again directly in opposition to the United States Constitution:

"This Constitution, and the Laws of the United States which shall be made in Pursuance thereof; …shall be the supreme Law of the Land; and the Judges in every State shall be bound thereby…" United States Constitution Article 6

The Constitution and subsequent laws are to be supreme, and the judges are to uphold them, not the Bible's laws. First in 2004 and again in 2005 the Religious Right got Senator Richard Shelby and Representative Robert Aderholt to sponsor the Constitution Restoration Act. CRA would have legislated "the acknowledgment of God as the sovereign source of law, liberty, and government." This bill is thought to declare that our judicial branch must uphold the Bible as the law of the land and nothing else, not our Constitution that is the basis of our laws, nor our very own Declaration of Independence's "decent respect to the opinions of mankind."

It would logically lead to establishing the Ten Commandments and all the Bible precepts as the one and only law of the country and all judges would be forced to rule accordingly. Lawyers would need a Bible degree, rather than legal degrees and constitution classes. It is also considered that CRA would essentially remove the ability of Federal courts to question the constitutionality of a State decision if it is cloaked in Religious Right beliefs. The Religious Right will be back with this legislation, never doubt that. They never take "no" for an answer; they persistently hammer to get their agenda through, and they tend to go state-by-state when they fail to get federal level legislation passed.

State courts

State Supreme Court Justices have increasingly come under fire from the Religious Right. The 2010 elections saw the Religious Right organization National Organization for Marriage run an expensive and successful campaign to remove the three Iowa state Supreme Court Judges because they ruled for marriage equality/same sex marriage.

> *"The Courage Campaign and Human Rights Campaign were quick to point out that NOM's goal was to intimidate judges throughout the country.*
>
> *NOM's president Brian Brown has admitted (here) that his group's effort in Iowa's judicial election was actually about intimidating judges around the country into ruling against equality for millions of loving American families. In Iowa, NOM spent an unprecedented $600,000 on TV ads and a 45-county bus tour. Despite NOM's mean-spirited and fear-driven campaign, same-sex marriage remains legal in Iowa.*
>
> *By their own admission, NOM's Iowa strategy was about sending a warning shot to judges nationwide," said HRC President Joe Solmonese. 'NOM and its secret donors will target judges around the country if they rule in favor of marriage equality and will foster an anti-gay, hostile environment in the process."* "Iowa Courts Hijacked By National Organization for Marriage Intimidation Campaign, Human Rights Campaign,
>
> http://www.hrc.org/news/15022.htm, Nov 3, 2010.

This cannot be driven home strongly enough. The Supreme Court, state and the higher federal courts, are to ensure our democracy's protection of citizens' rights under the Constitution, not Biblical mandates. This is under siege. Iowa become a battleground the instant that the judges made their ruling. Commercials started airing in 2009 called "A Storm is Coming" with actors portraying average people or professionals giving baseless claims of how giving marriage equality was going to destroy the fabric of the whole nation. Iowa has pretty much been under constant Religious Right assault ever since the judges made their decision. Apparently Iowans crumbled under the barrage.

"'What is so disturbing about this is that it really might cause judges in the future to be less willing to protect minorities out of fear that they might be voted out of office,' Erwin Chemerinsky, dean of the University of California at Irvine's School of Law told The New York Times. *'Something like this really does chill other judges.'*

The FRC, the National Organization for Marriage (NOM) and other Religious Right groups began taking aim at the judges months ago. They poured money into the state, organized in fundamentalist churches and blitzed Iowa with a bus tour.

The purple bus, emblazoned with the words 'Replace, Renew, Restore' and photos of the three targeted judges, made stops in 20 Iowa communities over four days in late October. FRC and NOM were so proud of the bus that they created a special Web site (judgebus.com) full of pictures and messages sent via Twitter. (You could even "like" the bus on Facebook.)

Some clergy jumped into the effort, heedless of the legal consequences of church-based politicking. In Sioux City, the Rev. Cary K. Gordon of Cornerstone World Outreach Church implored other preachers to attack the judges from the pulpit.

For years, Religious Right groups have fulminated against 'activist judges' who issue rulings the far right dislikes. Their success in Iowa will undoubtedly spur them to move on to other states and threaten more judges.

During the anti-judge campaign, FRC leaders railed against out-of-state gay-rights groups that they said were attempting to influence the outcome. But the FRC isn't based in Iowa either and featured Louis Gohmert, a member of

Congress from Texas, as one of its speakers.

The National Organization for Marriage, which is based in Princeton, N.J., poured $600,000 into the effort. The Christian Post reported that this was the largest donation made to the campaign.

The Des Moines Register *reported that the vote "triggered a battle never seen in Iowa's judicial history. Television, radio and Internet ads portrayed the justices as both activists and referees. Robo-calls urged a 'no' vote. U.S. Rep. Steve King embarked on a statewide bus tour to rally 'no' voters."*

Exulting in the victory, King remarked, 'It's something that will send a resounding message all across the country, and I think that every judge in the judicial branch of every state will learn about this decision by Iowans. We've been a little soft on the social issues lately, and we turned the corner last night.' " Rob Boston, "Iowa Supreme Court Judges Voted Out After Religious Right Smear Campaign," *Church and State,* December, 2010.

Do you get the picture here? Striking fear into local judges because they have thousands, even millions of dollars to manipulate the people's votes, and pastors preaching to a captive audience on politics. What judge will protect citizen rights in the future with that potential barrage waiting to rain down on them? When will single moms and un-married couples come under attack and lose rights?

Now we will examine the most influential ideologies within the Religious Right that give the more blatantly extremist edge to the movement. We will turn our attention to the Dominionists and Christian Reconstructionists who have become the pervasive philosophy of the Radical Right

Take With You From This Chapter

➤ The Religious Right has made tremendous headway in getting Supreme Court justices appointed who lean their way.

➤ Supreme Court rulings have been more and more conservative over the last several decades, essentially rewriting constitutional law as they go.

➤ The extreme 2010 Iowa campaign to oust several judges was meant to intimidate judges who would vote against Religious Right views.

➤ Ultimately, they want the legal system in the U.S. to follow the Bible, particularly the Old Testament and Ten Commandments.

Chapter 5
Add Dominionists & Reconstructionists

<u>What to Expect From this Chapter</u>

➢ The entrance of the agenda to take Dominion of the nation.

➢ Dominionism, Christian Recontructionists and Rousas J. Rushdoony explained.

➢ The Seven Mountains of Influence Mandate (or Blueprint) is introduced.

<u>Who and what are they?</u>

Dubbed Dominionists because they: 1) believe they are mandated by God to have dominion over the entire nation, and over every aspect of American life, and 2) they adamantly insist, despite any evidence to the contrary, that the U.S was started as a Christian nation and must return to being such. Christian Reconstructionists (Reconstruct America based on the Bible, including our legal structure) are reportedly the parent movement to Dominionism. Where one ends and the other begins is often fuzzy. *"Not all dominionists are Reconstruction apostles — but the differences are a matter of theological finesse, and political strategies are largely indistinguishable."* John Sugg, "A Nation Under God," *Mother Jones*, December, 2005. They do not acknowledge the legitimacy of other faiths, or even varying Christian expressions. They staunchly believe that the Ten Commandments and Old Testament laws should rule the country, and the U.S. Constitution should advance this extremist Christian view.

"Reconstructionists criticize the "conflation" of spheres of government. They draw clear distinctions between various forms of government they believe to be delegated by God. There is self-government, and then there are three forms of institutional government: family, church and state. So when the Constitution Party platform uses the phrase "civil government," it does so to draw a distinction between what the party sees as the mistaken idea that all government is civil government and its view that there are distinct biblical spheres of government —

civil government being only one.

The Constitution Party platform opposes marriage and/or legal partnerships for gays and lesbians. No surprise there, but the plank regarding family articulates a notion of family as one of three governing institutions established by God. Likewise, the platform articulates support for Christian schooling and homeschooling. But it does so on the basis of Reconstructionist framing: the family is understood as a form of government, given by God, with a specific sphere of authority that includes the raising of children, without the interference of the civil government. Opposition to welfare, in the platform, is not based in more common conservative view, such as "welfare allows people to be lazy," or "it's unfair (or even inefficient) to tax productive people to care for those who are not." Rather, it is based in the argument that welfare is more properly understood as charity and is legitimately within the authority of the church, not the civil government." Julie Ingersoll, "Rand Paul and the Influence of Christian Reconstructionism", *Religion Dispatches*, May 25, 2010.

This limited government view is seen more and more in the Republican platform. The Republican platform is "less government, more capitalist free market" but it is Religious Right through and through. The emphasis on family, church, (or values, absolute truth, and conservative Christian leaders), and state rights over and above the unifying Federal role, is the foundation for the Republican platform these days.

"Christians have an obligation, a mandate, a commission, a holy responsibility to reclaim the land for Jesus Christ – to have dominion in civil structures, just as in every other aspect of life and godliness.... World conquest. That's what Christ has commissioned us to accomplish. But it is dominion we are after.   Not   just   a   voice.
It is dominion we are after. Not just influence.

It is dominion we are after. Not just equal time.

It is dominion we are after.

World conquest. That's what Christ has commissioned us to accomplish. We must win the world with the power of the Gospel. And we must never settle for anything less...

Thus, Christian politics has as its primary intent the conquest of the land – of men, families, institutions, bureaucracies, courts, and governments for the Kingdom of Christ." George Grant and Gary North, *The Changing of the Guard: Biblical Principals for Political Action,* Dominion Press,1987.

~ ~ ~ ~ ~ ~ ~

"This is our land. This is our world. This is our heritage, and with God's help, we shall reclaim this nation for Jesus Christ. And no power on earth can stop us." D. James Kennedy, *Character & Destiny: A Nation In Search of Its Soul,* Zondervan, 1994.

~ ~ ~ ~ ~ ~ ~

"As the vice-regents of God, we are to bring His truth and His will to bear on every sphere of our world and our society. We are to exercise godly dominion and influence over our neighborhoods, our schools, our government, our literature and arts, our sports arenas, our entertainment media, our news media, our scientific endeavors — in short, over every aspect and institution of human society." Bob Moser quoting D. James Kennedy, "The Crusaders," *Rolling Stone*, April 7, 2005.

Seven Mountains Mandate – the blueprint

This *dominion* impacts every man, woman, and child in the United States because it is dominion over every aspect of life. A strategic blueprint to accomplish such dominion has been specified and categorized since 1975 by the Seven Mountains of Influence Mandate. This blueprint is the product of Loren Cunningham, founder of Youth With a Mission (YWAM) and Bill Bright, founder of Campus Crusade for Christ. To gain dominion, you must wrangle seven spheres of influence, or mountains, and gain control in order to mold the nation and advance the literal, physical kingdom of God. The seven strategic areas of influence are: 1) government and law; 2) business and finance; 3) education; 4) media and communication; 5) arts and entertainment; 6) the family; and 7) spirituality and the church. They have a tremendous focus on control of the business and finance section, which is why they are fervently sponsoring one another into leadership positions.

> *"The one mountain they all depend on. The mountain that fuels and funds all the other mountains, the mountain of business: where people build for the glory of God or the glory of man. Where resources are consecrated for the kingdom of God, or captured for the powers of darkness. Those who lead this mountain control what influences our culture...As long as the business mountain is held by the enemies of the Gospel, funding for the other mountains will always be constrained, and any efforts to advance the kingdom of God will be hindered.*
>
> *Imagine God's people reclaiming their cities and government, in the arts and entertainment, in the media, in education, in the family, in religious influence – but only limited by their imagination and not by a lack of finances."*

O.S. Hillman, "Reclaim the 7 Mountains of Culture," http://youtu.be/wQtB-AF41p8.

This worldview is personal and immediate. How do you feel about such dominion over your family life, the education system from kindergarten through graduate school, your entertainment, your books and magazines, your news and your science, that impacts the quality of your health care? How do you feel about the applying of Old Testament principles of biblical law to your family, government, laws and every aspect of your life? How do you feel about every aspect of your life being controlled by the Religious Right? We aren't talking about Christian principles affecting our society here. Let us be very clear. This is a radical movement within Christianity, who is promoting a take over, a hijacking of the country.

> *"For anyone wondering what the 'culture' would look like if the Christian Right achieved its dream of 'taking it back' from secularists, feminists, and the other dread enemies of God's plan for a Christian America, the San Antonio*

Christian Film Festival ... provides a telling window.

...Replacing godless Hollywood with a Christian film industry is one piece of the Christian right strategy known as dominionism: creating 'biblical' alternatives to, and ultimately replacements for, secular political, cultural, and economic institutions.

Whether through homeschooling or Christian schools, the goal is to 'replace' public education, which...is considered unbiblical... They have long been proponents of dismantling the federal Department of Education...and reducing funding for public education at every opportunity...

The goal of a rival film industry to replace Hollywood, though is merely an interim goal. Reconstructions' long-term goal is to produce a rival culture based in 'Biblical Law,' and through what they call 'multi-generational faithfulness' to the dominion mandate, to ultimately replace every aspect of our existing culture. They've obviously got a long way to go to accomplish that goal in its entirety, but for anyone who thinks that the Tea Party is an essentially secular libertarian movement with no connection to that dominion mandate, take note: last year, the Best of the Festival Winner, the film The Widow's Mite, was about the evils of taxation." Julie Ingersoll, "Replacing Godless Hollywood with Bible-Based "Cultural Dominion", *Religion Dispatches*, October 30, 2010.

In regards to home-schooling and the Religious Right, we go into more detail about the role it plays in their plans for public schools in a later chapter. Not all parents who decide to home-school may be part of the Religious Right, but home-schooling organizations have proven fertile ground to recruit earnest people into Dominionism and the larger percentage are home-schooling for religious reasons. The point to the quote is that the Reconstructionists and Dominionists are standing up replacements for the secular world to transition everything in our nation to a Christian based alternative.

Rushdoony's impact

Christian Reconstructionism, or Dominionism, regards Rousas John Rushdoony and his 1973 book *The Institutes of Biblical Law* as a defining work that has illuminated the path forward. This book is still loudly praised, and the idea of taking dominion over every aspect of life is applauded by radical Christians. Theologians, the Christian academics and researchers, have widely criticized his scholarship, but that has not stopped the movement that he began. Rushdoony himself is credited with being in the front lines of the fight in the '60s and '70s for legalizing private and home schooling.

"The racist and brutal intolerance of the intellectual godfathers of today's Christian Reconstructionism is a chilling reminder of the movement's lust for repression. The Institutes of Biblical Law by R. J. Rushdoony, written in 1973, is the most important book for the dominionist movement. Rushdoony calls for a Christian society that is harsh, unforgiving and violent. His work draws heavily on the calls for a repressive theocratic society laid out by Calvin in Institutes of the Christian Religion, first published in 1536 and one of the most important works of the Protestant Reformation. Christians are, Rushdoony argues, the new chosen people of God and are called to do what Adam and Eve failed to do: create a godly, Christian state. The Jews, who neglected to fulfill God's commands in the Hebrew scriptures, have, in this belief system, forfeited their place as God's chosen people and have been replaced by Christians. The death penalty is to be imposed not only for offenses such as rape, kidnapping and murder, but also for adultery, blasphemy, homosexuality, astrology, incest, striking a parent, incorrigible juvenile delinquency, and, in the case of women, 'unchastity before marriage.' The world is to be subdued and ruled by a Christian United States. Rushdoony dismissed the widely accepted estimate of 6 million Jews murdered in the Holocaust as an inflated figure, and his theories on race often echo those found in Nazi eugenics, in which there are higher and lower forms of human beings. Those considered by the Christian state to be immoral and incapable of

reform are to be exterminated.

Rushdoony was deeply antagonistic toward the federal government. He believed the federal government should concern itself with little more than national defense. Education and social welfare should be handed over to the churches. Biblical law must replace the secular legal code. This ideology, made more palatable for the mainstream by later disciples such as Francis Schaeffer and Pat Robertson, remains at the heart of the movement. Many of its tenets are being enacted through the Office of Faith-Based and Community Initiatives, currently channeling billions in federal funds to groups such as National Right to Life and Pat Robertson's Operation Blessing, as well as to innumerable Christian charities and organizations that do everything from running drug and pregnancy clinics to promoting sexual abstinence-only programs in schools." Chris Hedges, *American Fascists: The Christian Right and the War on America*, Free Press, 2008.

Followers of Rushdoony for you to be aware of include, but are not limited to, his son-in-law Gary North, Howard Ahmanson Jr., Greg Bahnsen, David Chilton, Gary DeMar, Kenneth Gentry, George Grant, Andrew Sandlin, John Eidsmoe, Donald Lutz, Gary Amos, O.S. Hillman, and David Barton. While highly visible Religious Right figures may not want to be openly linked with Dominionism, many within the movement endorse Dominionist books and espouse the Dominion philosophy openly. Rushdoony has been on D. James Kennedy's television program and the 700 Club several times.

Influential Pat Robertson, Tim LaHaye, Tony Perkins and James Dobson all support the view of taking dominion over the United States of America. Robertson is often heard spouting revisionist history and saying Bible believing Christians **must** direct the U.S. government.

Stealthy maneuvers

"These values, democratic and Christian, are being dismantled, often with

stealth, by a radical Christian movement, known as dominionism, which seeks to cloak itself in the mantle of the Christian faith and American patriotism. Dominionism takes its name from Genesis 1:26-31, in which God gives human beings 'dominion' over all creation...Dominionists now control at least six national television networks, each reaching tens of millions of homes, and virtually all of the nation's more than 2,000 religious radio stations, as well as denominations such as the Southern Baptist Convention.

Dominionism seeks to redefine traditional democratic and Christian terms and concepts to fit an ideology that calls on the radical church to take political power...Dominionism seeks to politicize faith. Dominionism is a theocratic sect with its roots in a radical Calvinism. <u>It looks to the theocracy John Calvin implanted in Geneva, Switzerland,</u> in the 1500s as its political model. It teaches that American Christians have been mandated by God to make America a Christian state." Chris Hedges, *American Fascists: The Christian Right and the War on America,* Free Press, Jan 8, 2008. (Underline added.)

Notice in the preceding quote how stealth is used, a cloaking of their message, and intentions, in appeals to the mainstream while packaging it all in patriotism. "But fascism, [Dr. James Luther] Adams warned, would not return wearing swastikas and brown shirts. Its ideological inheritors would cloak themselves in the language of the Bible; they would come carrying crosses and chanting the Pledge of Allegiance." Chris Hedges, "Feeling the Hate with the National Religious Broadcasters," *Harpers' Magazine,* May, 2005. This is mentioned only to illustrate that packaging can be used to manipulate people. Any marketing executive knows this full well, and so do the Religious Right. The marketing, or manipulation in this case is to propagate the myth that only extremist Religious Right adherents are the true patriotic Americans.

John Calvin and Geneva 1541–1549

Not many are aware of John Calvin, nor his connection to Geneva Switzerland that is cited in the above quote, and is a role model for Dominionists and

Reconstructionists alike. John Calvin was a contemporary of the church reformer Martin Luther and like Martin Luther was a key player in the great reformation. The Reformation was a time when the Catholic Church witnessed a large number of members leave the church and started the Protestant faiths. The reformation generally started with Martin Luther and then others like John Calvin became noteworthy. Calvin's connection to Geneva Switzerland is that Geneva, for a time, was a town completely run by the new Protestant church. The church regulated every aspect of life with Calvin at the head (after some political struggles.) Every aspect of life was monitored including all social aspects. Sermon attendance was mandatory, and there are even some reports of home visitations to verify that an individual's personal life was in compliance to biblical laws. Schools existed solely to teach biblical doctrine. This is the shining example the Christian Reconstructions and Dominionists look to for how to shape the U.S.

In an effort to make such Geneva-like dominion over American politics, everyday life, and culture legitimate, they actively promote that the U.S. is a Christian nation, founded upon Christian ideals and the Bible. If you accept that premise, then it would seem only natural to introduce more Bible–focused politicians, with more and more laws based on biblical views. We go into the deliberate re-writing of our nation's history with this very intention in a later chapter.

Dominionism dresses up anti-Democracy views as being a good Christian's mandated duty while also selling strict intrusive and controlling national policies as the country's only hope for a bright future. The "smaller government" chant sounds nice, but whether it is the state or national level, they want dominion over it. Their role model of Calvin's Geneva (home inspections to see if personal lives were in line with the Bible) shows how intrusive they think the government should be. The dislike of a Federal government that provides the uniting glue doesn't mean they are against intrusive government, the two are not mutually exclusive. They wish to take dominion of the federal and state levels and keep the court system strictly in line with the Bible.

This chapter introduced the Dominionists and Christian Reconstructionists who are the primary forces driving the Religious Right. The seven mountains mandate, the blueprint to accomplish such dominion, was introduced. Each of the seven mountains will be detailed later. Now let us get to the people and organizations headline the Religious Right movement at the moment, including who appears to be holding the reins and directing the massive network.

Take With You From This Chapter

➤ Who are Christian Reconstructionists and Dominionists and what is their agenda.

➤ Rushdoony is the father of the two groups.

➤ John Calvin and his reign in Geneva are viewed as a model for America.

➤ Seven Mountains Mandate is a blueprint to accomplish dominion.

Chapter 6
Naming Names

What to Expect From this Chapter

➤ Who are some of the key Religious Right figures.

➤ What organizations are advancing the Religious Right agenda.

➤ James Dobson, once the leader.

➤ The new leader, David Barton.

Just exactly who are the power brokers of the Religious Right, anyway? It isn't easy to point out the Religious Right because individuals don't typically identify themselves that way. A Religious Right person commonly identifies him or herself as a member of a specific denomination such as Catholic or Baptist. The leadership of the movement has debated how the movement should be referred to. It is even harder to find those who would say they are Dominionists or Christian Reconstructionists since that is a title bestowed upon the primary movements found within the Religious Right and not a label some appreciate.

Religious Right Characteristics

The Religious Right is identified by two main characteristics. The first identifying marker is their core religious beliefs or tenets. These are inflexible absolute truth, and biblical values they feel they alone posses, and all else is relative and humanist. They hold the most conservative of evangelical creeds with the Bible being inerrant and infallible. Also, there is a common, shared belief that the United States was deliberately and specifically founded to be a Christian nation, and separation of church and state was only meant to protect Christian churches from government interference in their matters, never to restrict the church from directing the government.

Secondly, the Religious Right fervently holds that their beliefs and Bible interpretations be imposed upon the nation, and all within the nation, utilizing political or legal means. The Old Testament is particularly emphasized for how to rule and less the New Testament, except for Revelation. The end goal is to forcibly create God's kingdom right here, right now. If it were just the first part of the equation, there would be no need for this book, or others on the Religious Right. This second marker is the critical one. This is where a spiritual belief becomes a political agenda.

So you can identify a Religious Right follower by his or her beliefs and the politicizing of those beliefs. The following are just the top Religious Right people and their organizations, there exist many more, but these are the leaders of the pack, so to speak.

<u>The Religious Right main players are:</u>

The following quote is taken from a much longer article. The highlights of the article are presented in a quick view format but maintain the original wording.

> *"The Religious Right in America is lavishly funded and politically well connected. … Collectively, these groups raise more than three-quarters of a billion dollars annually, the bulk of it tax-exempt.*
>
> *- The Pat Robertson Empire*
> *1) Christian Broadcasting Network: Budget: $295,140,001*
> *2) Regent University: Budget: $60,093,298*
> *3) American Center for Law and Justice: Budget: $13,375,429*
> *4) Christian Advocates Serving Evangelism (TV preacher Pat Robertson) Budget: $43,872,322*
> *a) The flagship operation is 'The 700 Club'*
> *b) Runs a global television network*
> *c) Founded a university*
> *d) Founded an influential right-wing legal outfit ACLJ.*
>
> *Despite his extreme views, Robertson remains well connected with the GOP power structure in Washington, and congressional leaders and presidential*

candidates often appear on his show. House Speaker John Boehner, for example, gave an exclusive interview in February [2011].

- The Falwell Empire

1) Liberty University Budget: $395,898,255

2) Jerry Falwell Ministries Budget: $4,208,989

3) Liberty Counsel Budget: $1,371,795

- Family Research Council / FRC Action / FRC Action PAC Combined Budget: $14,569,081

1) The Family Research Council has become the nation's top Religious Right group in Washington, D.C. Led by former Louisiana state representative Tony Perkins, the FRC seeks to merge fundamentalist Christianity with government.

2) The FRC is so extreme that this year it was designated a 'hate group' by the Southern Poverty Law Center.

3) FRC sponsors an annual 'Values Voter Summit' that draws leading GOP congressional figures and presidential hopefuls.

4) While managing the U.S. Senate campaign of Louisiana state legislator Woody Jenkins, [Perkins] paid former Ku Klux Klan Grand Wizard and notorious white supremacist David Duke $82,000 for his mailing list.

- American Family Association Budget: $21,408,342

1) The group says it owns and operates nearly 200 radio stations across the country.

2) The AFA is the leading group promoting the Religious Right's phony claim of a 'war on Christmas.'

3) An AFA staffer, Bryan Fischer calls church-state separation a 'myth' and an invention of Adolf Hitler.

4) The AFA has underwritten a series of 'pastor policy briefings' in Iowa, California, Texas and other states intended to organize fundamentalist churches into a potent political machine.

- Alliance Defense Fund Budget: $30,127,514

1) Formed by a group of TV and radio preachers in 1993

2) It was conceived as a funding pool for organizations that worked in the courts to promote theocratic views and undermine church-state separation

3) The organization began engaging in direct litigation and formed a network of sympathetic attorneys nationwide.

4) President Alan Sears says there is no such thing as church-state separation in the Constitution and that the bricks in the church-state wall are being removed "one by one."

5) the ADF sponsors 'Pulpit Freedom Sunday,' a ploy to openly defy federal tax law by encouraging pastors to endorse or oppose candidates from the pulpit.

- Focus on the Family Budget: $130,258,48

1) Although it poses as a family-oriented ministry, the group has always been political

2) FoF is opposed to church-state separation and secular government

3) Although Daly said he wanted to tone down some of the ministry's harsh attacks on gays and others, much far-right political content remains.

4) FOF has a network of 35 state 'family policy councils' that lobby in the state capitals.

- Southern Baptist Convention Ethics & Religious Liberty Commission Budget: $3,236,000

1) The lobbying arm of the nation's largest Protestant denomination, takes stands virtually identical to the Religious Right.

2) The SBC's government action office presses for school-sponsored religion, tax aid to religious schools, reductions in gay rights, limits on legal abortion and other far-right social issues.

3) In the early 1980s became the target of a takeover by Religious Right-style fundamentalists.

4) President of SBC Richard Land works hand in glove with Religious Right organizations to promote a theocratic agenda.

5) Despite the denomination's tax-exempt status, President Richard Land openly meddles in Republican Party politics.

- *Traditional Values Coalition Budget: $9,888,233*

1) Founded by the Rev. Louis P. Sheldon originally to work on 'culture war' issues in California but eventually expanded to become a national organization.

2) Sheldon's daughter, Andrea Lafferty, serves as TVC executive director. She is as partisan and as shrill as her father.

- *Coral Ridge Ministries Budget: $17,263,536*

1) Was founded by D. James Kennedy, a Dominionist TV preacher who died in 2007.

2) Coral Ridge also produced a number of books, DVDs and pamphlets attacking church-state separation. It was known for insisting that America was founded to be a "Christian nation."

3) Since Kennedy's death, the ministry has continued pumping out right-wing political material. Its website looks more like a far-right political site than a portal to a ministry.

- *WallBuilder Presentations / WallBuilders Budget: $1,091,531 (plus*

proceeds from a for-profit arm)

1) Founded by David Barton, a Texan who makes his living promoting bogus 'Christian nation' history to fundamentalist groups.

2) Barton insists that church-state separation is a myth and was never the intention of the founders. He markets books, DVDs and other materials that promote this view and speaks in fundamentalist churches and other venues.

3) Barton helped rewrite Texas' social studies standards, which downplay church-state separation and elevate the 'Christian nation' view.

4) The budget figures for WallBuilder Presentations are somewhat misleading. This organization is a small non-profit Barton runs – but he makes most of his money through a separate organization called simply WallBuilders. This group, which is a for-profit business, is not required to make its financial statements publicly available.

- Concerned Women for America Budget: $11,772,009

1) Founded in 1979 by Tim LaHaye and his wife Beverly to counter the growing women's rights movement, it claims to be the largest women's organization in the country.

2) Today, the group focuses mainly on opposing abortion, gay rights and public education, although it often attacks the United Nations.

3) Like a lot of Religious Right organizations these days, CWA has been adding fiscal issues to its agenda, demanding that government reduce spending. Its current targets include Planned Parenthood, the National Endowment for the Arts, Public Broadcasting and NPR.

4) It sponsors a legislative action committee that is a 501(c)(4) organization and an allied political action committee that in 2010 spent nearly $300,000 endorsing conservative candidates.

- Faith & Freedom Coalition Budget: Unavailable

1) A relatively new Religious Right group founded by Ralph Reed, former executive director of the Christian Coalition.

2) The organization already has developed enough clout to sponsor an Iowa forum for would-be Republican presidential candidates in March of 2011.

3) During the March forum, Reed discussed the possibility of 'replacing the government by force.'

4) The line is apparently part of Reed's stock speech. He also used it at an earlier gathering of Tea Party activists, telling the crowd, '[W]e have not only the right, but the moral obligation to overthrow that government by force if necessary, and form a new government that will protect our rights.'" Rob Boston, "The 12 Worst (and Most Powerful) Christian Right Groups," *Alternet*, May 2, 2011. (Numerical bullets are key points from the original longer text.)

Don't forget: Chalcedon Foundation, Heritage foundation, National Association of Evangelicals (NAE), Center for National Policy (CNP), The National Council on Bible Curriculum in Public Schools, Eagle Forum (founded by Phyllis Schlafly who spearheaded the "Stop the ERA" Movement) and the Eagle Forum Education and Legal Defense Fund as well as the Eagle Forum Political Action Committee, The Home School Legal Defense Association, National Organization of Marriage, National Center for Constitutional studies, Center for Christian Statesmanship, the Institute for Christian Economics, the Center for Reclaiming America, Vision Forum, the Howard Center, and the Family First Foundation just to name a scant few of the multitudes of Religious Right **political** organizations that are successful and very well funded.

The Catholic Church has long been involved in the abortion debate and still maintains its anti-birth control position. A simple vasectomy, or tubal ligation, cannot be obtained in a Catholic church owned hospital (roughly six hundred in the U.S. and growing). Increasingly the Catholic Church has been entering into the Religious Right fight, leveraging their vast resources towards anti-gay stances. They were involved in

California's Proposition 8 alongside the Mormon Church and evangelicals. The Catholic Church in Colorado distributed postcards to congregants to mail to their state representatives asking for a "no" vote on a civil unions bill. They form alliances with recognized Religious Right organizations routinely, and sound progressively more like the Religious Right's choir, singing the same song but with the Vatican's size, influence, and wealth. It is hard to judge just how much they are driving the agenda since they are happy to remain somewhat in the shadows and let the evangelicals be the face of the message. The February 2012 issue of *Church and State* magazine featured an article on it's cover titled, "The Bishops, Obama and Religious Freedom: The Catholic Hierarchy's Bold new Church-State Lobbying Blitz – and How It Might Affect Your Rights". Consider that the Supreme Court has become more Religious Right leaning with more openly devout Catholic justices in the majority.

<u>Religious Right is a network</u>

"*American evangelicalism has mobilized its resources to build networks of powerful people. Through political influence, academic respectability, creative inspiration, and financial capital, evangelicals have put significant resources into not only advancing their goals but also building the movement. More money can lead to the establishment of new organizations, which, in turn, can generate sources of political power. These resources build social networks and fuel cultural production, both essential to the movement. Almost all of this activity has begun within elite networks, within webs of interpersonal relations at the highest levels. Evangelicals would not be nearly as influential as they are today without these powerful networks...Also, being an evangelical can have an empowering advantage: Fellow believers help each other rise in power.*" D. Michael Lindsay, *Faith in the Halls of Power: How Evangelicals Joined the American Elite*, Oxford University Press, 2008.

A social network of "like-minded" people isn't a new idea and in-and-of-itself isn't a bad thing, until it leads to individual rights being violated. Networking by helping other like-minded people obtain opportunities is a common practice (fraternity brothers or sorority sisters help each other to obtain jobs etc.) whether it is a good thing or not. However, when it becomes discrimination based on your personal and private spiritual belief system then it is a caste system and against the U.S. Bill of Rights in our Constitution. This is the Business sphere of the Seven Mountains Mandate and the crucial aspect that is to finance the other six spheres of influence in taking over the culture from the government and courts all the way down to media and entertainment.

That was then

The head to this massive web of Religious Right programs and organizations for many years appeared to be James Dobson, founder of Focus on the Family. The 2008 book *The Jesus Machine: How James Dobson, Focus on the Family, and Evangelical America are Winning the Culture War* goes into detail about Dobson truly being the head to this Religious Right movement. Is there evidence that it is a consolidated effort? That is hard to say. The agendas all seem to take the same drives in the same directions and Dobson certainly appeared to be the most influential among them at that time. But was Dobson the conductor leading the train? All that can be said is – it appears that was the case.

> "*Dobson now* [2008] *works out of an eighty-one-acre campus in Colorado Springs that has its own zip code. He employs 1,300 people, sends out 4 million pieces of mail each month, and is heard on radio broadcasts in ninety-nine countries. His estimated listening audience is* **more than 200 million worldwide**; *in the United States alone, he appears on* <u>100 television stations **each day**</u>." Chris Hedges, "*Feeling the Hate with the National Religious Broadcasters,*" *Harper's Magazine*, May 2005. (emphasis added.)

James Dobson stepped down February, 2009 as the Chairman of the Board for Focus on the Family. Many started shouting how this signaled the end of the Religious Right and their influence. Initially all reports said Mr. Dobson was keeping his radio show and would still be active.

Interestingly, not even a full year passed before James Dobson announced that he was splitting off from Focus on the Family and starting a new radio ministry to be called *James Dobson on the Family*. *"Translation: Dobson wants to pass the torch to his son, Ryan, and couldn't do it at Focus because Ryan Dobson went through a divorce in 2001."* Barry Noreen, "Call it splits: Focus faces competition from Dobson," *The Gazette*, January 3, 2010.

Now we have the Focus on the Family media empire challenged in their position by its creator starting his own radio show to build another empire to pass along to his son. Who will take over as the heir to the Religious Right political web of influence? At the time, son Ryan was believed to inherit that power. Granted Ryan Dobson is a mini-me of his father. Ryan had written the book *Be Intolerant* which promotes an in-your-face-extremism as being the only way for an authentic Christian to live in this world.

Some suggested Rick Warren of Saddleback church who hosted the first 2008 presidential candidate debate, in his church, testing each candidate's worth to lead the nation based on a Christian litmus test. But as popular as Rick Warren has become with his books, he isn't one of the inner circle in the Religious Right. His position on global warming doesn't cut the mustard from the reports.

Not only is the question whether Focus on the Family will continue to be a power broker with James Dobson directly competing for funding with his separate radio show, but will this leave a power vacuum in the Religious Right, and who will fill that vacuum? From all appearances, Focus on the Family and Dobson's new endeavor, James Dobson on the Family, has taken a back seat to the new leader of the Religious Right.

<u>This is now</u>

All indications scream that David Barton who has been dubbed the Religious Right Cowboy has taken the role as the driving force of the Religious Right. Many have not heard of him, so here is an introduction to David Barton:

✗ He created "Wall-builders" with an express mission of rewriting America's history

74

to reflect the U.S. as a Christian product. This is the same message Rushdoony started.

✗ He has made appearances on the 700 club, James Dobson's radio shows, and now has his own radio show.

✗ He is against separation of church and state as being anything more than keeping the government out of the churches, but not the church out of running the government.

✗ He successfully got the Texas Board of Education to require the Bible in public school texts as well as striking references to separation of church and state from public school American history textbooks. The textbooks now cite Religious Right persons, such as Phyllis Schafly, as being important persons of our history.

✗ He was the former co-chair of the Texas Republican Party for eight years.

✗ He is a favorite on the Fox cable channel, having been featured by Mike Huckabee and Glen Beck, and even spotlighted as an expert commentator.

✗ Mike Huckabee said, in his speech at the Rediscover God in America conference on March 26, 2011 (a Christian supremacist conference) "I wish ... all Americans would be forced -- forced at gunpoint no less -- to listen to every David Barton message...And I think our country would be better for it.'" Bob Allen, "Huckabee defends praise for controversial historian," *The Baptist Standard*, April 8, 2011. Accessed May 21, 2011.

✗ The Republican National Committee requested Barton be a liaison to Evangelicals during the 2004 election season.

✗ He is a full-fledged Dominionist / Reconstructionist, pushing that biblical law should be the only law in America.

✗ Barton doesn't believe the First Amendment applies to the states, and that states and localities ought to be able to establish an official state religion.

✗ He was included in a February 7 2005 Time magazine article titled "The 25 Most Influential Evangelicals in America. "

✗ The same 2005 Time article claims "His books and videotapes can be found in churches all over the U.S., educating an evangelical generation in what might be called Christian counter-history. The 51-year-old Texan's thesis: that the U.S. was a self-consciously religious nation from the time of the Founders until the 1963 Supreme Court school-prayer ban (which Barton has called 'a rejection of divine law')."

David Barton has filled the power vacuum left by James Dobson. He has attained celebrity super-star status among the Religious Right, and particularly those far right politicians who have no regard for the First Amendment separation of Church and State.

"Mr. Barton is a self-taught historian who is described by several conservative presidential aspirants as a valued adviser and a source of historical and biblical justification for their policies. He is so popular that evangelical pastors travel across states to hear his rapid-fire presentations on how the United States was founded as a Christian nation and is on the road to ruin, thanks to secularists and the Supreme Court, or on the lost political power of the clergy.

Through two decades of prolific, if disputed, research and some 400 speeches a year on what he calls the forgotten Christian roots of America, Mr. Barton, 57, a former school principal and an ordained minister, has steadily built a reputation as a guiding spirit of the religious right. Keeping an exhaustive schedule, he is also immersed in the nuts and bolts of politics and maintains a network of 700 anti-abortion state legislators....

But many professional historians dismiss Mr. Barton, whose academic degree is in Christian education from Oral Roberts University, as a biased amateur who cherry-picks quotes from history and the Bible.

'The problem with David Barton is that there's a lot of truth in what he says,' said Derek H. Davis, director of church-state studies at Baylor University, a Baptist institution in Waco, Tex. 'But the end product is a lot of distortions, half-truths and twisted history.'

One of his most contested assertions is that the Supreme Court has misconstrued Thomas Jefferson's statement that the First Amendment erected a 'wall of separation between church and state.' According to Mr. Barton, Jefferson meant that government should not interfere with the public exercise of religion — not that public spaces should be purged of prayer. He also cites biblical passages that, he says, argue against deficit spending, graduated income taxes, the minimum wage and costly measures to fight global warming.' " Erik Eckholm, "Using History to Mold Ideas on the Right" *The New York Times*, May 4, 2011.

The article about David Barton in The New York Times came under considerable criticism because it downplayed Barton's skewed history and emphasized instead how sought after he is by Republican candidates. A side effect of the May 4, 2011 New York Times article was Barton was invited on the Jon Stewart's Daily Show. Barton refused to listen, denied the facts Jon Stewart (a shrewd interviewer) presented, and steamrolled his revisionist claims on air. At one point, he proudly claimed nobody has refuted him. Yet, an entire book titled *Liars for Jesus: The Religious Right's Alternate Version of American History* by Chris Rodda was written refuting his twisted claims. After his appearance on Jon Stewart, Rodda's book was offered free to combat his growing propaganda sweep of the nation.

"After watching Jon Stewart's interview of pseudo-historian David Barton last night, and the extended interview online this morning, I wasn't sure what to do. Jon did as good a job as he could against the fast talking Barton -- better than anyone else I've seen debate this very slick character – but missed several opportunities to really nail him.

After nine years of battling Barton's lies, the first three or four of which were spent writing my book, Liars For Jesus: The Religious Right's Alternate Version of American History, *I'm at a point of utter frustration as I watch this Christian nationalist liar get more and more influential. Jon Stewart's interview was the tipping point. If Jon couldn't nail this shameless and obvious history revisionist to the wall, I don't know who can.*

A lie can be told in a few words. Debunking that lie can take pages. That is why my book (which is only the first volume of what will be a three volume series) is five hundred pages long. ...

Then, staring up at the face of Ben Franklin, it was his words, 'Do well by doing good,' that suddenly popped into my head. 'Do well by doing good.' The words of a man who could have become outrageously wealthy by patenting his inventions, but decided to just let everybody have them for the public good have now been stuck in my head for hours, and aren't going to leave until I do what I'm about to do: give my book away for free.

[http:// www.liarsforjesus.com/downloads/LFJ_FINAL.pdf]

Can I afford to do this? No. Do I need to do this? Yes! Will lots of people download it and read it? I have no freakin' idea. It's just what I need to do to be able to look Ben Franklin in the eye on that poster on my wall." Chris Rodda, "Do Well By Doing Good," *Huffington Post*, May 5, 2011.

Chris Rodda has been debunking David Barton for a long time, spending years on laborious research, and personal money to keep the truth alive in the wake of David Barton's misinformation campaign. Please visit her website at www.liarsforjesus.com, and if her book is still free for download, it would be valuable get it immediately.

In the wake of The New York Times article and his appearance on The Daily Show, it seems official that David Barton is now the conductor, the leader of the Religious Right.

So what? Why is any of this important? Why is this religious movement that insists on getting into politics matter, even if it is a radical, extremist movement? Why should you as a mother or father, son or daughter care one little bit? How does this really make any difference? Glad you asked.

Take With You From This Chapter

➢ What the main Religious Right characteristics are.

➢ Who the Religious Right's main players and organizations are and the money at their disposal.

➢ How the Religious Right is a network of influential people and organizations.

➢ How James Dobson was once the leader of the network and how he faded out of the picture.

➢ Who the new leader is and what he has been doing to rise to such super star status in the ranks and his blatant rewriting of the U.S. history.

Chapter 7
Democracy's Greatest Threat

What to Expect From this Chapter

➢ Overview of the United States' form of Democracy.

➢ Religious dominion of the nation is not democracy and why.

➢ Theocracy or theonomy, what are they?

➢ Or something else?

Representative democracy

Democracy is a mix of ancient Greek philosophy of Plato and French political philosopher Rousseau in his treatise The Social Contract. Think of democracy as a contract, where you and I agree upon the rules we will be subject to. In our case, we elect officials to represent us for our overall good. It is consent of the governed, as Rousseau phrased it, or as Abraham Lincoln said in his Gettysburg Address, it is a government "of the people, by the people, and for the people."

The third sentence in the Declaration of Independence says "To secure these rights, Governments are instituted among Men, deriving their just powers from the consent of the governed" clearly linking our founding fathers to Rousseau and his ideal of "The Social Contract". It is important to note here that the Declaration of Independence says that governments are instituted among men. This promotes that our nation was seen as being instituted by men, on the best ideas available from the realm of man. Not inspired by God as the Religious Right have been elevating the United State's founding. Characteristic to the concept of democracy is the idea of equality for all citizens and of a constitution that has a mechanism to be updated (amended) as times change, not an absolute or unchanging legalistic creed.

This idea of a government deriving its power from the consent of the people in a representative democracy places an emphasis on people shaping their country. Democracy invests much in the idea of "the people" having a voice in the direction of the country, voting, and petitioning etc. This idea is just so...humanistic, man centered. Once you get behind their flag waving you find this fundamental difference with the Religious Right.

Contrast the concept of people having a say in their government, with the rigid nature of the Religious Right, and the mandates they want to institute from the Bible. The Religious Right eliminate the possibility of the general consent of those being governed. In fact, they don't care what the people or the citizens want, for that doesn't matter. Rules and laws are predetermined in the Bible, including Old Testament laws. There is a completely different emphasis that says people are sinners, thus untrustworthy to have any say in governing, and the unchanging God has laid out exactly how you are to live, in every aspect. There are no amendments, voting, or petitioning for change, in such a system.

> "*I think Rushdoony revived the Puritanism of John Winthrop and the early New England settlements, which goes back to Calvin's Geneva. He didn't write anything new.*
>
> *Many have never heard of Rushdoony or my dad. Nevertheless, the debate has been framed by the Reconstructionist agenda. Most don't want to hang, stone or burn people like Rushdoony did, but they do believe in doing away with the US Constitution and Bill of Rights and replacing it with theocracy.*
>
> *We should be concerned. This history is the reason that Republicans are so opposed to anything public—public schools, transport, infrastructure, even Amtrak. They believe the government is illegitimate and question everything it does.*" Kristin Rawls, "An Interview with Frank Schaeffer", *Global Comment*, September 8, 2011.

The Bible recognizes governments as necessary to provide structure and order for society, but Jesus never championed that the existing Roman government (pagan to the core) be chucked out for a Jehovah-based government. That probably would have been a popular message for his audiences of the time. Jesus preached about the inner person finding spiritual peace and personal salvation. This is common among the Religious Right, a focus on the Old Testament and its rigidity, laws, economics and only minimally on the New Testament when it's convenient.

In spite of the New Testament's admonition in Romans 13 that all governments are in existence because God established them. The Dominionist agenda mandates nothing less than the government of the United States to be run according to Biblical laws of the Old Testament. It is interesting how Christians who have been released from Old Testament laws by Christ's sacrifice want to put themselves and the entire nation back under that system. The following quote is from a former Religious Right member. She was home-schooled and taught what is increasingly the mainstream evangelical position.

"We were raised to fight the enemy, be that Satan or the environmentalist, socialists, and feminists, to come against them in spiritual warfare and at the polls. This is why Michael Farris, a proponent of Christian Patriarchy and the leader of the Home School Legal Defense Association, founded Patrick Henry College in 2000 to train homeschooled youth in the law and government. There were more interns from Patrick Henry College in the Bush White House than from any other college. Put simply, their goal is to take over the country, instituting godly laws ruling according to Christ's dictates.

While the goal is to take back the world for Christ through the polls, force is never completely ruled out. I was taught that someday the government might take away our rights entirely, become a dictatorship, and crack down on everything we believed in. My father used to point out the armory to us and tell us that that is where we would mount the resistance when this happened. Force, though, was to be a last resort. In the meantime, my family campaigned tirelessly for conservative political candidates and attended marriage rallies, pro-life marches, and second amendment rights meetings. I dreamed of someday being a politician's wife, supporting him in his bids for office and attempts to restore the country to its godly foundation. The world was framed in terms of good versus evil, and I had a role and a purpose." Libby Anne, "My Life as a Daughter of Christian Patriarchy," *Butterflies and Wheels Blog*, September 3, 2011.

It is much closer than the American public thinks. Some people argue that this is just being alarmist, pay no attention to the man behind the curtain. As more time passes, more followers are leaving the Religious Right fold and sounding the alarm. Vyckie Garrison, former Quiverfull and Religious Right adherent, states it bluntly in my interview with her.

"I see the Quiverfull movement accelerating the implementation of patriarchal and Dominionist ideas and policies using an impressive marketing savvy, which is proving frightfully effective among the Evangelical population.

... believers have no interest in maintaining America's democratic political system. Their lives are centered on living 'biblically' and they are determined that all of America follow suit." Vyckie Garrison, email interview with author, August, 2011."

Frank Schaeffer is another voice among several who are speaking out about the danger from first hand knowledge. How many will need to shout from every street corner and venue that this is dangerous to the very structure of our society before citizens, reporters, servicemen, judges and politicians etc. take this seriously?

"America becomes, in this militant biblicism, an agent of God, and all political and intellectual opponents of America's Christian leaders are viewed, quite simply, as agents of Satan. Under Christian dominion, America will no longer be a sinful and fallen nation but one in which the 10 Commandments form the basis of our legal system, creationism and "Christian values" form the basis of our educational system, and the media and government proclaim the Good News to one and all. Labor Unions, civil-rights laws and public schools will be abolished. Women will be removed from the workforce to stay at home, and all those deemed insufficiently Christian will be denied citizenship. Aside from its

proselytizing mandate, the federal government will be reduced to the protection of property rights and "homeland security." Some Dominionists would further require all citizens to pay "tithes" to church organizations empowered by the government to run our social-welfare agencies and all schools. The only legitimate voices in this state will be Christian. All others will be silenced." Chris Hedges, *American Fascists: The Christian Right and the War on America*, Free Press, Jan, 2008.

You and I would in no way be represented or have a voice, we would be specifically told how life will be organized, with no opportunity for amending the rules as situations change over the decades or centuries, because simply put – God's word doesn't change.

The Bible in no way contains even a whisper of a democratic society with no avenue to voice objections or petition for change of those mandated laws. The Bible shows tribal rule (Abraham etc.), then rule by judges and priests mandating laws, and finally a king (Saul, David, and Solomon etc.) ruling over the people. There is no sign of consent "by the people" as to how they will be governed, no contract, no give and take, but rather rigid, set in stone.

"*...Reconstuctionists believe that the Old Testament contains a blueprint for a model society. Accordingly, they would have the government enforce Old Testament dictates through the law. They have no use for democracy as we understand the concept today. They are quick to label those who do not agree with them 'apostates,' 'blasphemers,' or even 'tools of Satan.' The society they burn to create would severely restrict religious freedom for most Americans.*" *...forthrightly call for scrapping the First Amendment and reordering government along the lines of the Bible's Old Testament.*" Robert Boston, *Why the Religious Right is Wrong*, Prometheus Books, 1993.

Democracy's line in the sand

The grand experiment of democracy celebrated two hundred years in America back in 1976. We are one of the youngest countries on this planet, but it would be unforgivable to let democracy quietly slide into a theocracy because the public did not see the incremental shift. Theocracy is a rule by God, or his representative. Although, the Christian Reconstructionists insist that it would be more theonomy, if you have to pin it down. Theonomy is rule by the Bible and its precepts provided by God for all human governments covering civil, church, family, and individuals. It is a fine difference, isn't it? It all amounts to the same thing, not a democracy.

Democracy and the Religious Right's agenda for our political system are polar opposites. The more the Religious Right succeeds in advancing their extremist political concepts, the less and less this country is a democracy.

Power shifts from "the people" having a say, even via the proxy of elected officials, to a few elite religious leaders who direct everything. We move from personal choice to having everything decided for us, from how our children are educated, what our media (TV, movies, books, music, art, magazines etc.) can or can not generate, and how we are governed with biblical laws. The political, social and scientific advances made in the last two hundred years will be rolled back. One might call it the coming of the next Dark Ages. The Religious Right is the greatest threat to democracy. Period.

<u>Taboo</u>

Why isn't the Religious Right recognized as such a serious threat? I believe the answer is in three parts. Religious liberty is ground into us along with a taboo of criticizing anything resembling Christianity to the point that we would rather turn a blind eye than point out this confederation of Religious Right adherents are opposed to a government "of the people, by the people, and for the people." Few people want to be accused of persecuting Christianity or Christians, so they remain silent. However, many evangelicals are saying they don't recognize much of Christ in the Religious Right to begin with. The tactic of proclaiming they are being persecuted for the slightest scrutiny of their intentions continues to be a highly successful deterrent.

"The old left — the Communist Party and its many splinters — used organizing tactics called popular fronts, in which people were recruited through

specific causes into a movement tacitly guided by the Party. Reconstruction has married those Leninist tactics to the causes of the right — abortion, evolution, gay marriage, school prayer. Gary North wrote in 1982, in an effort to reach Baptists, 'We must use the doctrine of religious liberty...until we train up a generation of people who know that there is no religious neutrality, no neutral law, no neutral education, and no neutral civil government. Then they will get busy constructing a Bible-based social, political, and religious order which finally denies the religious liberty of the enemies of God.'... 'All governments are theocracies,' he [Gary DeMar] said. 'We now live in a secular humanist theocracy. I want to change that to a government with God at its head.'" John Sugg, "A Nation Under God," *Mother Jones*, December, 2005.

The taboo of spotlighting an extremist movement, operating under the title "Christian", allows them to freely move into all aspects of culture to influence us. This is called the Seven Mountains Mandate mentioned earlier with the specific goal to take over seven strategic areas of influence (government and law, business and finance, education, media and communication, arts and entertainment, the family, and the church.) Whoever controls the culture controls the thinking and creativity of the people. Southern Baptist Convention Ethics & Religious Liberty Commission puts the cultural brainwashing this way: *"President Richard Land has stated, 'When we convince a majority of Americans that we are right, that's not called a theocracy, that's called the democratic process.'"* Rob Boston, "The 12 Worst (and Most Powerful) Christian Right Groups," *Alternet*, May 2, 2011.

Cold War legacy

Secondly, a public relations campaign dating back to the cold war of the 1950s has been taking place. The idea that Christianity is the basis of American patriotism has taken center stage. The concept that to be a true patriot and good American citizen you must be a Christian began back during the bomb shelter era and McCarthy witch-hunts for communists behind every tree. We see evidence of this with the pledge of allegiance adding the line of "under God" as a patriotic response to Communism.

The Original Pledge of Allegiance read, "I pledge allegiance to my Flag and the Republic for which it stands, one nation, indivisible, with liberty and justice for all."

"Half a century ago, at the height of anti-Communist fervor, Congress added the words "under God" to the Pledge of Allegiance. It was a petty attempt to link patriotism with religious piety. But after millions of repetitions over the years, the phrase has become part of the backdrop of American life, just like the words "In God We Trust" on our coins and "God bless America" uttered by presidents at the end of important speeches." Opinion, <u>The New York Times</u> June 27, 2002.

Rather than stress our government "of the people, by the people and for the people" as our greatest achievement for liberty, to be held up against the communist threat, it shifted to a specific spiritual belief system as our brightest distinction against the communists. In adding the "under God" to the pledge of allegiance, a violation of the First Amendment was taught every day to our children in our federally funded schools.

Religious–Patriotism has been gaining momentum each passing year, shifting the focus away from consensual government as our genius and perhaps best ideal thus eroding our nation's democratic structure. More and more the belief that a true patriot must be a Christian is promoted, that we are only a great nation in proportion to how "Christian" we are.

Please note that the man who was the most damaging spy of all time to the U.S. was a devout Christian, attending mass daily. Robert Hanssen, an FBI agent, sold American secrets to our biggest enemy, the Russians, for 22 years. Robert Hanssen did so much damage with his access to, and subsequent selling of classified information, that we may never tally the damage, nor the lives taken due to his traitorous acts. The fact that he was a Christian did not make him a good citizen.

Being a Christian, or a Religious Right adherent, doesn't make you a good American. Being a patriotic American who loves this country and is willing to give your life for it doesn't mean you are necessarily a Christian either. Sgt. Stewart was killed in action in 2005 when his helicopter was shot down in Afghanistan. He was Wiccan and the request to have the symbol of his faith, a pentagram, on his tombstone, had been denied. Roberta Stewart sued the Veteran Affairs on behalf of her husband, a war hero. Veteran Affairs finally settled the lawsuit, and now the Pentagram is an accepted symbol of faith to be put on service member's grave markers. There are many good citizens who are patriotic to their core who are not Christian. They may follow traditional Native American beliefs, for example. One of the most cunning decisions in World War two was to use the Navajo language as the basis for a code that has never been broken. Would those very same World War II code talkers be any less patriotic because they are not Christian but rather follow their traditional faith?

The Unites States Air Force Academy in Colorado Springs announced in January of 2010 that the chapel had added a worship area for Earth-centered religions (i.e. pagan, Wiccan, and Druid) on a hill in the Academy grounds. To be a good citizen one does not have to be a Christian, and being a Christian does not automatically mean one is a good citizen.

"'*Every servicemember is charged with defending freedom for all Americans, and that includes freedom to practice our religion of choice or, for that matter, not to practice any faith at all,' said Chaplain (Lt. Col.) William Ziegler, Cadet Wing chaplain. 'Being in the military isn't just a job -- it's a calling. We all take an oath to support and defend the Constitution, and that means we've all sworn to protect one another's religious liberties. We all put on our uniforms the same way; we're all Airmen first.'* Staff Sgt. Don Branum, "Academy chapel to add outdoor circle to worship areas", *Unites States Air Force Academy official Website News*, January 26, 2010.

A democratic republic

Thirdly there has been a shift in speaking about our nation. Have you noticed the subtle change in politician's speeches from our being a democracy to our being a republic? In actuality, we are currently a mixture of both democracy and republic with elected representatives providing a structured form of consensual government. The government makes the laws, not a ruling king, and that is the hallmark of a republic. In a republic the government has the power to make laws that all persons, theoretically, are equally subject to, but – and here is the tricky part, may not have been according to the people's consent. The idea of a social contract with the citizens, that "of the people, by the people, and for the people," may not exist in a republic by definition. China is a republic, as was the Soviet Union (Union of Soviet Socialist Republics) consisting of fifteen republic states.

"A government, in which all men, rich and poor, magistrates and subjects, officers and people, masters and servants, the first citizen and the last, are equally subject to the laws

As you start reading this definition, you get the impression that it's going to be egalitarian – based on the equality of all people. But the last phrase gives the game away. Republicanism, according to this definition, isn't about any power that the people have but about the power that they are under. In a republic, says [John] Adams, everybody is equally under the law." Dr. Michael Arnheim, *U.S. Constitution For Dummies,* Wiley, 2009.

This shift in referring to the country as a Republic rather than a Democracy may seem subtle, but it is critical. The Religious Right has the laws for this country ready and waiting via the Bible, the Old Testament, which would still make this a republic, but not a democracy. Again, it would move into a theocracy or maybe a theonomy at best, and many see it as a fascist state at worst. This subtle shift that has taken place progressively in the last ten or so years, of referring to the U.S. as a republic in many political speeches, is important and needs attention. In the United States dealings with other nations, even in armed conflicts, we often hear how our country wants to spread democracy. We aided Iraq to set up a democracy. Democracy always has been the great ideal of our nation. But it appears it has been taken for granted, and complacency has set in.

Theocracy

A theocracy is a form of government with God or another deity recognized as the state's supreme civil ruler or is governed by divine guidance such as the Bible – possibly by officials who are supposedly divinely guided. A republic can be operative within a theocracy, but democracy and theocracy do not go together as easily primarily because of the flexibility of the people in having a voice and even amending the governing rules. Just how would a person amend an Old Testament law from God's unchanging Word? Some current examples of theocracies operating right now would be Iran, Saudi Arabia, Vatican City under the Pope, and Israel. A historical example of a theocracy would be John Calvin-ruled Geneva that Rushdoony and the Dominionist's favor that very closely resembles Iran of today, only with the Bible generating laws.

One of the biggest and perhaps wealthiest advocates and defenders for Rushdoony and Dominionist rule are Howard Fieldstead Ahmanson, Jr. and his wife Roberta. Howard is an heir of the Home Savings bank fortune built by his father, Howard Sr. The junior Ahmanson was revealed as a major lobbying force for Christian conservatives in California and is even called the "financier" of the Evangelical movement. He and his wife have financed school voucher initiatives in California and Colorado, and are primary backers of the Institute on Religion and Democracy, which is attributed with tearing apart more inclusive churches. According to the Los Angeles Times they contributed a reported $1,395,000 to the "YES on 8" campaign in the Proposition 8 campaign to deny marriage equality. They also helped establish Marvin Olasky who made it to George W. Bush's administration and proposed turning federal social outreach endeavors over to churches via the creation of the new White House Office of Faith-Based and Community Initiatives. The Office of Faith-Based and Community Initiatives will be covered more in the Tactics section. This background information is provided so you can understand the next quote, from wife Roberta in an interview to Christianity Today:

"Max Blumenthal took pains to show that the Ahmansons' ultimate goals

are theocratic, a charge that has been widely disseminated. Roberta at once denies and defends the claim: 'I never was, and I don't know if Howard ever was either. I'm afraid to say this, but also, what would be so bad about it?' " Christine A. Scheller, "Connoisseur for Christ: Roberta Green Ahmanson," *Christianity Today*, January 2011.

What would be so bad about it? What is the big deal really? Well it would not be a Democracy for one. Interesting that it is openly suggested in Christianity Today, one of the largest Evangelical magazines, that somehow not having a democracy wouldn't be such a big deal, somewhat like breaking out of your rut and trying a different brand of toothpaste. This shouts that the Religious Right is consciously aware that they are moving away from a democracy.

"The Ahmansons supplied crucial early support to Rushdoony's writing, his early efforts in the creationist movement, and to the establishment of his Chalcedon Foundation (which Rushdoony's son Mark now runs). In 2004 Max Blumenthal traced the Ahmansons' contributions and argued that they were key financial backers in the effort to bring about theocracy as envisioned by Rushdoony. In the Christianity Today piece, though, Roberta Ahmanson is quoted as saying 'I never was (a theocrat), and I don't know if Howard ever was either. I'm afraid to say this, but also, what would be so bad about it?'

...but Christian Reconstructionism is much broader, advocating a very specific ordering of family, church and civil society. It undergirds the religious right's agenda in far more sweeping ways than [just] the anti-gay movement.

When Roberta Ahmanson suggests theocracy wouldn't 'be so bad,' we want to know what she's talking about." Julie Ingersoll, "Theocracy: 'What Would Be So Bad About It?,'" *Religion Dispatches*, January 21, 2011.

Yes, the Religious Right and their agenda to have complete dominion over all aspects of government and life in the United States is in complete opposition to the democratic concept of a government of the people, by the people and for the people.

Religious Right: The Greatest Threat to Democracy

This country is just over 125 years old when European countries have been around centuries longer. Will the Religious Right effectively transform the nation into a theocracy?

"I was a Liberty University-trained evangelical pastor. I was sure that I was right and that every other person not of my faith was going to burn in hell forever. I was taught that we as Christians should take this nation back, only to find out later that we never had it to begin with. ...

I want you to know that the fundamentalist political movement is the beginning of a cultural revolution that will take our nation to a very dark place. You have to understand that this has been methodically planned and is being carried out with the utmost vigilance. In accordance with their worldview, my old friends do not in the least care about what you think. They are against democracy, and they are seeking to end the rule of the majority in our great country.

They truly believe that if you have not been "saved," you are living under a curse and are incapable of knowing what is best and that because of this you should be ruled over. You should also know they do not believe that even centuries-old Christian communities (Catholics, Anglicans, Greek Orthodox, etc.) are "saved," only those who think like they do.

You might be thinking that a minority fundamentalist group of zealots can't really take over the direction of a society. Just look at Iran, or the countless other places where people have allowed this to happen. Are you all really going to sit back and watch this happen? They will begin to attack all sources of accurate information. Public radio was first, next will be museums and then science books. Just listen to them argue against the scientific facts about the peril our planet is facing, because it does not fit in with their ideas. They represent a clear and present danger to our union. ...

The consequences of not acting are dire. We are not just fighting for ourselves. We are struggling to protect the future generations of Americans who will suffer from these ruthless actions of the far right. We are speaking out against the measures being taken against those in our community who can least afford to be marginalized." Jason Childs, "A Former Jerry Falwell Follower Reflects On How The Religious Right Gets It Wrong," *Church and State Magazine*, May, 2011.

Theocracy is the obvious end game, but there are several people who are raising a red flag that it is worse than even that. There are those who are warning of potential fascism resulting from such extremism. The "F" word gets tossed around a lot, but when a respected journalist, Chris Hedges, along with a minister, Robin Meyers, caution of this outcome, it is worth noting.

"Two years ago, in newspaper columns, on the radio, and from the pulpit, I began applying the term Christian Fascism to the direction in which America is headed. Some of my friends and colleagues found the terminology too strong. Others called it 'deeply offensive.' But when Oklahoma Senator Tom Cole's chief of staff recently said that we should not just impeach judges who make the wrong decisions, but 'impale them,' more people started using the f-word without apology.

Fascism, after all, comes in many guises. It was once brown shirts, banned books, and the Holocaust. But it can take many forms, so long as vested interests control the government. All that is required is a nation full of uninformed people whose religion makes them more fearful than enlightened. Fascism thrives on a worldview that is black and white and co-opts the name of a partisan God to fight crusades that pretend to be about moral values but are in fact about preserving and protecting wealth and power.

Christian fascism corrupts both politics and religion by stifling political dissent and debate and by regarding kindness and compassion, the heart of religious faith, as naïve. It dresses up as the savior of Western civilization, asking the rest of us to place our trust in the ability of the Appointed Ones to defend us while actually turning back the clock of human progress." Robin Meyers, *Why the Christian Right is Wrong: A Minister's Manifesto for Taking Back Your Faith, Your Flag, Your Future,* Jossey-Bass, 2006.

Is the great democracy experiment about to fade into history in favor of yet another theocracy, or perhaps even fascism? It is up to you to decide how important a representative government really is and how much your liberties are worth to you.

Take With You From This Chapter

➢ The U.S. is a representative Democracy and a Republic.

➢ The Religious Right is pushing for a theocracy or theonomy, not a Democracy. The Bible and its unchanging laws would rule.

➢ The Religious Right is not recognized as a threat because: it is taboo to be seen persecuting anything Christian, the cold war legacy of claiming Christianity as our greatest strength went unchallenged, there has been more of an emphasis on America being a republic and leaves democracy out.

Chapter 8
Tactics

What to Expect From this Chapter

➢ The various tactics used by the Religious Right so you are not fooled.

➢ When and how they use established propaganda techniques.

➢ Tactics they have cleverly developed or perfected such as how to take over moderate churches.

In a previous chapter, a few of the Religious Right's tactics were introduced such as the "Pink Sheet" which has evolved into "action alert" letters and fund-raising pleas. Now we will look more closely at the tactics employed by the Religious Right. These are successful tactics used to manipulate Christians across the spectrum that the Religious Right may not otherwise consider friends.

The Nation's Conscience

The concept of being the nation's conscience is employed as a good Christian's reason for supporting "Bible" fueled politics. This would make a dictatorial stance appear more caring; it is for the people's own good they just don't know it. So much for a democracy. These extremists are the unsung heroes saving America.

"The culture did not ask for the standards we espouse; in fact, most people reject them. We are attempting to rescue a resistant society that essentially thinks it does not need help, and we must remember this.

In the face of skepticism from many of our fellow Americans, some whom paint us as passé moralists who are out of touch with the modern world, we must strengthen our right to be heard by the culture ... Anytime someone is so bold as to try to be the conscience of a nation, their motives and integrity will be closely examined by skeptics...

Evangelicals are poised to lead such a spiritual awakening. But in addition to seeing souls saved, Christians must aim to reform the culture. This implies new laws, new public policies, and a new focus upon Biblical justice." Tony Perkins, *Personal Faith, Public Policy*, Frontline, 2008.

God's Blessing on the nation in peril

Bible passages proclaiming God's blessing being withdrawn from a sinning nation etc. are abundant as reinforcement of the appropriateness and urgency of taking over politics, the courts, the schools, the media etc. Interestingly every one of those Bible promises to uphold the nation if it is faithful to the one true God are very clearly made to Jewish people – never anybody else. The Religious Right fully believes that passages from the Bible on grafting in the wild Olive branches (Romans 11:17) to mean not just that the Christians were brought into the promises of God but that the conditional blessings are now applicable to the nation United States. There is a big difference between a spiritual inclusion of individual's accepting Christ's salvation to a nation having the same promises as God's chosen Israel.

But such is the deceptive message to get Christians and others to invest into their message, to feel their mission and cause are righteous. Dominionism has no concern for being this nation's conscience. In later chapters, we will go into the Seven Mountains Mandate in more detail. They are seizing control to present a Christian nation to the returning Christ. It is about dominion. Presenting an unsung-savior-of-the-country mask to convince people in the pews that, when they donate money, they are martyrs and true patriots is a successful tactic.

Propaganda

The overall tactics the Religious Right use can be summed up with the terms propaganda and manipulation. But there are specific tried-and-true propaganda techniques that they employ to manipulate, and a few they have devised themselves.

Propaganda goes back to 1622 when Pope Gregory XV. established the "Sacred Congregation for Propagating the Faith" (or spreading the faith), hence the term propaganda – propagating an agenda! No doubt propaganda has been around far longer, just not in such an organized systematic approach. Propaganda traditionally is exercised most in justifying wars and in advancing religious control. Sometimes the more things change the more they stay the same. Propaganda became a household word due to Adolf Hitler's aggressive propaganda machine. In 1933, Hitler appointed a Minister for Propaganda, Joseph Goebbels who worked hard at his job. But it was a man named Edward Bernays, considered the originator of modern Public Relations, who has probably contributed the most to the Religious Right's efforts. He melded psychology and other social sciences to form science based opinion-molding techniques he called "engineering of consent."

> *"Those who manipulate this unseen mechanism of society* [the manipulation of the habits and opinions of the masses] *constitute an invisible government which is the true ruling power of our country."* Edward Bernays, *Propaganda*, Ig Publishing, September 1, 2005.

Propaganda has stood the test of time because it works by taking advantage of human emotions. But as we shall see, it would appear that the Religious Right have taken such concepts to new levels. We are going to dissect the propaganda and manipulation techniques of the Religious Right, so you are better armed to recognize and counter such attempts to control you.

Creeping Normalcy

Have you heard the ancient story of how to boil a frog alive without it ever jumping out of the pan? You gradually turn up the heat, so the frog doesn't realize anything is wrong from the subtle temperature change, until it is far too late. Have you seen the changes taking place around you?

This gradual change is also called "creeping normalcy" for the way a major change can be accepted as normal if it happens slowly, in steady increments, when it would be regarded as objectionable if it took place in a single step or short period. It would seem this is the entire Religious Right approach until recently. Also, affectionately called "death by a thousand cuts," which refers to a political tactic of making gradual changes over time so that nobody notices, or those that do notice do not sound an alarm.

Propaganda rhetoric is critical in this creeping normalcy, and it is rampant all around us. You have probably received emails full of it – and forwarded it on to all your friends and family. Have you gotten the email claiming that crosses are going to be banned from U.S. headstones – with pictures of a European cemetery included? Did you get the email claiming a lawsuit (or something similar) to forbid our soldiers from bowing their heads during prayers? All of them are lies. Many of these emails claim some injustice to Christian freedom or stripping God from this country. They are very deceptive and clever fabrications, along the very same lines as the Pink Sheets mentioned earlier. These emails are full of wild conjecture with no factual basis. Some even claim to have been verified. But unless you take the time and verify the validity of these emails yourself, then you really don't know it is true when you forward it on.

These emails employ a few propaganda techniques that are extremely effective and when combined are powerful.

First, it uses "assertion" that consists of simply stating a debatable idea as out right fact with no explanation or backing up with legitimate documentation.

Secondly, these emails use "testimonials" of a trusted person (your friend or family member who sent the email to you, or you forwarding it on) supporting the suppositions in the email as being truth. You are automatically setup to accept the message without careful scrutiny of the content, because the email sender is a friend or family member.

Thirdly, the "Bandwagon" technique builds upon the testimonial technique. You don't want to be the one in that long line of people in the address line who is not part of the gang.

Finally, the "False Dilemma" technique (also known as "false choice) *"consists of reducing a complex argument to a small number of alternatives and concluding that only one option is appropriate...One group intends to save the country, and the other is out to ruin it. In reality, however, there are usually many possibilities that go unmentioned."* Magedah E. Shabo, *Techniques of Propaganda and Persuasion,* Prestwick House Inc., 2008.

These email propaganda pieces play on people's "Desires and Fears." Your desire to be a good citizen or a good Christian are played upon, and your fear that our country's great legacy shall be corrupted or come to an evil demise, manipulate you toward the emotional reaction of outrage. Beware of emails you receive, and do not pass propaganda along to other unsuspecting people, no matter who sent it to you.

We have shifted without noticing

Before very long the U.S. has moved along the path intended by the Religious Right due to small, incremental and consistent steps. In politics, an often-used tactic is for a politician to try and have their platform be "centrist" or a "down-the-middle" approach. Not really Left or Right. Proof that the Religious Right has been successful in its incremental changes, or creeping normalcy is in how the middle ground in politics and culture has been moving farther and farther to the Right than it was just fifty years ago!

> "*The story of modern American politics writ large is the story of your father's and your grandfather's Republican Party now being way to the left of today's "lefty-est liberals'. If Dwight Eisenhower were running for office today he would have to run – I'm guessing – as an Independent and not as some Joe-Lieberman-in-between-the-parties Independent. He'd be a Bernie-Sanders Independent. In 1982, who passed the largest peace-time tax increase in U.S. history? That would be Ronald Reagan. Who called for comprehensive Health Reform legislation during a State of the Union address in 1974? A program that was well to the left of either what Bill Clinton or Barack Obama ultimately proposed? That would be Richard Nixon. Eisenhower and Reagan and Nixon - they were not the liberals of their day they were the conservatives of their own time. But the whole of American politics has shifted so far to the right in the last 50 years that what used to be thought of as Conservative position is now*

considered to be off-the-charts-lefty. Former Supreme Court Justice Stevens pointed out this whole phenomenon of American Politics shifting to the right. When he told the New York Times this - he said quote

'Including myself, every judge who's been appointed to the court since Lewis Powell [in 1971] has been more conservative than his or her predecessor. Except maybe Justice Ginsburg.' That is the one exception he could come up with. Over the past half a century the center in American politics has gone further and further and further to the right...Historically the process of a Democrat trying to find the center in politics has seen Democrats chasing the center as it moves to the right. The thing that is different about the "left" and the "right" in this country is that there isn't an equal and opposite force on the "left" that is anything like the conservative movement on the right. The Conservative movement exists outside the Republican Party and it serves to constantly pull the Republican Party further to the right.

The Rightward drift of Republican politics from Eisenhower to Nixon to Ford to Reagan to Bush Sr. to Bush Jr. – it's less of a steady drift now than a fast rightward jerking motion. The rightward movement in Republican politics is moving faster, I think, than it ever has before....Republican politics jerking so fast to the right that Republicans are being forced to turn against their own policy positions when the "new" rightwing position dictates it. They can't even keep up within their own careers." Rachel Maddow Show, *MSNBC*, January 26, 2011.

Have you seen the small changes taking place around you in the last fifty years? Have you noticed the Supreme Court justices appointed are farther and farther to the right (Religious Right influenced) of the spectrum?

One more example to demonstrate how a shift drastically to the radical right has been occurring with few noticing is clear in the following statistics. Kevin Coe is an assistant Communications professor at the University of Arizona and the co-author of *The God Strategy: How Religion Became a Political Weapon in America,* and shares these interesting facts:

> "*Examples of trends that are major shifts over the last several decades from FDR forward:*
>
> <u>*References to God in the typical major Presidential address:*</u>
>
> *- From Franklin Roosevelt to Jimmy Carter – about 1 reference to God or one invocation of God.*
>
> *- Since Reagan about 3 references in the typical address (Obama on par).*
>
> *- Jimmy Carter and prior would use broader faith terms (Bible, scripture, blessing, pray etc.) about 6 times typically.*
>
> *- Since Reagan took office use of broader faith terms jumped closer to 11 times typically (Obama is the highest with 13).*
>
> *- Number of times in a presidential term since Ronald Reagan took office that the President would go out and speak to a religious audience roughly tripled from the presidents that preceded Reagan.*
>
> *- The number of times a president would issue a proclamation that dealt with a religious topic roughly tripled too.*
>
> *-Looking at Christmas communications and references specifically to Jesus Christ quadrupled in average Christmas communications.*" Kevin Coe, "Tucson Festival of Books: Politics Panel," BookTV, <u>CSPAN2</u>, May 29, 2011.

The Religious Right has been succeeding quietly without many people raising a ruckus, so much so that the radical movements to the extreme right are occurring faster now. How about the divisiveness that has created a wider chasm between our political parties since the Religious Right entered politics? Have you noticed the center drifting more and more to the right? Do you recognize propaganda emails when you receive them in your inbox? What about fund raising letters or commercials from the Religious Right? The following will assist you to understand the other tactics used by the Religious Right even more.

Disaster is Eminent

To the average person the scariest specter is a vision of a Satan-inspired attack on their freedoms and their rights. Fear is a recurring theme for manipulating masses. Very rarely do people disregard the initial "fight or flight" instinct when they read or hear that they are being threatened and verify facts. The "I'm going to fight this," or the "I am so afraid of this" instantly takes over, and the person who is communicating the disaster has control over directing the person's raw emotion into a desired action.

When somebody believes that disaster is just a breath away, they allow immediate action that they would not otherwise have agreed with, because it is an emergency. The book *Shock Doctrine* by Naomi Klein shows how this immanent disaster fear is used on a national scale to get policies passed that would never pass otherwise. This is the approach to people on the mailing lists of Religious Right organizations. We are in crisis, we are under attack, and the country is about to have every evil take over everyday existence. This is the opposite of the Creeping Normalcy because it works best for getting money quickly, from kids to seniors, through fear.

Social outreach

George W Bush created the Office of Faith-Based and Community Initiatives which was one of many ways that he allowed the Religious Right to have political say and to funnel tax dollars to support faith-based charitable organizations. This government office was a violation of the separation of church and state that received little notice. But true to the creeping normalcy, not many even noticed or realized the massive implications.

There were high hopes that once the Obama administration had settled in, that this highly biased and unconstitutional political office would be disbanded – but no. President Obama has kept the office and continues to say (as he did during his campaigning) that he believes in giving faith-based charitable organizations federal funds. This is exactly what the Religious Right wants – to get tax dollars to distribute as they see fit. If you know what to look for, you can see this being played out on the national stage, as well as in your local government.

"*A similar pattern reveals itself on the state level across the country. More than half of state governments have established their own faith-based offices to distribute funds to religious groups. One of the leaders is Jeb Bush's Florida, home to Lawtey Correctional Institution, the nation's first faith-based prison. Lawtey is ostensibly open to all religions, but in practice almost all the volunteers, both clergy and laymen are evangelical Christians.*

Christian nationalist thinkers have long dreamt of replacing welfare with private, church-based charity that would be dispensed at the discretion of the godly. *Marvin Olasky, one of the chief theorists behind Bush's faith-based initiative...his ideas have helped shape an ascendant movement that is challenging not just church/state separation, but the whole notion of secular civil society and social services based on empirical research rather than supernatural intervention. While Olasky and other supporters of faith-based funding make gestures toward ecumenicism, they're driven by the conviction that the poor and addicted are sinners who need to be redeemed by Jesus Christ...*

Olasky's work thus serves as a valuable guide to the kind of society that Bush and his Christian nationalist backers are striving to create. His vision is a deeply radical one, heavily influenced by Christian Reconstructionism. He yearns for the days before the New Deal, ***when sinners could be denied aid until they repented.***" Michelle Goldberg, *Kingdom Coming: The Rise of Christian Nationalism,* W.W. Norton & Co., April, 2007. (emphasis added.)

Federal money, our tax dollars, should never go to a faith-based charity or faith-based anything because of the separation of church and state. It is unethical to take money from, let's say, a traditional Native American and funnel that money to organizations that believe completely differently. That is setting up a national religion, and it is showing favoritism, which is exactly what our founding fathers did not want.

Why would the Religious Right desire to have dominion over federally funded social programs? The thinking is that sinners are comfortable in their sin and get handouts, or rewards, for the consequences of their sin.

"There is a point when grace ceases to reap a reward, and we are to that point in many areas of societal sin. We have entered a time when His righteous judgments must be evident so that the wicked can learn righteousness....

Government services that assist families are one of our primary areas of need. The Department of Family and Children Services should be staffed entirely by pastors – not official, professional pastors, but those who see this mountain of society as their mission field." Johnny Enlow, *The Seven Mountain Prophecy: Unveiling the Coming Elijah Revolution*, Creation House, 2008.

Taking control of federally funded social programs would allow them to deny aid due to a person's perceived sinful life. You must repent and change your ways to get that helping hand. It seems hard to believe that anybody would actually be so hardened as to let somebody suffer over a perceived sin, but read this example of how this plays out:

"[Colorado] State Sen. Dave Schultheis was the lone "no" vote Wednesday on a bill requiring pregnant women to be tested for HIV so their babies can be treated to prevent the transfer of the virus if the mother tests positive.

He explained that if the babies are born HIV-positive, they will teach society about the risks of promiscuous sex. 'This stems from sexual promiscuity for the most part, and I just can't go there,' the Colorado Springs Republican said. 'We do things continually to remove the consequences of poor behavior, unacceptable behavior, quite frankly.' ...He explained that not protecting people from the consequences of sexual promiscuity can be more compassionate in the long run because others might end up changing how they live after seeing the impact it can have....

The sponsor, Sen. Lois Tochtrop...a nurse, said the risk of transferring the virus from mother to baby during the pregnancy or delivery can be reduced from 25 percent to 2 percent with medication and preventive care." "Springs Lawmaker causes uproar with HIV, promiscuity stand," *The Gazette,* February 25, 2009

This is the truth behind the views of the Religious Right and their politicians. This is just one aspect of the "Government Mountain" in the Seven Mountains Mandate that they intend to take over. You can be denied, for instance, food and clothing at an ecumenical community outreach program that received your tax money on the basis of some presumed sin in your life that has put you in desperate need. Faith-based programs funded solely by donations are one thing, but what is proposed is replacing non-religious social outreach programs with Religious Right run programs using religious criteria to receive tax payer funded federal money.

As an example, let's say out of the taxes you paid last year that $150.00 of your taxes goes to Washington and then gets distributed to a Southern Baptist charity. The charity refuses to give baby formula, diapers, and clothes to a struggling mother and child because she had the baby while single. The charity believes her sin is why she is in need and will not give her aid. If you don't agree with the faith-based-charity's view, and would otherwise have no objection to this child receiving assistance, then you just contributed money (and your agreement) to a form of religious test to receive aid. This is the issue of tax funds going to faith-based charities.

An additional example can be found in the city of Bay Minette, Alabama, that devised an alternative jail-sentencing program that gives non-violent offenders a choice to either go to jail or go to church every Sunday for a year. The Huffington Post reported it in the article "Bay Minette Lets Offenders Choose: Jail Or Church" on September 23, 2011. The recent move to privatize everything the government administers includes prisons. Wakita, Oklahoma may be the first private-for-profit, completely Christian prison, from administrators and guards down through its programs and counseling, all on the tax-payer's dime. Iowa had tried previously, but the separation of church and state prevented that faith-based prison from becoming a reality. As of December, 2010, the Wakita prison was mired in controversy for planning to pay the inmates less than the Federal PIECP program's specified wage-for-the-work program, even though the prison is applying to run under the PIECP federal program.

That President Obama has kept the Office of Faith-Based and Community Initiatives in existence is a bad precedent in light of the First Amendment of our nation's Constitution establishing a separation of Church and State.

What about using a network of hospitals, the epitome of helping your fellow man, as a bargaining chip in politics? It seems unthinkable – doesn't it?

"A proposed bill [Freedom of Choice Act] promising major changes in the U.S. abortion landscape has Roman Catholic bishops threatening to close Catholic hospitals if the Democratic Congress and White House make it law...

'It would not be sufficient to withdraw our sponsorship or to sell them to someone else who would perform abortions. That would be a morally unacceptable cooperation in evil,' said Bishop Thomas Paprocki...He was speaking at the bishops' annual fall meeting in Baltimore in November (2008).

According to the Catholic Health Association of the United States, Catholic hospitals make up 13 percent of the country's nearly 5,000 hospitals and employ more than 600,000 people." Tim Townsend, "Bishop threatens to close hospitals," *The Gazette,* March 5, 2009

Is that a bargaining chip, or is that blackmail? It seems inconceivable to shut down hospitals because the federal government didn't do as you insisted? Additionally, the February 20, 2012 New York Times article, "Catholic Hospitals Expand, Religious Strings Attached," reported that Catholic hospitals are buying up smaller hospitals across the nation. The article says: *"About one-sixth of all patients were admitted to a Catholic hospital in 2010. In many smaller communities, the only hospital within miles is Catholic."* But wait, there is more coercion to witness.

"The Catholic Archdiocese of Washington said Wednesday that it will be

unable to continue the social service programs it runs for the District if the city doesn't change a proposed same-sex marriage law, a threat that could affect tens of thousands of people the church helps with adoption, homelessness and health care... Under the bill, headed for a D.C. Council vote next month, religious organizations would <u>not</u> be required to perform or make space available for same-sex weddings. But they would have to obey city laws prohibiting discrimination against gay men and lesbians." Allison Kilkenny, "Catholic Church Threatens to Stop Feeding Homeless Over Gay Marriage," *The Huffington Post*, November 12, 2009.

This isn't necessarily new behavior; check out your history and the battle between kings and the church during the Middle Ages. The battles that raged in the Middle Ages were between ruling kings down the ranks to feudal lords on one side, versus the Pope, and local priests lined up on the other side. Not only were there power politics between and king and the Pope, but between local dukes and the bishops over any issue. It is the same power politics threatening to close hundreds of hospitals, or refusing to feed the multitudes of hungry and homeless, because the ruling democracy hasn't done as they want. Blackmail, coercion, whatever you call it, it is wrong.

What if all federally funded humanitarian service is handed to "faith based" organizations to run? Services could potentially be denied on grounds of sin in either the person or in a method/procedure. Does it seem that the lesson of the Good Samaritan has been lost somewhere in the political posturing? The story of the Good Samaritan in Luke 10:29-37, did not say that the care of the beaten man found along the road was dependant upon how moral his life was in the eyes of the Samaritan man who found him. The Good Samaritan didn't question the beaten man if he had done something to deserve his condition; the Samaritan man just instantly helped out without questions. Note the concept that denying aid is the best aid, which is actually the "Assertion" propaganda style, that is a highly debatable idea stated as fact. Welcome to the Religious Right's view of social outreach. Democratic? Not even slightly. Again, it is a step closer to a Theocracy.

Demonizing opponents

One long–standing tactic of the Religious Right is to spread propaganda demonizing those they are against or generally keeping the fear of anti-Christian forces up.

A popular method to demonize is the use of a boycott. There have been many boycott campaigns, such as the Disney boycott because they have supposed pro-gay cartoons influencing children, provide domestic partner benefits, and are generally gay-friendly. Proctor and Gamble was boycotted in the 1980s, because of the claim that their logo had demonic symbols. Teletubbies were not officially boycotted, but the effect was the same.

Sometimes it isn't officially a boycott, just spreading of rumors. Remember the claims of back masking rock and roll music with satanic messages? In 2009, we saw CBN and Pat Robertson claim that witches place time-released curses on Halloween candy, no joke.

Paranoid? Actually, it is a long-standing form of propaganda called "Pinpointing the Enemy," and the related practice of "Scapegoating." When religion is involved it elevates propaganda to an us-versus-them syndrome, with all others having an evil intention. The Religious Right excels at demonizing.

In April, 2009 a well-crafted lie in the form of a commercial dubbed "The Storm is Coming" was aired for a few weeks, that caused a great stir that combined demonizing with a couple of other techniques. The lie was that common people were portrayed in the video, people who had been hurt or are fearful because of gay marriage equality legislation. This form of propaganda is called "Plain Folk." *"People tend to distrust outsiders, and the plain folk technique takes advantage of these misgivings by helping the propagandist to appear more like the average citizen. Through this technique, propagandists gain the public's confidence, hoping to manipulate popular opinion..."* Magedah Shabo, *Techniques of Propaganda and Persuasion,* Prestwick House Inc.,

2008.

The Human rights campaign got hold of the actual audition tapes of the *actors* reading the lines for the commercial. That was the lie. The commercial did not portray real people; they were paid to say specific lines convincingly, as if they really were doctors or other professionals. The commercial also painted a doom-and-gloom storm of the century upon us because some people will be able to get married now, and enjoy the same rights as others. The art to the lie was the impending doom music with the near tornado skies in the background. This took advantage of the public's fears, implanting uncertainty and the thought of an unknown future holding terrible threats, because of their vote. The actors said their lines convincingly. The overall message warned the voters they had signed up for the worst times of their lives, for who will survive the dark storm of gay marriage equality! The end result was a glossy production claiming gay people were, without a doubt, the evil scourge upon the good citizens, not good citizens themselves.

Transcript of the commercial:

"There's a storm gathering.

The clouds are dark. the winds are strong.

And I am afraid.

Some who advocate for same-sex marriage are taking the issue far beyond same-sex couples.

They want to bring the issue into my life.

My freedom will be taken away.

I'm a California doctor who must choose between my faith and my job.

I'm part of a NJ church group punished by the government because we can't support same-sex marriage.

I'm a Massachusetts parent helplessly watching public schools teach my son that gay marriage is OK.

But some who advocate for same-sex marriage have not been content with same-

sex couples living as they wish.

Those advocates want to change the way I live.

I will have no choice.

The storm is coming.

Damon Owens (of NOM): 'But we have hope...a rainbow coalition of people of every creed and color are coming together in love to protect marriage. Visit Nation for Marriage.org. Join us.'

Paid for by the National Organization for Marriage, which is responsible for the content of this ad."

This commercial is perfect proof that demonizing, scapegoating, and plain folk propaganda tactics are alive and well in the Religious Right. Actors, not real people, are making statements without any proof or having to back up a single statement (Assertion: stating a debatable idea as proven fact.) The point is to manipulate people into fearing the enemy, in this case, gays. The Religious Right has elevated demonizing beyond propaganda to an art form of despicable lying. Lies, such as that commercial claiming concern, when in reality it covers a murderous mindset sweeping the nation. Perhaps the real storm about to unleash is the Religious Right.

Another classic example of the Religious Right demonizing those who differ, was seen at the Las Vegas event put on by Lou Engle, founder of The Call, on September 25, 2007. At this event, Engle tells how gay people are of the dominion of darkness, translation: part of Satan. This is more than saying they are in sin, just like the guy who has premarital sex. Lou Engle is not a fringe radical either. Lou Engle led the Family Research Council's Prayercast on December 16, 2009, attended by Republican Senators Jim DeMint and Randy Forbes. At a separate event, Lou Engle prayed over and blessed Republican presidential candidates Mike Huckabee and Newt Gingrich at a two day event at Rock Church (Bruce Wilson, *GOP's New Prayer Guru Says Gays Possessed by Demons*, <u>Alternet</u>, December 19, 2009.) Additionally, Lou Engle was the front man for the Mormon-Church–led Proposition 8. Lou Engle IS mainstream

Religious Right, and he believes and preaches that gay people are of Satan's realm. This is literal demonizing of your opposing viewpoint holders!

God is punishing America for sin

A standard tactic being used that may seem very obvious, but still needs to be addressed, is how natural disasters and tragedies of various kinds are claimed to be God judging an unrepentant nation. This is the most basic form of propaganda, pure fear. God's wrath is a most effective manipulation. The following is a quote of Jerry Falwell laying the blame for the 9/11/2001 tragedy:

"But, throwing God out successfully with the help of the federal court system, throwing God out of the public square, out of the schools. The abortionists have got to bear some burden for this because God will not be mocked. And when we destroy 40 million little innocent babies, we make God mad. I really believe that the pagans, and the abortionists, and the feminists, and the gays and the lesbians who are actively trying to make that an alternative lifestyle, the ACLU, People For the American Way - all of them who have tried to secularize America - I point the finger in their face and say 'You helped this happen.'" Jerry Falwell appearance, 700 Club, CBN, Nov, 2001.

~ ~ ~ ~ ~ ~ ~

"[re: Sept 11] How many Americans – let alone Britons or other Europeans – were told that nations are often judged with enemy attacks after God has removed His protection from them? ...Everything that happens has a spiritual root. Perhaps the reason America was attacked in September 2001 was that it had turned away from God, murdered forty-three million babies in abortion clinics, and endorsed homosexuality, among other perversions of God's perfect ways. As mosques were built all over the United States and false gods were worshiped everywhere..." Alan Franklin, *EU: The Final World Empire*, Hearthstone Pub. 2002.

Several Religious Right figures claim that not only the September 11 terrorist attack on the World Trade Center were God's punishment, but also 2004 Indian Ocean Tsunami, hurricane Katrina in 2005, the 2010 earthquake in Haiti, the 2011 tornadoes destroying large regions in the South, and even the BP oil spill, were all due to God's judgment.

This old behavior is seen in many superstitious cultures. Some ancient cultures thought they had to sacrifice virgins to placate their god(s) and keep such disaster from happening. What we see now is a resurgence of superstition and blaming that was commonplace in the Dark Ages when science could not explain why things happened. The Religious Right doesn't consider that there are rational explanations for why these events happen as viable. Do they truly believe that God is punishing regions, towns, areas etc., for not following the Bible and God closely enough, or for perceived sinfulness, or even for allowing sin to occur in their areas? Or is it a great scare tactic?

They are being persecuted

"Moreover, though evangelicals frequently claim to be marginalized and persecuted, they are curiously insensitive to the possibility that minority groups like Jews or atheists might see their efforts as a crusade for domination. For these groups, the alliance between evangelical fervor and power is a scary prospect that conjures visions of religious zealots ruling the country with intolerant force." D. Michael Lindsay *Faith in the Halls of Power,* Oxford University Press, October, 2009.

It was pointed out previously how the Religious Right feel laws and culture that are not in alignment with their belief system are limiting of their freedoms, and are an imposing of other beliefs on them. They actually believe *they* are the ones under attack.

Janet Folger echoes the standard Religious Right cry in her book, *The Criminalization of Christianity: Read This Book Before It Becomes Illegal,* in which gays and lesbians are the culprits, along with feminists, the Human Rights Campaign, the ACLU, etc. who are systematically persecuting *them*. That isn't the only book to promote such a mindset. There are scores of them authored by religious right persons: *Persecution: How Liberals Are Waging War Against Christianity,* by Limbaugh, *The Marketing of Evil,* by Kupelian, *The ACLU vs. America: Exposing the Agenda to Redefine Moral Values,* by Sears, and *The Homosexual Agenda: Exposing the Principal Threat to Religious Freedom,* by Sears etc. All these books promote the same sentiment, that anything good, pure, or wholesome (they believe they have a monopoly on) is under attack by the gays, feminists, pro-choice, and human rights people. The market place is flooded with Religious Right authored books that claim everything Christian is under attack and is being singled out. They claim they are the ones being victimized.

"Just like what Nazi Germany did to the Jews, so liberal America is now doing to the evangelical Christians. It's no different. It is the same thing. It is happening all over again. It is the Democratic Congress, the liberal-based media and the homosexuals who want to destroy the Christians. Wholesale abuse and discrimination and the worst bigotry directed toward any group in America today. More terrible than anything suffered by any minority in history." Molly Ivins, "Pat Robertson Interview", *Fort Worth Star-Telegram,* September 14, 1993.

~ ~ ~ ~ ~ ~ ~

"Chris Matthews: 'Evangelical Christians met up for a Washington event called 'War on Christians and Values Voters' of 2006 this week. Speakers gave impassioned testimonies about Christian persecution across the country...Tony, do you believe that Christianity is under active assault politically right now?

Tony Perkins, President, Family Research Council: ...Well, clearly, it's not a war on Christianity like we talked about last week with Abdul Rahman and what he was under, but it's a hostility nonetheless. I mean, just last week in San Francisco, 25,000 young evangelicals gathered there for a rally, and the board of supervisors passed a resolution. It's first time I've ever seen a legislature pass a resolution condemning them as a right-wing Christian fundamentalist group that spreads hate. That was the official language. I mean, you see that. You see Indiana where the legislature there is no longer allowed to open their sessions in prayer, if they pray in the name of Jesus.

I mean, you ask any parent in America today, they're concerned. Their kids cannot pray in school, graduations, football games, no prayer, even the pledge... Well I agree, there's none being thrown to the lions today but I'm not for allowing those cubs to grow up to become adult lions." Tony Perkins, "Chris Matthews Hardball," *MSNBC*, March 29, 2006. (Emphasis added.)

In the clamor about persecuting them, it reminded me of a term in Psychology – projection. Psychological projection (or projection bias) is a defense mechanism in which a person projects their own unacceptable or unwanted thoughts and/or emotions to others. Could it be that all their screaming about being persecuted is in actuality projecting their own tendency to be intolerant and dictatorial onto others? It may not be projection in the classic psychological sense, but most everything they take offense at, is exactly what they are doing, and in most cases, excel at.

"'Unwittingly, many people who preach pluralism offer us a new caste system that makes Christian citizens 'political untouchables.'" Tony Perkins *Personal Faith, Public Policy*, Frontline, 2008.

Michelle Goldberg shares in her book *Kingdom Coming: The Rise of Christian Nationalism,* an account of typical Religious Right twisting, or ignoring, of the facts. Jerry Falwell made a big issue of a Massachusetts school claiming that the American Civil Liberties Union (ACLU) had supported the suspension of seven high school students for sharing religious messages when passing out candy canes. This supplied lots of airplay blaming the evil ACLU. But the facts were actually that the ACLU defended, via a submitted brief, that those seven students had a right to their freedom of speech. But having the ACLU as the bad guys stirs up more anger and triggers more donations than the truth.

Marketing savvy

Many find the notion that the Religion Right and their aligned churches are utilizing hard-core marketing and public relations for their public face as ludicrous. You must be savvy and use stealth when you are trying to take over an entire culture. You need marketing, the ultimate tool for shaping minds. They have a very carefully constructed message that hides their agenda.

> *"Jerry Falwell, now dead, was a Southern Baptist, as is Rick Warren. Pat Robertson is Pentecostal. Using methods pioneered by Billy Graham, also a Southern Baptist, the so-called "evangelical" movement has put together a formula for building large churches that is less informed by the theology of the Reformation than a desire for cultural power, big audiences, nativistic religion, and a prosperity gospel (lots of money in the offering plates). The religious right has become an Americanized and commercialized form of religion, far from the historic traditions of the Protestant Reformation. It has over these past decades aligned itself with a particular political party in this country, the Republican Party, which has dominated politics since the 1968 election of Richard Nixon."* Ed Knudson "On Religion, Abortion, and Politics: Dr. George Tiller's Christian Ethics," *Religion Dispatches*, June 18, 2009.

"Family Values" is a marketing tactic picked up in the early years of the Religious Right's solidification of the many varying pieces and parts of Christianity in America. It is a romantic and nebulous term, and a dangerous one. When the term "traditional family values" is used, you think of happier times, perhaps subconsciously linking the phrase to the television programs "Leave It To Beaver," or "The Waltons," in your mind. They are counting on your fear of a complex and ever-changing world, and then deceptively offer to restore things to supposed simpler times. What the Religious Right is marketing to you under the guise of family values and what that conjures up for you is not at all what they intend with their political actions.

Public Relations and marketing strategies are very important to the Religious

Right, as the following quote shows.

> *"Pick a trend – megachurches, seeker churches, satellite campuses, vacation Bible school, children's church, affinity group ministries (e.g., ministries for singles, women, men, young marrieds), contemporary worship music, big screen projection systems, EFT giving, cell groups, downloadable sermons, sermon outlines in bulletins, Alpha groups. All of the above have simply been attempts to rely on marketing strategies to perform the same activities in different ways or places, or with particular segments of the aggregate population."* George Barna and Frank Viola, *Pagan Christianity: Exploring the Roots of Our Church Practices*, January, 2008.

Marketing strategies are not utilized just to build up attendance and membership, it is the face the Religious Right promotes with clever terms such as "traditional family values," "Jesus is the Reason for the Season," and "WWJD?" etc. They are marketing mantras, just like a fast food restaurant or a car insurance company.

Never underestimate the marketing prowess of the Religious Right. In *Shopping for God: How Christianity Went from In Your Heart to In Your Face,* James Twitchell points out that Evangelicals have marketing savvy and know how to package the goods for the greatest appeal. Thus, we see Mega-churches that have a sustained average weekly attendance of 2000 people or more at their church services (the largest US mega-church averages 35,000 weekly attendance) and Hartford Institute for Religion Research's 2005 poll of Protestant churches shows that 56% of mega-churches claim to be Evangelical. This amounts to a captive audience to market the Religious Right political agenda to…and a captive audience to get finances from, for the advancement of that political agenda.

Their fund-raising letters are professionally done to get your blood boiling, or get you scared so you will donate willingly to the cause. Pamela Mason in The Gazette newspaper article "Religious Extortion of our City," on July 3, 2009, printed that just the one city's churches and religious organizations spend $895,056 for professional fundraisers services, in one year. That $895,056 was most likely to professional companies to construct their mail out campaigns and other literature to utilize the standard deck of propaganda techniques to wrench money from each person receiving their fund-raising letters.

Consider the 2010 advertising campaign to repair the Mormon Church's suffering image after it was discovered they bankrolled California's infamous Proposition 8, a bill introduced to prohibit same-sex marriage. The ad campaign consists of several versions, all of which are high-end productions where the viewer is introduced to a plain folk person that they can like and identify with. At the very end of the commercial, the person admits "...and I am a Mormon." These are great works of marketing and public relations.

There you have a multi-million dollar marketing blitz for the Religious Right to sway average people that there is nothing out-of-the-ordinary in the Mormon Church.

"These new ads dodge religion almost altogether in favor of a simpler message: We're not weird. In the ad below, pro surfer Joy Monahan says, 'I'm a surfer, a woman, and a woman's longboard champion. And I'm a Mormon.'

...Campbell says the ads are a response to worsening public perception of Mormons over the past few years...Campbell says the media framed the controversy over the [California Proposition 8] *initiative (which a federal judge overturned last week) as 'Mormons vs. gays.' He said that the church 'has a lot of work to do to improve that reputation.'*

...LDS spokesman Scott Swofford said the church has run ad campaigns for 25 years..." Liz Goodwin, "In new TV ads, Mormons pitch message to Middle America," *Yahoo News*, August 11, 2010.

Another significant tactic is how the Religious Right is redefining our language. What "patriot" used to mean is no longer the case thanks to the Religious Right. It used to be that patriot meant keeping the nation's interests a priority, not keeping the Religious Right's drive for dominion as your priority. You can read Tony Perkins and think you agree wholeheartedly with him, but do you really agree with what he stands for?

"Dominionists and their wealthy, right-wing sponsors speak in terms and phrases that are familiar and comforting to most Americans, but they no longer use words to mean what they meant in the past. They engage in a slow process of 'logocide,' the killing of words. The old definitions of words are replaced by new ones. Code words of the old belief system are deconstructed and assigned diametrically opposed meanings. Words such as 'truth,' 'wisdom,' 'death,' 'liberty,' 'life,' and 'love' no longer mean what they mean in the secular world. 'Life' and 'death' mean life in Christ or death in Christ, and are used to signal belief or unbelief in the risen Lord. 'Wisdom' has little to do with human wisdom but refers to the level of commitment and obedience to the system of belief. 'Liberty' is not about freedom, but the 'liberty' found when one accepts Jesus Christ and is liberated from the world to obey Him. But perhaps the most pernicious distortion comes with the word 'love,' the word used to lure into the movement many who seek a warm, loving community to counter their isolation and alienation. 'Love' is distorted to mean an unquestioned obedience to those who claim to speak for God in return for the promise of everlasting life. The blind, human love, the acceptance of the other, is attacked as an inferior love, dangerous and untrustworthy.

'The goal must be God's law-order in which alone is true liberty' wrote Rushdoony in Institutes of Biblical Law:

Whenever freedom is made into the absolute, the result is not freedom but anarchism. Freedom must be under law or it is not freedom...Only a law-order which holds to the primacy of God's law can bring forth true freedom, freedom for justice, truth, and godly life.

Freedom as an absolute is simply an assertion of man's 'right' to be his own god; this means a radical denial of God's law-order. 'Freedom' thus is another name for the claim by man to divinity and autonomy. It means that man becomes his own absolute. The word 'freedom' is thus a pretext used by humanists of every variety...to disguise man's claim to be his own absolute...If men have unrestricted free speech and free press, then there is no freedom for truth, in that no standard is permitted whereby the promulgation or publication of a lie can be judged and punished..

As the process gains momentum – with some justices on the Supreme Court such as Antonin Scalia steeped in this ideology – America starts to speak a new language....

Terms such as 'liberty' and 'freedom' no longer mean what they meant in the past. Those in the movement speak of 'liberty,' but they do not speak about the traditional concepts of American liberty – the liberty to express divergent opinions, to respect other ways of believing and being, the liberty of individuals to seek and pursue their own goals and forms of happiness. When used by the Christian Right, the term 'liberty' means the liberty that comes with accepting a very narrowly conceived Christ and the binary worldview that acceptance promotes." Chris Hedges, *American Fascists: The Christian Right and the War on America*, Free Press, 2008.

It is important to recognize that every word the Religious Right speaks or writes must be scrutinized and questioned. If the common language we communicate with is hijacked, they can promote one vision in their campaigns and politics according to the old meaning of words but in reality mean something completely different. Communication basics are that the individuals communicating must be speaking with the same word meanings. This is deliberate miscommunication and deception.

As for the other side to the marketing coin, if Hollywood can expertly wrench a tear from you on every episode of a TV series (like classic "Little House on the Prairie" or "Touched by an Angel") then you know the hired marketing companies will get the Religious Right the maximum donations. You can bet your paycheck that marketing and fundraising companies are equally adept at getting the optimum emotional response from supporters, but facts are unimportant in the equation.

One state at a time, one issue at a time

Naturally, it is more effective to get federal laws that impact all states in one brush-stroke, rather than expend resources state-by-state. The Religious Right is very cunning in this. They try every back door method to legislate their worldview. This may not be propaganda in and of itself, but it is their strategic approach.

In the 2008 elections, Colorado had a ballot initiative to amend the state constitution to declare that "personhood" begins at the moment of conception. If it had passed, it would have guaranteed that fertilized eggs receive full rights secured in the Constitution. Because it was during a major election cycle, the initiative got a lot of attention and was defeated. In true Religious Right political fashion, they took this idea to Montana and got the first personhood amendment passed quietly through the house, but not the state senate. Also, the very same ballot initiative was on the ballot again in Colorado in 2010. The personhood movement felt that Mississippi, in the heart of the Bible belt, might pass such a state amendment. In 2011, Mississippi fought the same battle and the personhood amendment failed to pass again. They will continue until they hit upon the message that persuades voters to pass it. It is up to voters to be aware.

You see that team of lawyers and the massive network of Religious Right organizations at work here - as well as their well funded political action committees.

It is critical to understand that whoever the US President may be, does not stop the Religious Right. The President being non-Religious Right may potentially make them more deceptive, use more marketing to package their message. They fall back to the position that has been very successful, to fight each individual issue on a state-by-state basis. Enormous amounts of money, raised by these Religious Right organizations, are pumped into moral battles on a state-by-state basis. After all, this is a war to take the United States for Christ.

Religious Right: The Greatest Threat to Democracy

"The Religious Right has developed an extraordinary infrastructure especially at the state level, that will restore and replenish the movement as the founding generation of Religious Right leaders pass from public life, and will regroup in the wake of national Republican Electoral losses in 2008.

Win or lose from election to election, whatever its ups and downs, the Religious Right is on a mission, or rather a cluster of interrelated missions. The missions are religious in nature and transcend not only electoral outcomes but the lives of individuals and institutions. This is much of the source of both the movement's resilience and its development of a vast capacity to move people and shape events to raise up leaders, and to field effective organizations able to wage electoral campaigns at all levels and effectively use the process of state ballot initiatives to drive wedge issues and, ultimately, their legislative and constitutional agenda.

So let us be clear. The Religious Right will be a major factor in American politics for at least as long as the life of anyone reading these words." Frederick Clarkson, "The Culture Wars Are Still Not Over," *The Public Eye*, Winter, 2008 Vol. 23, No. 4.

The fight over the marriage rights is another example of this tactic. While attempting to pass a marriage amendment to the United States Constitution, they draft the same amendment legislation state-by-state. The Religious Right, the Mormon Church in this case, was successful in getting a marriage amendment to the Hawaii state constitution and then moved on to California with Amendment 8. The documentary *8: The Mormon Proposition,* by director Reed Cowan, details how the Mormon church is going from state-to-state with this agenda. The Mormon Church reached out to the Evangelical church to become the front people for Proposition 8, since it was perceived that the public in California wouldn't respond well to the Mormon Church leading the effort. It worked. In the 2008 elections, the Right won big in three states, getting state constitutional bans on same sex marriage. Who is in control of the national level House and Senate or who sits in the White House has little to no effect on how they are pushing their agendas through on the state levels. They move steadily forward proposing legislation state by state and an issue at a time. They have the funding to push legislation and corresponding media blitzes in several states simultaneously, that drains other activist resources trying to get their message out to counter the misinformation and scare tactics. But the prospect of handing the White House, and the nation, to a Religious Right President is perhaps the most counter-productive action that could be done, nonetheless.

Going International

The Religious Right isn't solely focusing on the United States, but is influencing other nations too. The Religious Right grasps that cultural influences easily cross borders with the advent of the internet and social networking websites. It is more than just a cross-pollination of cultures at work for the Religious Right.

"The Great Commission was to 'make disciples of all nations.' It was not to 'make disciples of all souls.' God is interested in the nations – a word mentioned over three hundred times in the Scriptures." Johnny Enlow, *The Seven Mountain Prophecy: Unveiling the Coming Elijah Revolution*, Creation House, 2008.

So they are ramping up their contact with the Catholic Church in Rome and other countries to safe guard their efforts here at home, or perhaps expand their power base. They want to be the ones who impact other nations (utilizing all the same tactics abroad.)

"The American Christian right, increasingly seeking influence abroad, has recognized that this anxiety over shifting national identities creates fertile terrain for spreading its ideology of traditional sexual morality as a quick fix for a postmodern age...

The WCF [World Congress of Families] is just one channel for this goal: a locus for heavyweight US conservative actors such as the Heritage Foundation, the Family Research Council, Concerned Women for America and James

Dobson's Focus on the Family – a Who's Who of the American Christian right – to network with representatives from the Vatican, conservative Christians from developing nations and a smattering of Muslim groups seeking allies to fight gay and women's rights at the United Nations. The result is the spread of US culture-war tactics across the globe, from the Czech Republic to Qatar – where right-wing Mormon activist and WCF co-founder Richard Wilkins has found enough common cause with Muslim fundamentalists to build the Doha International Institute for Family Studies and Development.

'The new view is that in order to create and defend a profamily culture, we also have to have a friendly international environment,' says Carlson. 'So you see something fundamentally new: the social conservative movement going global.'... [Austin] Ruse himself, not given to understatement, imagines the global Christian profamily alliance is 'unlike anything we've seen since the Reformation.' A bloc like this, he boasts, is capable of mayhem: 'Picture the documentaries about Africa; the hyenas going after the wildebeest. You're just surrounded. We are everywhere, doing everything.'" Kathryn Joyce, "Missing: The 'Right' Babies," *The Nation* February 14, 2008

For more on the Religious Right's global agenda, you might want to read the book *Born Again: The Christian Right Globalized* by Jennifer Butler, or the book *The Next Christendom: The Coming of Global Christianity* by Philip Jenkins. The following is from the inside cover of Mr. Jenkins' book, which is used here for its summation of such a bulk of information:

"Philip Jenkins' The Next Christendom: The Coming of Global Christianity is the first book to take the full measure of the changing face of the Christian faith....Within a few decades Kinshasa, Buenos Aires, Addis Ababa, and Manila will replace Rome, Athens, Paris, London and New York as the new focal points in the Church's universality....

Moreover, Jenkins shows that the churches that have grown most rapidly in the global South are far more traditional, morally conservative, evangelical, and apocalyptic than their northern counterparts. Mysticism, Puritanism, belief in prophecy, faith-healing, exorcism, and dream visions – concepts which more liberal western churches have traded for progressive political and social concerns – are basic to the newer churches in the South. And the effects of such beliefs on global politics, Jenkins argues, will be enormous, as religious identification begins to take precedence over allegiance to secular nation-states. Indeed, as Christianity grows in regions where Islam is also expected to increase – as recent conflicts in Indonesia, Nigeria, and the Philippines reveal – we may see a return to the religious wars of the past, fought out with renewed intensity and high-tech weapons far surpassing the swords and spears of the Middle Ages." Philip Jenkins, *The next Christendom: the Coming of global Christianity*, Oxford University Press, 2002. Bookjacket.

What do you think? As the preceding quote points out, the allegiance isn't so much to the country they live in, but to their conservative faith. This gives us a prime example of the need to keep church and state separate. It might sound like a way to global peace if the world were not so concerned about borders and rather were centered on spirituality. The world has been-there-done-that with the Roman Catholic Church in history, and it did not bring peace, but the horrific and bloody Crusades. Also, remember that it is not a Democratic structure they desire, either.

Canada is a close neighbor and is experiencing the Religious Right's easy access to their country clearly creating a political divide based on religion as in America.

"The cross-border distribution of [Stephen] Bennett's fiery speech is just one small illustration of the way dozens of powerful conservative Christian networks in the U.S. are helping shape Canada's cultural and political landscape.

Many U.S. evangelicals have been galvanized by recent developments in Canada -- particularly Parliament's July vote in favour of same-sex marriage, but also by Canadian political efforts to legalize marijuana and maintain wide access to abortion, as well as Ottawa's refusal to join the U.S.-led war against Iraq.

Scholars and pollsters who track the links between conservatives in the two countries say the American religious right has gained more clout in Canada in recent years, particularly by bolstering right-wing elements in the Conservative party.

Big-name American Christian conservatives are warning the faithful that what is happening in Canada could soon infect the United States.

'The U.S. religious right certainly sees Canada as a place where liberalism runs amok,' says Bruce Foster, head of the political science department at Calgary's Mount Royal College. 'And they're saying if Canada is going to hell in a moral handbasket, it will happen in the U.S. It's the slippery-slope argument,' says Foster, whose PhD explored the link between U.S. and Canadian religious groups.

Roger Robins, a political scientist at Marymount College in California, says the numerous American evangelicals trying to sway the Canadian scene want to remain below the public's radar.

'There's so much interaction between religious conservatives in the two countries. There are so many cross-border networks. So many groups,' says Robins, a former Mennonite pastor who has worked in Canada and specializes in North American religious politics.

'The Americans are smart enough to know not to be seen as too pushy. And Canadians also don't want to be viewed as clones of American evangelicals.'

Some of the more important Christian organizations that have direct or indirect cross-border links, say the scholars, include Focus on the Family, the Evangelical Fellowship of Canada, Real Women, the Pentecostal Assemblies of Canada, Campus Crusade for Christ, Youth for Christ, various Mennonite and charismatic denominations, and dozens of Canadian evangelical colleges that are well populated with American students and faculty." Douglas Todd, "U.S. Religious Right moving into Canada," *The Vancouver Sun*, July 30, 2005.

Canada has become the first, closest, and perhaps the easiest for the Religious Right to colonize. How is this obvious Religious Right colonization in established countries sold to the person-in-the-pew? Colonization is sold as advancing the moral fight wherever evil is found, even within another sovereign country, and securing the world from terrorists as only the Religious Right can effectively do. Let's see how Tony Perkins can spin it in his book:

"We recently attended a meeting in New York City with fifty or so bishops and church leaders from Europe and Africa. Their core message to us was this: radical Islam is on the march around the world, and the church in America is a key player in meeting this challenge. They asked us to redouble our efforts at personal evangelism around the world. This is a great example of what everyday believers can do to truly fight terrorism over the long term. We should support ministries that go into the Middle East and present the gospel and missionaries who evangelize Muslims in this country.

There is a strong public policy element to this as well. Many countries, including allies to the United States, do not allow Christians to live and move freely. An example is Saudi Arabia, which is a close ally but which will not even allow a church to be built within its borders...We have to flex our muscle, because if Christian witness is excluded from these countries, then radical Islam will grow and terrorism will flourish. We must demand that our government open doors for evangelism in places where Muslim rulers have slammed that door shut." Tony Perkins, *Personal Faith, Public Policy*, Frontline, 2008.

In this quote we see bishops, and other anonymous church leaders throughout the world, pleading for the American churches to save the world by evangelizing. Evangelizing in countries that specifically don't want that activity, under the guise of combating terrorism. That can create a holy war mentality. The quote also promotes missionaries to Muslims in America, beyond just sharing Jesus with your neighbor, but full-blown missionary work to the Muslim community in the U.S. Further, Tony Perkins believes the U.S. government should demand that our allies open their doors for missionary efforts, when those countries refuse them, thereby risking shaky critical international relations. What about saving this country from the Christian extremists here at home who would risk our country's precarious and delicate international relations that are aiding us with valuable reports on terrorist activities, just so they can go into a country that doesn't want them, to recruit more members?

The Religious Right has been on the move, and you didn't even know it. Well you know it now.

Recently, we have witnessed the Catholic Bishops rage over a law that already existed in several states, for birth control to be covered free of charge in health insurance plans. This is extremely important, and not for the reasons most have been led to believe. We already have several states with *conscious objection* laws for pharmacist technicians who claim moral objections to refuse filling prescriptions for birth control. Now, the Catholic Church is attempting to set a devastating precedent, by elevating the church as being exempted from a law, essentially above the law. The church wants to be excluded from a law. This is a serious violation of the first amendment.

It was discussed prior how America is a Democratic Republic. As a Republic, everyone is equally under the same laws. This is a direct challenge to the first amendment, because it shows favoritism to a church, and it is a death-blow to our Republic. Yet, some women are arguing against their own best interests of birth control, and claiming the church is being persecuted. This is a testament to the successful tactics of: 1) claiming they are the ones being persecuted and 2) the propaganda machine that is in place successfully manipulating people.

The results from such a precedent could be sweeping. Mormons could challenge laws keeping them from maintaining several wives. Child brides could be allowed again, child abuse under the spare-the-rod-and-spoil-the-child could be seen. When any church is viewed as above the laws we all must abide by, the basis for our cohesive legal system has been annihilated, and the nation handed over to the various churches.

The important thing is to protect your rights in your city, state, and nation. This book will help you to understand the signs and tactics, but it is up to each person to get involved locally, and nationally, in the schools, courts, and politics.

Take With You From This Chapter

➢ America has shifted to the right incrementally, and the shift went largely unnoticed.

➢ The Religious Right uses propaganda techniques and fear to gain finances and support quickly.

➢ They are great at demonizing their opponents, and claiming they are the ones being persecuted.

➢ The Religious Right uses marketing, has changed the meaning of words to further their agenda, and has moved to international meddling.

➢ They are unsung heroes saving America from itself; whether the citizens want it or not is irrelevant, for dominion is the end-game.

Section 3: The Resulting Worldview

In this section ...

The worldview that the Religious Right engenders and promotes is examined.

Chapter 9
We Obey a "Higher Law" Ethics

<u>What to Expect From this Chapter</u>

➢ The concept of violating national laws because they are at cross-purpose with biblical principles is examined.

➢ From religion in schools, to violence against abortion providers, how the Religious Right encourages civil disobedience.

➢ No other movement or group has so successfully flaunted the laws of the nation, and yet fervently proclaim themselves true patriots.

<u>Obey God rather than men</u>

The motto "live and let live" simply doesn't have any meaning within the Religious Right. They have made it clear that to give any ground whatsoever to feminists, gays, or humanists is unimaginable. And there in lies a huge danger.

"Tolerance is a kind of watchword of those who reject the concept of right and wrong. It's a kind of desensitization to evil of all varieties. Everything has become acceptable to those who are tolerant." James Dobson, Focus On The Family radio broadcast, Nov 4 1996

Acts 5:29, *"But Peter and the apostles answered and said, 'We must obey God rather than men.'"* This scripture verse has provided the Religious Right carte blanche to do as they see fit in their interpretation of what God would have them do. Civil law ultimately means very little because they feel they must answer first and foremost to God's laws and views. Even the hero of the reformation, Martin Luther, wrote in his pamphlet *The Freedom of a Christian,* that a Christian is free of earthly authority's claims on them. But Martin Luther's point was to do beneficial works for our neighbors and community as a "paying forward" for one's salvation and joy, rather than because a law says so.

As early as 1962, the US Supreme Court handed down rulings that prayer and reading of the Bible in public schools is unconstitutional, and ever since then there have been "*...hundreds of overt and intentional violations of those decisions, leading to dozens of federal court cases in which the judges and justices have reaffirmed the Court's original findings.*" Robert S. Alley, *Without A Prayer: Religious Expression in Public Schools,* Prometheus Books, 1996. They have blatantly disregarded what the laws have said.

Abortion and breaking the law

It is especially with abortion that the concept of not being held to a worldly legal system is seen starkly. Abortion may be legal, but they consider it so against God and the Bible, they feel justified in advocating and carrying out domestic terrorism, in all its ugliness. They have no regard for the people they kill or torment. They have no respect for the law they are breaking, because the legal system allows abortions, thus they are above the law.

How about the attacks against abortion providers? There have been 8 murders, 17 attempted murders, 41 bombings, 100 butyric acid attacks, 656 anthrax threats, and 176 arsons against abortion providers since 1977, at this writing. They are still occurring. Until the headline-grabbing murder of Dr. Tiller in his church, the incidences got very little press coverage in the last decade, considering that it is domestic terrorism. The perpetrators that have been caught and tried are following their extremist Christian consciences, rather than the law of the land.

In the wake of Dr. Tiller's not-so-surprising murder (Dr. David Gunn in 1993; Dr. John Britton and James Barret in 1994; two abortion clinic receptionists in 1994; Robert Sanderson and Emily Lyons in 1998 by nail bomb; Dr. Barnett Slepian in 1998; and lastly Dr. George Tiller in 2009), there is a clear message that the murderer is a hero carrying out justice. The Army of God organization has on their website a section titled "Prisoners of Christ," praising the jailed domestic terrorists who have waged this war against abortion clinics and providers. There is no feigned distaste; they are honest about their glorifying of shooters, bombers, and acid throwers etc.

Operation Rescue's founder Randall Terry held a press conference June 1, 2009 at the National Press Club. Just one day after the murder of Dr. Tiller, the world heard Mr. Terry saying *"George Tiller was a murderer, and he was doing something that was literally demonic...He was a mass murdered, he sowed death, and then he reaped death in a horrifying way...Roe vs Wade will be on the ash heap of history, and men like George Tiller will be remembered as one of the villains of history who met an untimely death. He was not a good man; he was an evil man. Mr. Tiller's untimely death can be a teaching moment for what child killing is really all about, and what he was doing behind those doors in his grisly trade."* There is no compassion for this Christian, only a talking point of how evil the man was in his life, a regular church attendee gunned down in his own church. Notice there was never a condemnation of the premeditated and cold-blooded murder, in spite of the Ten Commandments charge "thou shall not kill." That commandment apparently doesn't apply to them.

Randall Terry wrote a book titled *Operation Rescue* in 1988, that he dedicated to the scores of protestors who were arrested during 1988's anti-abortion protests in Atlanta. All the protestors refused to give their legal names, but identified themselves instead as either Baby John Doe or Baby Jane Doe. As a small side-note, Jerry Schwartz in the New York Times on October 5, 1988, reported the protests and arrests cost the city taxpayers $500,000. In the book *Operation Rescue*, the Religious Right luminaries of the time, Pat Robertson and D. James Kennedy each supplied a forward for the book. This links Operation Rescue to the Religious Right. One of the chapters in this book is clearly titled, "Higher Laws: Should We Obey God Rather Than Men?"

"If I asked, 'Should Christians break the law?' most Christians would quickly answer 'No!'

However, if I reframed the question, 'Should Christians obey God's Word even if it means disobeying the ungodly laws of men?' Many believers would say 'Yes.' Others wouldn't know what to do...

Numerous scriptural examples support two basic reasons to defy civil authorities:

1. Saving someone's life (Hebrew midwives, Moses' parents, Rehab, and the magi);

2. Remaining faithful to God (three Hebrew children, Daniel, and the Apostles)....

The actions of these courageous men and women [in cited Bible stories] are not heralded as civil disobedience, but acts of faith and obedience before God. Breaking man's law was incidental to walking out their convictions." Randall A. Terry, *Operation Rescue,* Whitaker House, 1988.

This is a common teaching in the Religious Right, obeying God first and foremost before any mere laws on this earthly existence. But where can that lead, given that the Religious Right leaders manipulate the vast majority of their followers? With such power, the leadership can direct followers down many paths by claiming they are following God's will rather than sinful man-made laws.

Frank Schaeffer's apology

In the Religious Right there are luminaries. Dr. Francis Schaeffer was such a one. My Religious Right church went through his books and DVDs during adult Sunday school. He was the intellectual evangelical. Therefore, you can imagine the ripples that took place when Dr. Schaeffer's son left the Religious Right fold to become an "other than Evangelical" Christian. Even more shocked when Frank Schaeffer apologized for his contribution to Dr. Tiller's murder.

"My late father and I share the blame (with many others) for the murder of Dr. George Tiller the abortion doctor gunned down on Sunday. Until I got out of the religious right (in the mid-1980s) and repented of my former hate-filled rhetoric I was both a leader of the so-called pro-life movement and a part of a Republican Party hate machine masquerading as the moral conscience of America...

In the early 80s my father followed up [Whatever Happened to the Human Race documentary] *with a book that sold over a million copies called* A Christian Manifesto. *In certain passages he advocated force if all other methods for rolling back the abortion ruling of Roe v. Wade failed. He compared America and its legalized abortion to Hitler's Germany and said that whatever tactics would have been morally justified in removing Hitler would be justified in trying to stop abortion. I said the same thing in a book I wrote (*A Time For Anger*) that right wing evangelicals made into a best seller. For instance Dr. James Dobson (of the Focus On the Family radio show) gave away over 100,000 copies...*

The same hate machine I was part of is still attacking all abortionists as 'murderers.' And today once again the 'pro-life' leaders are busy ducking their personal responsibility for people acting on their words. The people who stir up the fringe never take responsibility. But I'd like to say on this day, after a man was murdered in cold blood for performing abortions that I – and the people I worked with in the religious right, the Republican Party, the pro-life movement and the Roman Catholic Church, all contributed to this killing by our foolish and incendiary words.

I am very sorry.' " Frank Schaeffer "How I (and Other "Pro-Life" Leaders) Contributed to Dr. Tiller's Murder", *Huffington Post*, June 1, 2009.

Then to top off Frank Schaeffer's printed apology, he appears on national television and tells how behind the scenes the Religious Right advocates such radical acts.

"The book you mentioned earlier, Crazy for God, *has a number of chapters talking about the way we took the [Religious Right] movement from its early stages when it was more a moral concern, not so much about politics and not so much about changing the law and radicalized that movement. And I follow the step-by-step process: secret meetings with Pat Robertson down at the 700 Club, Jerry Falwell sending his jet up to me to bring me down to his church to speak a*

couple of times. And what we did was we talked one game to the large public and we talked another amongst ourselves and amongst ourselves we were very radical.

And I don't think it takes much imagination to guess that tonight there are people who are publicly saying 'This is terrible...we never advocated killing... abortion is murder but we didn't mean people to take us this seriously,' but in private you know if these people popped champagne bottles they would be drinking a toast to this murderer tonight. And I know that is the case because of the fact that I was part of the movement but also understood very well what we were doing back then was to attack the political issue when we would talk to people like Ronald Reagan and the Bush family and Jack Kemp...but on a private side we also were egging people on to first picket abortion clinics then chain themselves to fences then go to jail.

We knew full well that in a country that had seen the assassination of Dr. Martin Luther King, two Kennedy brothers and others that what we were also doing was opening a gate here. And I think there is no way to duck this. We live in a country in which guns are all over the place, we have plenty of people with a screw loose, plenty of people on the edge, it only takes one...We are a very divided nation coming out of this culture war...'" Frank Schaeffer "Rachel Maddow Show" *MSNBC*, June 2 2009.

Thank you Frank Schaeffer. Thank you for your true remorse, for telling the truth, and bringing it to light. Thank you for not white-washing it, or saying there is a higher law that the faithful are to follow. Thank you for being so courageous, and taking a stand.

There is yet one more comment from Frank Schaeffer that needs to be added to this section. In his book *Crazy for God,* he shares the repercussions from his defending a Virginia candidate for Senate, James Webb. Senator Webb he was under merciless attack by the Religious Right for his widely praised fiction books. Mr. Schaeffer received a flood of emails in response.

"When combined, the hundreds of e-mails seemed to boil down to: 'Do what we say Jesus says – and if you don't, we'll kick your head in!' The reaction confirmed why any sane person would run, and keep running from the right-wing/evangelical/Republican morass as far as their legs would carry them, something I'd been doing for more than twenty years." Frank Schaeffer, *Crazy for God: How I Grew Up One of the Elect, Helped Found the Religious Right, and Lived to Take all (or Almost All of It Back)*, Carroll & Graf, 2007.

<u>Religious Right are extremist</u>

Many people may read this and feel this can't be true. Christianity is about redemption, forgiveness, and helping one's fellow man. Earlier, the concept that the Religious Right are an extremist movement was set forth, and this section nails that description home. No longer can this radical movement be viewed as regular Christianity. No more excuses.

An Arizona pastor, Steven Anderson, reportedly gave a sermon where he prayed for President Barack Obama to die and go to hell. You read that correctly. This isn't as fringe as you might initially think. Pastor Anderson apparently confirmed his statement to TPmuckraker, a small online reporter/blogger and part of the TPM Media, showing he isn't in the least sorry for the hate he is spreading. The Religious Right, during Barack Obama's campaigning for president, promoted the concept that he was the Antichrist, so this is a logical by-product of such character assassination. Also a logical result is Chris Broughton, after hearing pastor Anderson's shocking prayers in his sermon, showed up at the President's appearance the next day with an assault rifle and a hand gun. This is the reality of the theory of following a higher law in action.

"But it's worth noting, again, that it is a rhetorical approach with inherent dangers. Whereas it's entirely immoral *to kill over a political disagreement concerning a medical procedure that's widely practiced around the world, it is, after all, entirely within the moral framework of all of the major Abrahamic*

religions [Judaism, Islam, Christianity] *to kill others to protect an innocent child. As such, it's a rhetorical strategy that fosters dangerous eliminationism.*

Which explains why the overwhelming majority of terrorist attacks in the United States since the 1980s have been committed by right-wing Christian fundamentalists." Joshua Holland, "Pastor of Gun-Toting Town Hall Protester Prayed for Obama's Death," *Alternet,* August 27, 2009.

In the wake of pastor Steven Anderson's Christ-like display of praying for the President of the Unites States' death and torment in Hell, (amazingly nobody is calling him a traitor) there are bumper stickers, mugs, t-shirts and even adorable stuffed bears that say "Pray for Obama: Psalm 109:8." People have not taken this little slogan very seriously. It reappeared when Kansas House Speaker Michael O'Neal sent two emails using this Bible quote to the Republican caucus. In January of 2012, O'Neal received a petition with thirty thousand signatures asking for his resignation over the emails. Two pastors representing the Faithful America organization delivered the petition. Here is the Bible quote in its full context:

"*Let his days be few; let another take his office. Let his children be fatherless and his wife a widow. Let his children wander about and beg; and let them seek sustenance far from their ruined homes. Let the creditor seize all that he has, and let strangers plunder the product of his labor. Let there be none to extend loving kindness to him, nor any to be gracious to his fatherless children.*'" Psalm 109:8-12.

Witness the love and compassion, loving of one's enemy, turning of the other cheek that apparently does not extend to anybody politically opposed to the Religious Right's righteous agenda.

Law Students taught God's law first

Jerry Falwell founded Liberty University in Lynchburg, Virginia. Liberty has an estimated 60,000 students enrolled, so it is the largest Religious Right college in the world. In 2004, the University started its law school, which instructs law students that

God's law is more important than man's laws. A real world headline-grabbing case was used in recent exams: an ex-Lesbian was aided and abetted by her pastor to kidnap her daughter and run to Nicaragua to keep her former partner and legal co-parent from exercising visitation rights with the daughter.

> *"That semester's mid-term exam, obtained by RD [Religion Dispatches.org], included a question based on Miller's case asking students to describe what advice they would give her 'as a friend who is a Christian lawyer.' After laying out a slanted history of the protracted legal battle, the exam asked, 'Lisa needs your counsel on how to think through her legal situation and how to respond as a Christian to this difficult problem. Relying only on what we have learned thus far in class, how would you counsel Lisa?'*
>
> *Students who wrote that Miller should comply with court orders received bad grades while those who wrote she should engage in civil disobedience received an A, the three students said. 'People were appalled,' said one of the students, adding, 'especially as lawyers to be, who are trained and licensed to practice the law—to disobey that law, that seemed completely counterintuitive to all of us.'*
>
> *. . . The Foundations class is unlike anything offered at secular law schools, its purpose being to guide students toward a 'Christian worldview' of the law. In the 2008-09 academic year, the required texts included David Barton's* Original Intent, *which Barton's website describes as an 'essential resource for anyone interested in our nation's religious heritage and the Founders' intended role for the American judicial system,' and Francis Schaeffer's* Christian Manifesto." Sarah Posner, "Exclusive: Liberty Law Exam Question on Notorious Kidnapping Case Pressured Students to Choose 'God's Law' over 'Man's'," *Religion Dispatches*, May 13, 2011.

Witness how law students are being indoctrinated with the same worldview that God's law trumps this democracy's laws, and that not everybody has rights that are to be protected. It is important to note the required textbooks cited were by pseudo-historian David Barton, renowned for rewriting America's history, and Francis Schaeffer known for drawing the battle lines in the war against humanism.

<u>Various examples</u>

There are instances where obstruction of justice has taken place. It is scary that a pastor, shepherd of a flock, can so easily defy the laws, such as the following case.

"A New Hampshire man was found guilty Friday of raping and impregnating his children's 15-year-old baby sitter, who belonged to the same church, more than a decade ago.

The case involving Ernest Willis, 52, of Gilford garnered national attention because the fundamentalist Baptist church he and the girl attended made her apologize to the congregation for accusing Willis. The pastor then helped ship the girl to live with a Colorado couple she didn't know and put her baby up for adoption. Concord police did not locate her until last year." Briefly, "Who's sorry now? Rapist convicted," *The Gazette*, May 28, 2011.

In July 2007, the *Colorado Daily* reported evolutionary biology professors at Colorado University in Boulder had received death threats in letters slipped under their office doors. The Religious Right has continually been pushing for every Christian to join the fight against the perceived secularizing of America and such death threats or even physical violence are the results of the call to fight.

In July, 1999, Matthew Williams and his brother, Tyler, murdered a gay couple, Gary Matson and Winfield Mowder, <u>in the couple's home</u> near Sacramento, California. Speaking to his mother from the Shasta County Jail, Matthew explained his actions in this way: "I had to obey God's law rather than man's law," he said. "I didn't want to do this. I felt I was supposed to. I have followed a higher law...I just plan to defend myself from the scriptures."

The *Oakland County Daily Tribune* reported on October 8, 2008, that a man felt his teacher at the Taft Education Center was a witch, and he threatened to "burn the witch" as he poured a liquid on her. He was following a higher law and claimed to be trying to purify the witch, but he is undergoing psychiatric evaluation, regardless.

Take notice, this is the Religious Right's mentality; it is no joke, and this is no exaggeration. The Religious Right is *dangerous*. If this were individual person, he or she would be evaluated for Antisocial Personality Disorder (which causes a person to feel no remorse and little regard for the feelings of others), or Narcissistic Personality Disorder (which causes a person to view him or herself as the center of the universe), plus a pathological liar, along with Histrionic Personality Disorder (which causes people to over-dramatize) – ultimately a textbook psychopath. But we are talking about a religious-political power broker movement with an agenda to dominate the United States.

<u>Take With You From This Chapter</u>

➢ The Religious Right teaches that God's laws from the Bible are a higher law to be followed, above man's laws.

➢ This "higher law" emphasis is even taught in Religious Right law schools.

➢ Use of the concept of a "higher law" is easily seen concerning abortion and gay people. Individual rights are not of concern.

Chapter 10
The End-Times Focus

<u>What to Expect From this Chapter</u>

➢ How the Religious Right has an end-times mentality, and how that impacts our society and politics.

➢ How Dominionism uses the Second Coming to endorse their agenda.

As a citizen, how our nation navigates complex and sensitive international situations, that rapidly change, is of vital importance to understand. One would hope our elected officials are well informed about all the factors and influencing conditions impacting any situation, and that they possess cool heads, and rationally approach solutions. The Religious Right feels positive that they know how it is all going to end, and any other outcome is unthinkable. This impacts politicians who approach international affairs believing they already have the answers because of what the Bible reveals. Is that sufficient to lead this country in volatile and intricate international dealings? Rationally, NO. It is not.

<u>Christ's second coming is the end game</u>

The Book of Revelation, and other scripture passages, describes a traumatic time. Revelation is a vision that John had. The Religious Right view this book as a prophecy of what is to come in the final days of Earth. The Old Testament book of Daniel is often used, in combination with the prophecy in Revelation, to construct a time-line of major events, that point to the End Days approaching.

The gentle and loving Jesus will come back with a vengeance in glory and power, displaying not love, but wrath. This is the Christ that the Religious Right focuses on, rather than the "turn the other cheek," "love thy neighbor," or "care for the orphans and widows" characterizations of Christ.

This is the Second Coming of Christ that many Religious Right wish to speed up, get the show on the road. This is what the Dominionists and the Seven Mountains

Strategy are ultimately about. They have a view of the Bible that Jesus' Second Coming will only happen once the Kingdom of God has been physically established here on planet Earth. This is a tremendous responsibility to put on the shoulders of believer, in claims that He has not returned yet because the faithful are not doing their part.

"MacDonald quotes liberally from the Book of Revelation, the only place in the New Testament where Jesus (arguably) endorses violence and calls for vengeance against nonbelievers. It is, along with the apocalyptic visions of St. Paul, the movement's go-to text. Rarely mentioned these days is the Jesus of the four Gospels, the Jesus who speaks of the poor and the marginalized, who taught followers to turn the other cheek and love their enemies, the Jesus who rejected the mantle of secular power.

'His eyes are like a flame of fire,' MacDonald tells us. 'Out of his mouth goes a sharp sword, and with it he can strike the nations. He treads the wine press of the fierceness and wrath of the Almighty God...'

MacDonald leaves little doubt that the convention [2005 National Religious Broadcasters Association annual convention] *is meant to serve as a rallying cry for a new and particularly militant movement in Christian politics, one that is sometimes mistaken for another outbreak of mere revivalism."* Chris Hedges, "Feeling the Hate with the National Religious Broadcasters," *Harpers*, May, 2005.

Yes, the End Times have become an obsessive focus. Dominion must be attained, Christ is waiting on dominion before He returns. It is this mindset that makes strange bedfellows with the Jewish community. On the one hand, they want those of Jewish decent to all become Christians, and that creates a tension. However, in the political realm they appear to be in agreement on international policies about Israel. Israel's status is a mutual concern, but not for the same reasons. To the Religious Right, Israel is still all about having specific conditions in alignment for Jesus' return to happen; for the Jewish community, it is a matter of ethnic identity, survival and even a sacred land bequeathed to them by their God. What appears to be a joint effort is situational coincidence, and the Religious Right is not concerned with anything but Christ's return and the conditions necessary for that to happen. On other issues of Jewish concern, they have very little warmth towards a "false religion" that is not in step with them. Beware such situational friends.

Knowing the future

Believing that you know what the future holds gives you a sense of control, no matter how false that knowledge may be. Horoscopes, Nostradamus, psychics, and prophecy all give us that illusion of control via knowledge of what is coming.

"Let's face it – the vast majority of people have no clue what's going on in our world today. Even most world leaders don't really understand what's happening. They grope around in the darkness, trying to figure out this world. But as God's children, we have a light that helps us see in the darkness of our world. That light is Bible prophecy 'We have...confidence in the message proclaimed by the prophets. Pay close attention to what they wrote, for their words are like a light shining in a dark place – until the day Christ appears and his brilliant light shines in your hearts.' Bible prophecy is a light that helps us understand our world and live as lights in the darkness (Phil. 2:15-16). Mark Hitchcock, *The Complete Book of Bible Prophecy*, Tyndale House Publishers, 1999.

~ ~ ~ ~ ~ ~ ~

"For evangelical Christians with an interest in prophecy, the headlines always come with asterisks pointing to scriptural footnotes. That is how Todd Strandberg reads his paper. By day, he is fixing planes at Offutt Air Force Base in Bellevue, Neb. But in his off-hours, he's the webmaster at raptureready.com and the inventor of the Rapture Index, which he calls a 'Dow Jones Industrial Average of End Time activity.' Instead of stocks, it tracks prophecies:

earthquakes, floods, plagues, crime, false prophets and economic measurements like unemployment that add to instability and civil unrest, thereby easing the way for the Antichrist. In other words, how close are we to the end of the world? The index hit an all-time high of 182 on Sept. 24, as the bandwidth nearly melted under the weight of 8 million visitors: any reading over 145, Strandberg says, means 'Fasten your seat belt.' " Nancy Gibbs, "Apocalypse Now," *Time,* June 23 2002.

The End Times prophesies appeal to those people who really are uncomfortable with the changes going on around them. Yes, sometimes it can be a bit scary in the world, but mostly it is the unknown that is frightening, and Bible prophecy seems to give assurance of what is coming. Who among us wouldn't want a promise of an approaching better world without crime, child abuse, hunger, and so on? It is getting there that is the issue.

Left Behind series

The fascination with the rapture and Christ's Second Coming is so pervasive a belief that a media empire has been built upon the *Left Behind* series of 12 books (55 million sold so far) based upon End Times events, and its success rivals Stephen King and John Grisham. The *Left Behind* phenomenon has spread beyond just books, and includes videotapes, audio books, graphics novels, children's books, study guides, weekly emails detailing how current events are fulfilling the book's view of prophecy, calendars, gift cards, apparel and a violent video game. In the following quote from Time magazine, notice the impact of such End Times focus on viewing world events, and consider how this shapes politicians actions and reactions.

"That is because among the best-selling fiction books of our times — right up there with Tom Clancy and Stephen King — is a series about the End Times, written by Tim F. LaHaye and Jerry B. Jenkins, based on the Book of Revelation. That part of the Bible has always held its mysteries, but for millions of people the code was broken in 1995, when LaHaye and Jenkins published [Book 1 in the

144

series] Left Behind: A Novel of the Earth's Last Days. People who haven't read the book and its sequels often haven't even heard of them, yet their success provides new evidence that interest in the End Times is no fringe phenomenon. Only about half of Left Behind readers are Evangelicals, which suggests there is a broader audience of people who are having this conversation. ...

The series has sold some 32 million copies — 50 million if you count the graphic novels and children's versions — and sales jumped 60% after Sept. 11. ...

Now the 10th book, The Remnant, is arriving in stores, a breathtaking 2.75 million hard-cover copies, and its impact may be felt far beyond the book clubs and Bible classes. To some evangelical readers, the Left Behind books provide more than a spiritual guide: they are a political agenda. When they read in the papers about the growing threats to Israel, they are not only concerned for a fellow democratic ally in the war against terror; they are also worried about God's chosen people and the fate of the land where events must unfold in a specific way for Jesus to return. That combination helps explain why some Christian leaders have not only bonded with Jews this winter as rarely before but have also pressed their case in the Bush White House as if their salvation depended on it.

*At the religious extremes within Islam, that means we see more suicide bombers: if God's judgment is just around the corner, martyrdom has a special appeal. The more they cast their cause as a fight against the Great Satan, **the more they reinforce the belief in some U.S. quarters that the war on terror is not one that can ever end with a treaty or communiqué, only total victory or defeat.** Extremists on each side look to contemporary events as validation of their sacred texts; each uses the others to define its view of the divine scheme.*

Even the horror of Sept. 11 was experienced differently by people primed to see God's hand in all things. [Todd] Strandberg (of raptureready.com) admits

145

that he was "joyful" that the attacks could be a sign that the End Times were at hand. "A lot of prophetic commentators have what I consider a phony sadness over certain events," he says. "In their hearts they know it means them getting closer to their ultimate desire." Nancy Gibbs, "Apocalypse Now," *Time,* June 23, 2002. (Emphasis added.)

This book series is so prevalent in our mindset that Minneapolis radio show host Chris Baker repeatedly called then presidential candidate Barack Obama "Nicolae Carpathia" who is the anti-Christ character in the series. Yes, this series has reached pop culture status in its own right and has a huge following. The Religious Right loves the success of the series, for it crossed over from just Christian readers to the general public, which in the Seven Mountains is the Arts and Entertainment ground being taken. But they hate it as well because it doesn't put forth that believers must establish the kingdom of God on earth for Christ to return.

Like so many Bible matters, there are differing views about the End Times. Rushdoony was a postmillennialist. This simply means they believe that Christ's kingdom on earth will be, must be, established for a millennia before Christ returns. Thus believers must have dominion and create that kingdom, or Christ will not return. This is a key to their insistence and feverish need to gain dominion over all areas of the culture.

Self-fulfilling prophecy

Are you familiar with the concept of a self-fulfilling prophecy? A self-fulfilling prophecy is when a person's belief causes the person to act in such a way as to bring about the exact situation the person believed in. For the rest of us it is important to consider the Religious Right worldview in terms of manifesting reality. What reality are they manifesting in the sense of self-fulfilling prophecies?

Consider a Religious Right president who so strongly believes in only a certain conclusion in the Middle East and Israel, that the president actually brings it about from his or her actions. That foreign policy regarding and the volatile Middle East area could be driven by an interpretation of Armageddon prophecies is a dangerous policy position for our nation's leaders. That is a very real possibility, and illustrates yet again why the separation of church and state is so critical. For Dominionists, an End Times focus fuels the mandate to take over the seven mountains of influence and set the stage for the Second Coming. Everything else fades to unimportance in comparison.

As a citizen you need to be aware, involved, and actively encourage our governmental representatives to act in the best interests of this country, not in fulfilling prophesy, and not assuming they foreknow the outcome.

Take With You From This Chapter

➢ An End Times focus can color people's actions and perceptions of world events. Politicians with this worldview may not act for the best of our country, believing they know how matters will ultimately end.

➢ Rushdoony was a postmillennialist, and this fuels the Dominionist agenda to create Christ's kingdom now, so Jesus will return.

Chapter 11
Religious Caste System

What to Expect From this Chapter

➢ The Religious Right views all non-Christians as not being covered under the U.S. Constitution, and therefore not having rights.

➢ How non-Christians should not hold any public office.

➢ How they view anybody who is not a Christian as not a full citizen with full rights.

The United States and democracy bring to mind equal rights for its citizens. As a country we have had some blemishes on that ideal historically, but we have improved, and have tried to better our nation. This very concept is under attack by the Religious Right.

Not all citizens are created equal

"We hold these truths to be self-evident, that all men are created equal," was one of our first important declarations as a nation, but is being invalidated by the Religious Right. Only Christians are equal, the rights secured in the U.S. Constitution are for Christians, and if they are feeling generous, Jews are included. No Buddhists or traditional Native Americans are covered, let alone an agnostic or, *gasp*, an atheist.

> *"They truly believe that if you have not been "saved," you are living under a curse and are incapable of knowing what is best and that because of this you should be ruled over. You should also know they do not believe that even centuries-old Christian communities (Catholics, Anglicans, Greek Orthodox, etc.) are 'saved,' only those who think like they do.'"* Jason Childs, "A Former Jerry Falwell Follower Reflects On How The Religious Right Gets It Wrong," *Church and State Magazine*, May 2011.

If you are not recognized as a true believer in their eyes, you are meant to be ruled over. You are disqualified from public office because you are living "under a curse" of

148

sin and damnation. It is common to believe that no one other than the strictly Religious Right is to be trusted and is not fit to lead this country nor even have input into it. Former Religious Right adherent Libby Anne explains further.

"It didn't help that I was taught that those outside of our beliefs, including humanists, environmentalists, socialists, and feminists, were evil selfish people who were destroying our society, and that Christians who did not share our beliefs were 'wishy-washy' and 'worldy.' There is a very 'us versus them' mentality at work in Christian Patriarchy. They were the enemy, the agents of Satan out to destroy belief in God and pervert the world. They cared only for themselves and their own desires and were not to be trusted." Libby Anne, "My Life as a Daughter of Christian Patriarchy," Butterflies and Wheels Blog Article, September 3, 2011.

Labeling the non-Religious Right as evil people who are destroying our society essentially says they are traitors to the nation. If you aren't one of them, then you are an enemy of the nation. How long do you think the average person will maintain basic rights, the more influential and powerful the Religious Right grows?

Only Christians should hold public office

There is a growing clamor from the extremist right that a religious test be applied to every single candidate for any public office anywhere in the nation. An agnostic, atheist, or an earth-centered spirituality such as a traditional Native American for example can serve in the armed forces and sacrifice his or her life for the nation, but aren't worthy to hold a public office. Seriously?

There are seven states (Texas, Arkansas, Mississippi, Tennessee, North Carolina, South Carolina, and Maryland) that have in their state constitutions that a person is not eligible to run for a public office in that state unless they believe in the Almighty God. That means the God of the Bible, and increasingly it means the God of the Religious Right. The Bible Belt is alive and well, but in Maryland, as well?

Unconstitutional?

Those state constitutions can be viewed as violating the higher law of the United States Constitution with the First Amendment Establishment Clause. Add to this that the U.S. Constitution article VI. clearly states, "but no religious test shall ever be required as a qualification to any Office or public Trust under the United States." Additionally, the Supremacy Clause, Article VI., Clause 2 of the U.S. Constitution states that U.S. Treaties and Federal Statutes are the "supreme law of the land." The Supremacy Clause puts the "united" in the United States. We are all under the same federal laws, and that is not an amendment, but in the text of the original Constitution.

James Madison expressed in the Federalist Paper number 44, that having the Federal government subservient to the various states would be like the brain taking orders from the various limbs of the body. Our founding fathers intended for no religious test for public office whatsoever, in any part of the nation. Yet we currently have seven states that intentionally violate that unity with, and supremacy of the Federal government. In this, they are purposely thumbing their noses at our Founding Fathers and their express wishes for the country. How patriotic is that?

On August 16, 2008, at Saddleback Church in Lake Forest, California the two presidential candidates were asked the following questions by a pastor before a live audience, and broadcast on national television. Question such as: What does it mean to you to be a follower of Christ? Does evil exist and, if so, should we ignore it, negotiate with it, contain it or defeat it? Would you insist that faith-based organizations forfeit the right to hire people with incompatible beliefs in order to access federal funds? History was made that night when presidential candidates violated the U.S. Constitution, and citizens didn't protest. We had the usual pundits commenting on who won the debate, a debate that was brazenly geared towards the Conservative Christian vote, but not a word was uttered about the violation to our Constitution and Bill of Rights. These same values voters feel very patriotic in examining a candidate on his or her spiritual beliefs. What a shame that the U.S. Constitution was made a mockery of during 2008 Saddleback Church presidential debates, and barely anyone noticed.

Qualifications be damned

The Religious Right has grown bolder in expressing their feelings about "others" or "non-believers," that they are unfit, no matter if they are the only qualified person in the state to save it from certain ruin; they are unfit, and should have no official positions. Thus they are not equal citizens, but less than full citizens. A caste system based upon very personal spiritual beliefs is being enacted and promoted.

A good example of this is the case of Joe Straus. State Republican Executive Committee member John Cook began a campaign to remove the Texas State Representative and House Speaker Joe Straus, because he was not a Conservative Christian. Speaker Straus is Jewish, you know, the first part of that "Judeo-Christian" heritage.

> "*When I got involved in politics, I told people I wanted to put Christian conservatives in leadership positions,' he told me, explaining that he only supports Christian conservative candidates in Republican primary races.*
>
> *'I want to make sure that a person I'm supporting is going to have my values. It's not anything about Jews and whether I think their religion is right or Muslims and whether I think their religion is right. ... I got into politics to put Christian conservatives into office. They're the people that do the best jobs over all.'*" Abby Rapoport, "SREC Member: 'I got into politics to put Christian conservatives into office,'" *Texas Observer*, December 3, 2010.

John Cook's position had mixed responses, but it is a viewpoint that has become more prevalent. It should be noted that in the "tactics" chapter under the "going international" subsection it was mentioned that the Religious Right had worked with Muslims against their perceived common enemy of gays and feminists. This in no way colors their belief that those very same people they worked with are not to be considered equals. They may forge situational alliances to strategically win a battle, but at the end of the day if you aren't one of them don't expect any favors. This

Christian exceptionalism and superiority is particularly vivid with David Barton's worldview that he preaches, and that Rushdoony had pushed in his book.

Alisa Harris was raised Religious Right, home-schooled and trained in the correct worldview. She is the author of the book, *Raised Right: How I Untangled My Faith from Politics,* and shares this account of going to a Religious Right Student Conference that taught her Christian exceptionalism in every area of life.

> *"I attended Summit Ministries' Student Worldview Conference as a 15-year-old.*
>
> *They gave us a handy worldview chart that had a vertical column for every area of life - economics, politics, psychology, law – and a horizontal column that showed how Muslims, humanists, Marxists and New-Agers were wrong on every count."* Alisa Harris, "I could have become Michele Bachmann," *CNN Religion Blog,* August 14th, 2011.

Constitution is for Christians

David Barton, the pseudo-historian of the Religious Right and founder of WallBuilders, promotes the position that the separation of church and state was only for the Christian expressions of faith that the Founding Fathers guaranteed religious liberty, not all religions inclusively.

> *"A case currently before the 9th Circuit Court of Appeals in California could establish that some faiths are indeed more equal than others – and that minority faiths are not entitled to First-Amendment protection.*
>
> *In a previous post, I wrote about Patrick McCollum and his suit to gain equal standing for Pagan chaplains in the California prison system. Currently, only chaplains who represent one of five faiths – Catholic, Protestant, Jewish, Muslim or Native American – can have staff positions and the full access that affords in the system.*
>
> *A new amicus brief was filed this week by a group called Wallbuilders, Inc. The Wallbuilders brief calls on the court to state that the First Amendment itself*

does not cover Paganism. Or really, anything but Christianity or some other monotheistic faiths." Kathy Nance, "Is your faith about to be demoted?" *STLToday.com*, January 30, 2010.

Bryan Fischer, the American Family Association radio talk-show host, wrote an opinion piece at the Religious Right media site Renew America that reinforces that religious liberty is only for Christians. Mr. Fischer's piece is titled "Islam and the First Amendment: privileges but not rights" and was posted on March 24, 2011. In his opinion, *"The First Amendment was written by the Founders to protect the free exercise of Christianity."* He uses Islam as his sole example of a non-Christian religion that should be obstructed. He continues with, *"While there certainly ought to be a presumption of religious liberty for non-Christian religious traditions in America, the Founders were not writing a suicide pact when they wrote the First Amendment."* And this ironic statement, *"They have that privilege at the moment, but it is a privilege that can be revoked if, as is in fact the case, Islam is a totalitarian ideology dedicated to the destruction of the United States."* This is ironic because of the dominion mandate that can easily be seen as an extremist danger to our democracy, but they themselves are pointing towards others as the threat.

The following quote is from John Ragosta, an instructor at the University of Virginia School of Law and author of *Wellspring of Liberty: How Virginia's Religious Dissenters Helped Win the American Revolution and Secured Religious Liberty,* and clearly shows that the revolution-era people knew how far reaching the religious liberty they were seeking would extend.

> *"From these Virginia people I'm talking about, and I had three quotes and I can give you many more, people were saying we understand that what we are fighting for is going to affect the Jews, the Mohammedans, which is the term they would use, Turks. Jefferson actually talks about Hindus at one point that this is going to apply to Hindus. Now we don't have a lot of Hindus in eighteenth century Virginia but there's recognition that that's what we are talking about.*

Now there are many other people, for example, during the Constitution and ratification process – people recognize that there is no reference to Christianity in here. And in fact the reference John [Fea] makes about 'In the year of Our Lord' – that was actually added by a clerk after the Constitution was voted on and the fifty-five delegates had left. Okay." John Ragosta, "The Founding Fathers and Religion Panel," 2011 Virginia Festival of the Book, *CSPAN2-BookTV*, March 18, 2011.

Remember the "we hold these truths to be self-evident, that all men are created equal" statement from our Declaration of Independence? As a country we have amongst us those who don't see it that way. We have the Religious Right advancing the concept that only Christianity should have constitutional protections and a religious test of faith to hold public office. It would seem that at the age of 235 years old, the country is losing its memory. Perhaps senility has set in?

Francis Schaeffer is credited with sparking some of the initial fire in the early Religious Right especially against humanism and abortion with his book *The Christian Manifesto* and *How Should We Then Live*. Several Religious Right luminaries cite Francis Schaeffer as inspiring them to political involvement. Now, years later, son Frank Schaeffer has certainly come into his own and in an interview on CNN with DL Hughley in March 2009 he shared this about the true Religious Right:

"...And the people, for instance like William F. Buckley, who was a friend of my dad's, or Barry Goldwater. You could have disagreed or agreed with them. But these were not crazy people. These were not Fruit Loops.

HUGHLEY: They wanted a separation of church and state.

SCHAEFFER: Right. They wanted a separation of church and state. They were not using politics to beat people over the head with a moral crusade. They were not looking to start wars for no reason. We moved from a period when the Republicans represented something you could agree or disagree with, to a period where it represents a kind of fundamentalist Christianity on one side and a view of the world, which sees everyone who is other, whether that is black, white, Arab, Muslim, a different country, gay, as the enemy. And basically that's a very dangerous position." Frank Schaeffer interview, DL Hughley Breaks the News, CNN, March 7, 2009.

This sets up a caste system; Christians are the full citizens with full rights and protections under the Constitution and then there are the others with some "courtesy privileges." Witness a country viewed and run with your most personal spiritual beliefs determining if you get full citizen rights rather than your being a law abiding American born-or-naturalized person securing your rights.

Once upon a time, a person's religion was a very private matter, not something to be cheapened on tee shirts or bumper stickers. Not only are people's most intimate thoughts on religious matters now on parade, but your rights may be demoted if you don't believe the correct way.

Take With You From This Chapter

➢ Only "true" Christians should be allowed to hold any public office.

➢ Religious Right Christians get full citizen rights, and others don't. It is that simple.

➢ A caste system based on personal spiritual beliefs is being promoted.

Section 4: The War is On

In this section ...

The practical results of the Dominionist agenda in our culture will be examined in light of the Seven Mountains Strategy. Taken as a whole it is a recipe to take control of the nation from the inside. We will look at the various "mountains of influence" and how that truly impacts citizens of the nation.

Chapter 12
The Seven Mountains of Influence

<u>What to Expect From this Chapter</u>

➤ An introduction to the Seven Mountains of influence and how this is a blueprint infiltrating every aspect of American life.

➤ How the Seven Mountains Strategy has already been successful in furthering an extremist Christian dominion.

There is a culture war being waged that is reaching a frenzied pitch. Every area of life is being assaulted, but few know there are battles raging around them.

"Something far more significant than money is behind the contest for the hearts and minds of children. Nothing short of a great Civil War of Values rages today throughout North America. Two sides with vastly differing and incompatible worldviews are locked in a bitter conflict that permeates every level of society.

Bloody battles are being fought on a thousand fronts, both inside and outside of government. Open any daily newspaper and you'll find accounts of the latest Gettysburg, Waterloo, Normandy, or Stalingrad.

Instead of fighting for territory or military conquest, however, the struggle now is for the hearts and minds of the people. It is a war over ideas." James Dobson, *Children at Risk*, Word Pub., 1990.

<u>The Seven Mountains of a culture war</u>

The term culture war was first coined in the 1870s in Germany, but it became part of American life in the 1990s. First with the publication of the book *Culture Wars: The Struggle to Define America,* by James Davison Hunter and then Pat Buchanan's speech at the 1992 Republican National Convention that was dubbed the "culture war speech" where Buchanan defined the war and its battle lines. He named the enemies in the war; the environmental extremists and radical feminists and public morality were the front lines of the battle. The everyday lives of the populous are now a major battlefield.

Yet this does not begin to describe the intense war that is actually being waged. From Dominionist Rousas Rushdoony came the call to arms in 1973, claiming Christians must, absolutely must, take dominion of the United States. That was the call for an army to assemble. Marching orders were defined in 1975 with the Seven Mountains Strategy, courtesy of Bill Bright, founder of Campus Crusade for Christ, and Loren Cunningham, founder of Youth with a Mission. Seven strategic areas of influence were identified for staking their flags of victory, including business, government (politics, courts, military), media, arts and entertainment, education, the family, and religion. It was significant that these two men dealt with youth who would take this message into the world almost immediately.

"The favor to 'invade' these seven mountains is already upon us as part of God's end-time strategy to establish Him as Ruler of the Nations. ...

Some are recognizing the strategic sovereignty of God in promoting them to heights heretofore unseen. Many, however, do not fully grasp the opportunity God is giving us. That is the central purpose of this book: to help Christians understand that this favor is divinely strategic and constitutes the place of each person's ministry assignment. Every believer needs to understand his or her work is not a 'secular' calling, but rather a God-assigned mission!

I believe this book can be a helpful resource for Christian high school and college students to assist them in pursuing a biblically mandated career opportunity. Imagine beginning your adult life, focusing your passion for God on a specific area of study, knowing that you are called to transform it through supernatural, Holy Spirit-inspired strategies that would blow the world's mind. ... It is crucial that young adults who are passionate for God be shown valid options for their futures besides going into typical ministry-related fields. ... The seven mountains or areas of influence are not the only seven in our societies, but they are the specific arenas that God is giving us favor to retake and bring under the influence of Christ. In order to become 'the head and not the tail' (Deut. 28:13), we must capture the areas of influence at 'the head' of our society. It is our spiritual poverty of vision and poor eschatology that have kept us as 'the tail' and out of our Promised Land." Johnny Enlow, *The Seven Mountain Prophecy: Unveiling the Coming Elijah Revolution*, Creation House, 2008.

"Poor eschatology" has kept the Religious Right from leading rather than being the leader. Eschatology is the study of the End Times, the Rapture and the coming apocalypse, and most importantly Christ's Second Coming. Not having the correct End Time's concept has supposedly kept Christians from taking dominion of the culture and nation before now. In other words, belief in Post Millennialism is critical. Post Millennialism says that Christ's Second Coming is waiting for His kingdom to be established before He can return. Christianity must reign in the nations for Christ to return. This is at the core of Dominionism and the Seven Mountains strategy.

An interesting note is that the Coalition on Revival, a dominionist organization that works to bring mainstream Evangelicals together with dominionists, has identified seventeen major human life and activity spheres of influence: law, government, economics, business and professions, education, art and media, medicine, science and technology, psychology and counseling, Christian unity, local and world evangelism, discipleship, helping the hurting, educating Christians about social and political moral issues, revitalizing Christian colleges and seminaries, marriage and the family, and pastoral renewal. This strategy to bring every aspect of America's culture and thinking under Religious Right influence is not confined to just Bill Bright and Loren Cunningham with their Seven Mountains Mandate strategy. Others, such as the Coalition on Revival, have also defined the areas of American life that must be brought under biblical authority. For our purposes we will address the seven "mountains" for simplicity.

A note of clarification is due at this point. Rushdoony, the father of Christian

Reconstruction and thus Dominionism, declared that Christians are mandated to take dominion of the nation, but he drew a distinction between dominion and dictatorship. Christians must work to bring every area, every thought, into captivity to Christ. Dictators use armies to keep the masses under control. This is why the concept of mountains or spheres of influence goes along with Dominion ideals. The difference is really subtle; instead of armies, there is cultural pressure to conform.

A cultural dictatorship

When the nation has: only doctrinally correct presidents, politicians, judges, military leaders, and police along with media uplifting a Christ-focused bent on all news and magazines, music, books, photography, artwork and fashion reinforcing proper values and roles, churches are all brought into alignment to the proper doctrine, all children are indoctrinated in the proper world-view through education centers, and the work place reinforces all these correct values and thinking, then you have a complete cultural domination that in itself creates a dictate about how you are to think and act. That is different than a dictatorship only in that force is not used, but rather a complete cultural indoctrination and brainwashing similar to what cults put recruits through, is in place. Disobedience will be swiftly dealt with under much stricter laws to quiet those rebellious voices. This seems contrary to the popular mantra of "government so small you can drown it in a bathtub," that Grover Norquist coined. Again, small government is their marketing slogan, but this is the reality. They loudly proclaim one thing, and act completely differently.

How seriously is this "war" really taken? It is all just metaphor for the spiritual war, right?

> *"Equally striking as the agenda itself is the rhetoric that leaders of the Religious Right use to motivate their followers. In the course of these travels, I was impressed anew by the pervasiveness of the language of militarism among leaders of the Religious Right. Patrick Henry College, according to Michael Farris, 'is training an army of young people who will lead the nation and shape*

the culture with biblical values.' Rod Parsley, pastor of World Harvest Church in Ohio, issues swords to those who join his Religious Right organization, the Center for Moral Clarity, and calls on his followers to 'lock and load' for a 'Holy Ghost invasion.' The Traditional Values Coalition advertises its 'Battle Plan' to take over the judiciary. 'I want to be invisible. I do guerilla warfare,' Ralph Reed famously declared about his political tactics in 1997. 'I paint my face and travel at night. You don't know it's over until you're in a body bag. You don't know until election night.' The Family Research Council tries to enlist evangelicals to 'fight the battle' against a 'powerful alliance of leftists.' And in Longview Texas, I heard strains of triumphalism: 'The army of God is taking America back!' I wonder how this sounds to the Prince of Peace.

This rhetoric and these policies are a scandal, a reproach to the gospel I honor and the Jesus I love." Randal Balmer, *Thy Kingdom Come, An Evangelical's Lament: How the Religious Right Distorts the Faith and Threatens America,* Basic Books, 2006.

It is not a metaphor; it is real, and yet the elusive "liberal" media is ignoring this blatant challenge to democracy because nobody wants to be perceived as persecuting Christians by pointing out this danger. It is a sobering war for the existence of democracy, and for this nation to continue to stand as a beacon of rule-by-consensus of the governed. With all the allusions to war, America is a religious battlefield that could easily turn bloody in the streets, like in Norway's Anders Breivik case. The tensions certainly are running high. The real question is, what will it take to wake up the American people? Saddam Hussein remarked that America would ultimately fall due to its complacency. Letting democracy slowly and insidiously be replaced is the ultimate complacency and failure.

"The best lack all conviction, while the worst are full of passionate intensity." William Butler Yeats

We covered the governmental aspects to some degree, during the discussion of the infiltration of the courts and the Republican Party. Shortly, we will cover how the Religious Right have been active in the armed forces. The true success of any take-over depends upon the military being on your side, even in a subtle cultural takeover. But this following quote reminds us of the significant government influence they have acquired already.

"At the same time, evangelicals have sponsored a number of organizations and initiatives that train future evangelical leaders. These include new universities like Patrick Henry College in Virginia and year-long educational and internship programs sponsored by Trinity Forum Academy and the Falls Church Fellows program, both based in the Washington area. Outside the capital, evangelicals have built local infrastructures for everything from school board decisions to mayoral and congressional races to presidential campaigns.

Though they are now firmly entrenched within the Republican Party, there are indications that Democrats, too, want to bring evangelicals into the fold. ...

Still, evangelicals have, for the most part aligned themselves with the conservative Republicanism, perhaps to their political disadvantage." D. Michael Lindsay, *Faith in the Halls of Power: How Evangelicals Joined the American Elite*, Oxford University Press, 2007.

~ ~ ~ ~ ~ ~ ~

"'The federal government's relationship with faith-based groups is stronger than ever,' said the Rev. Peg Chemberlin, president emeritus of the National Council of Churches. '...government partnerships with faith-based groups are expanding,' she said. ...

The faith-based office created under President George W. Bush has expanded during Obama's presidency, broadening partnerships between the government and faith-based groups. ...

According to a recent article in Mother Jones, Catholic religious charities have received more than $650 million during Obama's presidency from the

Department of Health and Human Services, one of the largest government funders of faith-based groups. The Conference of Catholic Bishops has received $81.2 million in federal grants from the HHS during Obama's first three years, almost $10 million more than during the last three years of the Bush presidency.'' Jaweed Kaleem, ''President Obama's Faith Inspires Pastor's Defense of White House Religion Policies," *Huffington Post,* February 23, 2012.

How successful is this Dominion mandate and seven mountains strategy? Since the 1970s the youth of that time and subsequent graduates have been incorporating this ideal into the major cultural spheres of influence.

"From major motion pictures to the National Council on the Arts, evangelicals are involved in the mainstream culture. I encountered them at the highest levels of television, film, graphic and video arts, music, publishing, poetry, short and long fiction, theater and the performing arts, visual arts, fashion, modeling, professional athletics, journalism, broadcasting, advertising, architecture, interior design, and urban planning....

Social groups can gain power in a variety of ways – by voting a candidate into the Oval Office, by assuming leadership of powerful corporations, or by shaping the mainstream media. Evangelicals have done them all since the late 1970s, and the change has been extraordinary. ... For many of them, the evangelical imperative to bring faith into every sphere of one's life means that they cannot expunge faith from the way they lead... In this way, the evangelical vision is sweeping and significantly more comprehensive than outside observers realize. How have evangelicals – long lodged in their own subculture and shunned by the mainstream – achieved significant power in such a short time? " D Michael Lindsay, *Faith in the Halls of Power: How Evangelicals Joined the American Elite,* Oxford University Press, 2007.

Evidence of how successful the government takeover has progressed can be seen in the 2012 Republican candidates campaigning, not on job creation or foreign policies, but on who is the most extremist Religious Right. This is historic, and yet most of the American people sit idly by as though this were normal. It is not normal; it is evidence of our democracy falling apart before our eyes. Additionally, a large part, if not all, of the Republican platform on financial policies are exactly as Rushdoony prescribed and David Barton actively preaches.

<u>The Family's influence</u>

Other evidence of the successful takeover of our government is the power of The Family. The Family is said to also go by the names The Fellowship, The Fellowship Foundation, National Fellowship Council, Fellowship House, The International Foundation, National Committee for Christian Leadership, International Christian Leadership, C Street, and the National Leadership Council. It has a pact of secrecy with members that appears to have been ironclad until recently.

"In 1985, President Ronald Reagan said about the Fellowship, 'I wish I could say more about it, but it's working precisely because it is private.'" Jeff Sharlet, *The Family*, Harper Perennial, 2008, p.19.

Abraham Vereide founded The Family and was the originator of the National Prayer Breakfast that is hosted by the United States Congress. The Family maintains a townhouse on C Street in Washington D.C. near the U.S. Capitol, and has several members of Congress living there very inexpensively. Their mission is to bring about a Godly government, like the Religious Right. The Family has been instrumental in influencing several Democrats to vote more like far right Republicans. Democrats such as Bart Stupak, Joe Pitts, Ike Skelton, Mike Mcintyre, John Tanner, Lincoln Davis, Dan Boren, and Heath Shuler, for example, all of which live at the Family's C Street house. Could this be an indication of the influence that has been built by the Dominionist ideal in the nation's capital?

"One group has been particularly important to the spiritual lives of political leaders: an entity known as 'the Fellowship.' In 1944 Abraham Vereide started an organization called International Christian Leadership that hosted prayer

breakfast groups for business and government leaders. This group eventually became the Fellowship. Vereide organized the first annual National Prayer Breakfast in 1953. President Eisenhower attended that year, as has every U.S. President since. Vereide died in 1969 and passed the reins to Douglas Coe. Coe, who avoids the limelight, has been closer to more U.S. presidents than any other religious leader, including Billy Graham. Indeed, he has been called a 'stealth Billy Graham.'

Of the leaders that I interviewed, one in three mentioned Coe or the Fellowship as an important influence. Indeed, there is no other organization like the Fellowship, especially among religious groups, in terms of its access or clout among the country's leadership.

Several people I interviewed referred to the Fellowship as an 'underground State Department.'" D. Michael Lindsay, *Faith in the Halls of Power: How Evangelicals Joined the American Elite*, Oxford University Press, 2007.

The cover story is that they provide a Christian support group of sorts. Bible studies and moral support for busy politicians is one thing, but it is quite another to use such influence to promote extremist agendas, whether they be social or economic. The Family on C Street is heavily involved in both. The shocking "Kill the Gays" bill presented in Uganda has been traced back to this organization. The tremendous anti-workers' rights movement that has reappeared in the last few years is the cornerstone of the Family's economic push since 1933. They are not simply ministering to those with difficult jobs; they are shaping our national politics without our consent via their influence.

Mr. Sharlet, a research scholar at New York University's Center for Religion and Media, published his book in May of 2008, titled *The Family: The Secret Fundamentalism at the Heart of American Power* based upon his personal experiences while living among The Family, as well as research he conducted. He terms the Family, currently lead by Doug Coe, as a special brand of extremist Right wing

Christian agenda, characterized by terms such as "Economic Evangelism" or "Biblical Capitalism". This is the Religious Right Tea Party economics with major political juice behind it.

Jeff Sharlet wrote a follow up book to his *The Family*, titled *C Street: The Fundamentalist Threat to American Democracy*. These two books are recommended as further reading on the topic of this powerful religio-political group. The Family is an example of the extreme influence that the Religious Right has over our politicians.

In the remainder of the book, the family mountain is covered in the upcoming section titled The Traditional Family, with chapters addressing the role of women, and children, and an explanation of just how gay individuals are believed to be impacting the family. This includes information on the Quiverfull movement, and features an interview from a former insider.

Education is covered in its own chapter. It shows how and why public education is under attack and their ultimate goal for the education system. In a separate chapter we will spotlight the rewriting of American history to reflect a Christian nation from its inception that supplies validity to their actions in this takeover.

That leaves business, media, religion itself, and finally arts and entertainment that we will cover as well in the immediately following chapters.

The Seven Mountains Mandate gives a strategic blueprint of how to infiltrate and take control over areas of influence throughout our nation, and it has had nearly forty years in practice. Do the executives, artists, movie producers etc., know that they are part of this strategy? Not necessarily. But they view their careers as a mission field to advance their faith, a calling to shine their worldview into the workplace and culture, to impact their career field like any missionary sent into a foreign culture.

Take With You From This Chapter

➤ The Seven Mountains of influence are government, the family, education, business, media, arts and entertainment, and religion.

➤ Taken together, the Seven Mountains constitute a cultural dictatorship.

Chapter 13
Religious Right and Our Military

What to Expect From this Chapter

➢ How Dominion of our military has been taking place and few have noticed.

➢ The Religious Right extremism in the armed forces is examined.

➢ Why our military has regulations to keep a separation of church and state in the ranks.

Ever since the Crusades, the idea of Christian soldiers waging a holy war is nightmarish to most. George W. Bush referred to the military response to the September 11 attacks as a "crusade" and Europe collectively cringed. American citizens should be particularly nervous at the thought of the armed services answering to religious direction, rather than answering to our elected officials and the citizens of the nation to uphold the Constitution and thus protect the nation. This is yet another beautiful aspect to our democracy, that the politicians, and even the military, work for the people ultimately.

Michael Weinstein versus the U.S. Air Force Academy

Within the pages of the book *With God On Our Side,* by Michael Weinstein, you will find how Mr. Weinstein, a US Air Force Academy graduate, discovered that the Academy had become an Evangelical Crusaders training camp and his subsequent fight to expose it is discussed. He took a stand against "intolerance, intimidation, and inappropriate evangelism in the armed forces" according to Richard Schlosberg, retired CEO of the *Los Angeles Times.*

Mr. Weinstein and his charges are controversial. Many contend that the military is not consciously pressuring members to conform to a specific religious belief system, it just hasn't occurred to them how one-sided they are.

The following is part of the much longer formal charges that Michael Weinstein filed in court against the United States Air Force (In United States District Court For the District of New Mexico, October 6, 2005).

"Over the course of at least the last decade, a pattern and practice has developed at the Academy where senior officers and cadets have attempted to impose evangelical Christianity into arenas that are clearly United States Air Force venues in violation of the Establishment Clause of the First Amendment to the United States Constitution. ...

Despite claims by the USAF that it has changed its policies regarding evangelizing at the Academy and throughout the entire USAF, USAF officials have made it clear that they have no intent to actually remedy the unconstitutional practices of the USAF.

Shockingly, as recently as July 12, 2005, Brig. General Cecil R. Richardson, the Air Force deputy chief of chaplains, had the audacity to say in an interview carried on the front page of the New York Time's 'We will not proselytize, but we reserve the right to evangelize the unchurched.'

Despite being repeatedly asked by Plaintiff to repudiate Brig. General Richardson's statement and to make a clear statement that this is not its policy, the United States Air Force and Defendant Geren have refused to do so, thereby ratifying this policy."

LA City Beat on May 24, 2007, published an interview with author Michael Weinstein. In the interview with LA City Beat, Mr. Weinstein shares his belief that Dominionists have infiltrated the armed forces and have been given leeway, in spite of the fact of the general orders against proselytizing in the military. Mr. Weinstein also tells what has happened to him, at the hands of extremists in the aftermath of his book and lawsuit against the Air Force.

"We've had dead animals on our front door. We've had feces and beer bottles thrown at our house. Our tires have been slashed. They burned a church down when the head of a church came out to support me when I spoke in Kansas. We had a synagogue that was desecrated. There's a group of Christian women who

call me and chant 'Mikey Weinstein, bullet in the head, praise the lord he's finally dead.' They call my wife up and say they're going to blow her head off. ...

What I found was that it wasn't just the Air Force. We now have 737 U.S. military installations scattered around the world as we garrison the globe in 132 countries. And in every one of them, we have this Christian Taliban. It's the Officers Christian Fellowship for the officers, and the Christian Military Fellowship for the enlisted. And they have a tripartite goal – a goal that they view as much more critically important than merely the oath that they all swore to protect and to serve the Constitution: Number one, they want to see a 'spiritually transformed military;' number two, with 'ambassadors for Christ in uniform;' and number three, 'empowered by the Holy Spirit.' ...

Well, the Air Force's attack F-16 squadron, at Cannon Air Force Base in my home state of New Mexico, they're called the Crusaders. Their official Air Force logo on their F-16s, which are equipped to carry laser-guided conventional and nuclear weapons, is a giant crucifix and a giant crusader's helmet from the year 1096, the year of the first of the nine crusades; the helmet is surrounded by three yellow stars in the shape of a crucifix to represent the trinity, and a giant crusader's broadsword. ...

This is all part of a passion play, now. Commanders in the field are censoring the soldiers' DVD libraries, leaving only the movies that have appropriate Christian content. Battle staff meetings are being diverted into evangelical prayer sessions. I had a Captain JAG tell me that he recently tried to stand up to the colonel to refuse this, but the colonel grabbed him by the lapels of his battledress uniform in front of all the troops, and said, 'Boy, we're here to do two things: spread the gospel of American democracy and spread the gospel of our lord Jesus Christ. And if you don't like it, I'll send you home now.'" Interview with Michael Weinstein, *LA City Beat*, May 24, 2007.

Mr. Weinstein is an Air Force Academy graduate (Magna Cum Laude) and a former Air Force Judge Advocate General, or JAG, and White House counsel to President Ronald Reagan, and to two-time presidential candidate Ross Perot. This is not a man who cries wolf easily nor flippantly.

Perhaps Mr. Weinstein believes this is bigger than the reality, a mountain out of a molehill situation? Yet the Colorado Springs Gazette on April 26, 2009 is still reporting on the issues surrounding the Air Force Academy. The article titled "Christian Speaker's AFA Visit Canceled." The speaker was Maria Anne Hirschmann, an Evangelical Christian who was on the speaker list for a February 2009 conference at the Air Force Academy, for which attendance was mandatory for the student body. It wasn't just that she was an evangelical speaking at a military academy, but that she has taken a political stand against the President, and speaking at a military academy that was the icing on the cake.

Most tax payers are unaware of how much of their money is spent on religion in the military. Slowly facts have been brought to light; it paints a disturbing picture.

"When the average American thinks of military spending on religion, they probably think only of the money spent on chaplains and chapels. And, yes, the Department of Defense (DoD) does spend a hell of a lot of money on these basic religious accommodations to provide our troops with the opportunity to exercise their religion while serving our country. But that's just the tip of the iceberg when it comes to the DoD's funding of religion. Also paid for with taxpayer dollars are a plethora of events, programs, and schemes that violate not only the Constitution, but, in many cases, the regulations on federal government contractors, specifically the regulation prohibiting federal government contractors receiving over $10,000 in contracts a year from discriminating based on religion in their hiring practices.

About a year ago, the Military Religious Freedom Foundation (MRFF) began an investigation into just how much money the DoD spends on promoting religion to military personnel and their families. What prompted this interest in

DoD spending on religion was finding out what the DoD was spending on certain individual events and programs, such as the $125 million spent on the Army's Comprehensive Soldier Fitness program and its controversial 'Spiritual Fitness' test, a mandatory test that must be taken by all soldiers. The Army insists that this test is not religious, but the countless complaints from soldiers who have failed this 'fitness' test tell a different story... But the term 'Spiritual Fitness' is not limited to this one test. The military began using this term to describe a variety of initiatives and events towards the end of 2006, and this `code phrase' for promoting religion was heavily in use by all branches of the military by 2007....

As mentioned above, what MRFF is looking at does not include chaplains or chapels -- not even the excessive spending on extravagant 'chapels' like the $30,000,000 mega-church at Fort Hood, or the 'Spiritual Fitness' centers being built on many military bases as part of what are called Resiliency Campuses. The examples below are all strictly from DoD contracts, with the funding coming out of the appropriations for things like 'Operations and Maintenance' and, somehow, 'Research and Development.' Chris Rodda, "Why Is the Military Spending Millions on Christian Contractors Bent on Evangelizing US Soldiers?" *Alternet,* August 21, 2011.

This article could not be quoted in its entirety, but it continues to outline the extent of the "Spiritual Fitness" program, a program that is shocking and disturbing. The military has been getting bad press over such violations, which are met with denials by the military hierarchy. Despite the public outcry, tax-payer funds continue to support overt evangelizing in the armed forces.

Not a new phenomenon

There exists a book, *American Evangelicals and the U.S. Military 1942-1993,* published in 1997 by Anne Loveland, that traces this trend as far back as 1942 for our modern military forces, not just the Air Force Academy. The following is about her book:

> *"Until the Vietnam War, it was the traditionally moderate mainline protestant denominations (Methodists, Presbyterians, Episcopalians), together with the Catholic Church, that dominated the religious life of the military. But as leading clergymen in these denominations spoke out against the war, evangelicals who saw the struggle in Vietnam as God's work rushed in. In 1967, the Assemblies of God, the biggest Pentecostal denomination in the world, formally dropped its long-standing commitment to pacifism, embracing worldly war as a counterpart to spiritual struggle. Other fundamentalists took from Vietnam the lessons of guerrilla combat and applied them to the spiritual fight through a tactic they called infiltration, filling the ranks of secular institutions with undercover missionaries."* Jeff Sharlet, "Jesus Killed Mohammed: The crusade for a Christian military," *Harpers Magazine,* May 2009.

You may remember these "infiltration" tactics being mentioned earlier. Jeff Sharlet's article, "Jesus Killed Mohammed: The crusade for a Christian military," in Harpers Magazine, details how our military has become *"spiritual warriors — 'ambassadors for Christ in uniform,' according to Officers' Christian Fellowship; 'government paid missionaries, according to Campus Crusade's Military Ministry....they must bring this 'Lord of all' to the entire armed forces. 'We will need to press ahead obediently,' the [OCF Bible] study concludes, 'not allowing the opposition, all of which is spearheaded by Satan, to keep us from the mission of reclaiming territory for Christ in the military.'"* It is driven from the top down, and through every branch of the armed forces.

This is the Seven Mountains Strategy in action, and it has apparently been successful. Barbara Starr and Jennifer Rizzo reported in the CNN article, "Air Force: Bible and nukes don't mix," on August 3, 2011, how the Air Force had just stopped a twenty year run of an ethics briefing at Vandenberg Air Force Base, after many complaints. The briefing was intended to address the ethics and morality issues of launching nuclear weapons, but it heavily used Christian justifications for war, with many biblical references. Jennifer Rizzo reported in the August 9, 2011, CNN article "Air Force's use of Christian messages extends to ROTC," that ROTC cadets were instructed on the Air Force's core values with lessons on the Ten Commandments, the Sermon on the Mount, and the Golden Rule, until an instructor blew the whistle to the Military Religious Freedom Foundation. In 2009, the news broke that Donald Rumsfeld would interject Bible quotes regularly with war images in his daily digest, "Secretary of Defense Worldwide Intelligence Updates." Major General Glen Shaffer, a director for intelligence serving the Joint Chiefs of Staff and Rumsfeld, was reportedly the person who started the practice, that continued for years.

"Evangelicals looked at the military and said, 'This is a mission field,' explains Captain McLinda Morton, a Lutheran pastor and former missile launch commander who until 2005 was a staff chaplain at the Air Force Academy and has since studied and written about the chaplaincy. They wanted to send their missionaries to the military, and for the military itself to become missionaries to the world. ...

The most zealous among the new generation of fundamentalist chaplains didn't join to serve the military; they came to save its soul. One of these zealots is Lieutenant Colonel Gary Hensley, division chaplain for the 101st Airborne and, until recently, the chief Army chaplain for all of Afghanistan...

He [Lt. Colonel Bob Young] seemed to feel that the military was now the only safe place to be. 'In the military, homosexuality is illegal. I don't want to get into all the particulars of 'Don't ask,' but you can't act on homosexual feelings. And adultery is illegal. Really, arguably, the military is the last American institution that tries to uphold Christian values. It's the easiest place in America to be a Christian...'

In its principal battle, the front lines are not in Iraq or Afghanistan but right here, where evangelical militants must wage spiritual war against their own countrymen. In a lecture for OCF [Officers' Christian Fellowship] titled 'Fighting the War on Spiritual Terrorism,' Army Lieutenant Colonel Greg E. Metzgar explained that Christian soldiers must always consider themselves behind enemy lines, even within the ranks, because every unsaved member of the military is a potential agent of 'spiritual terrorism'...What they mean is the very idea of diversity, its egalitarianism – the conviction that my beliefs have as much right to speak in the public square as do yours; that truth, in a democracy, is a mediated affair." Jeff Sharlet "Jesus Killed Mohammed: The crusade for a Christian military," *Harpers Magazine,* May, 2009.

This will not have changed simply because "Don't Ask, Don't Tell" has been repealed. If anything those who have been entrenched in this mentality that the armed forces are their haven will not adjust well. The preparedness that the armed forces underwent to make the transition from the repeal of DADT most likely had more to do with protecting gay service members from the Religious Right element than any other human element involved.

The Officers' Christian Fellowship

The Officers' Christian Fellowship mentioned in the preceding quote states on their website that, "We believe God calls military believers to be His ambassadors to the armed forces. OCF exists to help you become a more effective ambassador, integrating faith and profession with excellence." As the name indicates, it is made up purposefully of military officers who are the leadership of the armed forces. Leading up to the repeal of Don't Ask Don't Tell, there have been several instances that have reached the media, of military leaders exhibiting virulent anti-gay sentiments.

The worldview of the Religious Right fits well with the military, but more importantly, it is seen as a critical territory to be won for Christ. According to Chalmers Johnson in his book *Nemesis: The Days of the American Republic* there are approximately 737 U.S. military bases in *other* countries all around the globe [2005 data] with more than two and half million military personnel. That is a considerable missionary network allowing for access to nearly every nation, with government footing the bill via your tax dollars for missionary transport and lodging.

To the Religious Right's viewpoint, this is supposed to be a Christian nation in the first place, so there is no conflict with utilizing the military complex. Any historian will tell you that the military is critical in the leadership of a country. Many takeovers of a country were dependent upon the military backing the person maneuvering to take over. It seems unlikely that such a fact has escaped the Religious Right in their bid to make this a Christian nation, according to their vision of Dominion. Let us not forget the atrocities of the Crusades by a militarized faith. Combining the Religious Right with our military can easily lead to feminists and science teachers, among others, being counted as enemies of the state.

Take With You From This Chapter

➢ Over the last several years, more evidence has been unearthed about the strong impact of the Religious Right on the armed forces.

➢ Michael Weinstein filed a lawsuit in United States District Court for the District of New Mexico against the United States Air Force, on October 6, 2005.

Chapter 14
The Mountain of Religion

<u>What to Expect From this Chapter</u>

➢ Why religion is a mountain of influence in the first place.

➢ How the war has extended to moderate or progressive Christian churches.

➢ Hear from the Evangelical Left and their lament over the damage to the faith.

In the Seven Mountains Mandate to take over areas of influence, it is interesting that there is a mountain dedicated to religion. We have seen how there is a religious caste system in the Religious Right view. But what about those Christian churches that claim to love and follow Jesus, but who just don't share the same extremist stance? They are why there is a Mountain dedicated to religion; those churches that do not mesh with the Religious Right must be influenced and won over.

<u>Fighting a common enemy</u>

"You say you're supposed to be nice to the Episcopalians and the Presbyterians and the Methodists and this, that, and the other thing. Nonsense! I don't have to be nice to the spirit of the Antichrist. I can love the people who hold false opinions, but I don't have to be nice to them" Pat Robertson, 700 Club, <u>CBN</u>, Jan 4, 1991.

That quote shows very starkly that the many Evangelicals came from a position of no surrender; either you were with them or against them. Since that time, the Religious Right has made a great effort to cooperate in political endeavors, even with those formerly not in doctrinal alignment, for the sake of fighting against common enemies. Focusing on a common enemy has been a tried-and-true method for centuries, and works very well to unite warring factions. In this case, the common enemies uniting unfriendly denominations are feminists and homosexuals, who are "breaking down family values," and reproductive health services which include sex education, contraceptives, abortion, and science. Thus we see Catholics and Protestants fighting abortion together, or evangelicals and Mormons fighting gay rights. The Religious Right lumps all of these under the label "Secular Humanism," which is viewed as man supplanting God's will with man's tainted desires and reasoning, one of the lessons from the Garden of Eden.

The problem of moderate churches

But that only goes so far towards an immediate political end. What do you do about those troublesome churches who are more moderate or (gasp) liberal? In the book *Steeplejacking: How the Christian Right is Hijacking Mainstream Religion*, Rev. Dr. John Dorhauer of United Church of Christ's Missouri Mid-South Conference, blows the lid off of how the Religious Right has very effective and insidious tactics to take over those churches that aren't in line with their core tenants or their political agenda.

This important book exposes the Institute on Religion and Democracy, that uses "conservative renewal groups." The "renewal groups" systematically enter mainstream churches that have more progressive views or are more tolerant and inclusive, and purposefully infiltrate the congregations to cause division and strife over social wedge issues like abortion or gay rights, with the express goal of ripping the congregation apart to take over the church leadership and shift the church to the Religious Right way. This works towards the goal of taking over entire progressive or liberal thinking denominations.

This is a cunning and deceitful way to get everybody in line, and is much less bloody than was the Spanish inquisition. But, it shows that tolerance isn't practiced towards brothers and sisters who differ. Rev. Dr. John Dorhauer is not a conspiracy theorist; he is a level-headed minister who is fighting the Religious Right for the right of churches to practice their Christian faith as they see fit. This is a prime example of why Christians should be supporting the Separation of Church and State with their every waking breath. Individual Christian expressions will be ground into the dust when that wall of separation goes tumbling down.

> *"The traditional evangelicals, those who come out of Billy Graham's mold,*

are not necessarily comfortable with the direction taken by the Dominionists, who now control most of America's major evangelical organizations, from the NRB [National Religious Broadcasters] to the Southern Baptist Convention, and may already claim dominion over the Christian media outlets. But Christians who challenge Dominionists, even if they are fundamentalist or conservative or born-again, tend to be ruthlessly thrust aside." Chris Hedges, "Feeling the Hate With the National Religious Broadcasters," *Harper's Magazine,* May, 2005.

Churches under attack

Two other books exist that expose the underhanded tactics of the Religious Right. *Hard Ball on Holy Ground* by Stephen Swecker, dated 2005, is a collection of interviews, research, and essays on the efforts of the Religious Right to undermine mainline churches. Also, the book *United Methodist @ Risk: A Wake-up Call* (2003) by Leon Howell, details the battle in the Methodist Church between left and right and issues a challenge to church moderates and liberals to fight or loose their churches.

"Journalist Leon Howell in his recent book, 'United Methodism at Risk,' warns that the UMC [United Methodist Church] must recognize the danger of this tightly organized, highly motivated, and well-financed 'take-no-prisoners' crusade to take over the churches and turn them in a right-wing direction. He called on the church leaders and laity to rise up in a 'fighting mood' to repel the attack." Tim Wheeler "Bush, Religious Right Target Churches," *People's Weekly World,* July 3, 2004.

Leon Howell gives us a great history lesson that clearly shows the Religious Right's propaganda appearing in mainstream media, as far back as the early 80s when the assault on inclusive Christians had begun.

"The stories began like hand grenades in the ecumenical world.

They began in Reader's Digest. In August 1982, it blasted the World Council of Churches with an article that asked, 'Karl Marx or Jesus Christ?' In January 1983, Reader's Digest had another question: 'Do you know where your church dollars go?' The ominous subtitle: 'You better find out because they may be supporting revolutions rather than religion.'

Also in January 1983, CBS's '60 Minutes' carried harsh and distorted attacks on the World and National Councils of Churches, especially their ties to Third World liberation groups such as the anti-apartheid South African Council of Churches. False accusations of giving funds to armed insurgents were framed as questions, an apparent attempt to avoid slander charges.

Twenty years later, Don Hewitt, creator and still producer of the program, was asked on Dec. 2, 2002, 'Larry King Live' show if he regretted any show in '60 Minutes' 36-year history. 'Yes' he answered. 'We once took off on the National Council of Churches (NCC) as being left-wing and radical and a lot of nonsense.'

The morning after the NCC '60 Minutes,' he got congratulatory calls from several right-wing sources. He thought: 'We must have done something wrong last night, and I think we probably did.'

Four articles appeared in the New York Times within 15 months with headlines like: 'New Church Group Assails Aid to Leftists.'

All these stories had been initiated by the Institute on Religion and Democracy (IRD). It had hit the ground running after its 1981 founding. It and some of its founders were featured in each of the stories. Who are those guys, asked the ecumenical participants from around the world? And what motivates them?" Leon Howell, *United Methodist @ Risk: A Wake-up Call*, Information Project for United Methodists, 2003.

Leon Howell shares that the initial key players in the 1980s in the Institute on Religion and Democracy (IRD) were Richard John Neuhaus, Michael Novak, Penn Kemble, David Jessup, George Weigel and Edmund W. Robb Jr. He also shares that they started a "public-television documentary with Ben Wattenberg (still on television in *Think Tank with Ben Wattenberg*) attacking church leaders called *Protestants Protest*. Mr. Howell states that Penn Kemble produced it, and in reality Edmund Robb

Jr. was the only "protestor" in the *Protestants Protest* title. This provided a media mouthpiece to assault inclusive churches.

> *"Their long-time leadership means IRD's core vision remains. The board has continuity and strong connections with other conservative renewal groups.*
>
> *[Diane] Knippers became the institute's president in **1993**. She oversees the Episcopal effort. Mark Tooley – a CIA employee for eight years – has been at IRD since **1994**. He directs UMAction, the IRD subsidiary focusing on The United Methodist Church. Alan Wisdom, who has been on the IRD staff since **1983**, heads the Presbyterian committee."* Leon Howell, *United Methodist @ Risk: A Wake-up Call*, Information Project for United Methodists, 2003.

Mr. Howell also states that the Institute on Religion and Democracy was created and sustained by right-wing corporate foundations that supplied more than 80% of their income in the first decade.   He claims IRD's 2001 revenues were $1,120,508. That is a substantial budget for "influencing the governing church conventions of three denominations" mission as stated in the 2000 funding proposal called "Reforming America's Churches Project: 2001-2004."

This is what is meant in the Seven Mountains Mandate concerning the Religion Mountain. Dominionists believe that the church itself must be reclaimed, the people brought back to proper worship and cultural power. The Religious Right doesn't like Christians who aren't on board with their extremist agenda, and may challenge them. They utilize conservative renewal groups in this attack on moderate or progressive churches.

> *"We will annually prepare resolutions for local and regional church conventions in the three major denominations. These resolutions will call attention to egregious behavior by radical church leaders and will be important tools for grassroots organizing. They will also focus on positive, proactive initiatives that unite traditional religious believers and discredit the Religious Left. Working with other renewal organizations, we will identify electable*

conservative candidates for national church conventions. We will help train elected delegates to be effective at church conventions. We also will assist conservatives who serve on the boards of key church agencies so as to have direct influence over the permanent staff." "Reforming America's Churches Project: 2001-2004," Institute on Religion and Democracy.

From this quote you see a strategy to takeover inclusive churches by:

— Ferreting out "egregious behavior" of leadership to discredit them (shades of Carl Rove.)

— Discrediting the Religious Left in positive ways, thus bringing together the "traditional" believers. Amazing how they can use positive and discredit in the same sentence and not be embarrassed.

— Identifying the candidates for denomination leadership positions that they like and then training delegates "to be effective at church conventions," meaning help the delegates to swing votes to their preferred candidates.

— They will "assist" their approved and placed board members on strategically important denomination boards so they can have "direct influence" on the policies and decisions that govern all the churches in that denomination.

Voilà, you have just one small lesson in how to takeover moderate or inclusive churches and bring them in line with the Religious Right. This is the religion mountain in the Seven Mountains Mandate, and how they are taking dominion of the religion mountain.

Where did the Religious Left go?

Has the Religious Left been completely destroyed and overrun? Within the Evangelical church, there are many who disagree strongly with the Religious Right but feel their voices are not heard. Randal Balmer, devout Evangelical and editor-at-large for the magazine *Christianity Today,* wrote the book, *Thy Kingdom Come, An Evangelical's Lament: How the Religious Right Distorts the Faith and Threatens America.* In this book he shares the frustration of Evangelicals who view the Religious

Right as taking over the faith and drastically distorting it.

"The evangelical faith that nurtured me as a child and sustains me as an adult has been hijacked by right-wing zealots who have distorted the gospel of Jesus Christ, defaulted on the noble legacy of nineteenth – century evangelical activism, and failed to appreciate the genius of the First Amendment. They, appear not to have read the same New Testament that I open before me every morning at the kitchen counter. When they do quote the Bible, they wrench passages out of context and offer pinched, literalistic interpretations – of Genesis account of creation, for instance – that diminish the scriptures by robbing them of their larger meaning.

The effect of this right-wing takeover has been a poisoning of public discourse and a distortion of the faith. Leaders of the Religious Right have managed to persuade many of my fellow evangelical Christians that it is something akin to sin to vote for anyone who is not a Republican...

Although the numbers are hard to come by, there are more politically liberal evangelicals than you might think, for one of the great delusions perpetrated by the Religious Right in recent years is that all evangelical Christians are politically conservative. ...

I'm not alone, although sometimes it feels that way. Other evangelicals have similar views, though we have trouble making our voices heard – at least, we haven't been very skilled at doing so. Part of the problem lies in the fact that, unlike the Religious Right, we don't have radio or television programs, let alone entire media networks. Our views don't lend themselves easily to sloganeering... Unlike the Religious Right, we cannot tap into the vast reservoirs of corporate money available to conservative causes.

As an evangelical Christian, someone who takes the Bible seriously and who believes in the transformative power of Jesus, I want to reclaim the faith from the Religious Right. I also want to protest that most of the Religious Right's agenda is misguided, even ruinous, to the nation I love and, ultimately, to the faith I love even more.

I don't find much that I recognize as Christian *in the actions and policies of the Religious Right."* Randall Balmer, *Thy Kingdom Come, An Evangelical's Lament: How the Religious Right Distorts the Faith and Threatens America,* Basic Books, 2006.

More evangelicals who don't agree with the Religious Right are standing up and speaking out. Alisa Harris was raised Religious Right with home-schooling mixing religion with a political worldview. She was a toddler at conservative-right rallies and anti-abortion demonstrations. She has since written the book, *Raised Right: How I Untangled My Faith from Politics,* chronicling her parting from the extremism she was raised in, to find a progressive Christian path that she felt was closer to what Jesus taught.

"Over the years I began to doubt what I'd been taught — that we could find in the Bible the final answers to our questions about the minutiae of 21st century tax policy and the path to economic growth. I saw Christians yell at gay activists, obsess over sex, and enforce ideological purity instead of reducing abortions or helping the poor.

I began to think that our Christian duty was not to make our country's laws conform to our private morality but to heal the broken-hearted and bind up their wounds. The political principles I now embrace – human equality, human dignity, and human rights — align less with Schaeffer and more with King, who not only marched for civil rights for African-Americans but also launched the Poor People's Campaign and fought for the economic rights of all, black and white.

These principles come from a Christian passion for justice but are not, like Bachmann's worldview, exclusive to Christianity. I have abandoned neither politics nor my Christian faith but the idea of a 'worldview' where all spiritual

183

questions have political answers, and all political problems have spiritual solutions." Alisa Harris, "I could have become Michele Bachmann," *CNN Religion Blog*, August 14th, 2011.

In spite of the presence of moderate or progressive churches and politically left evangelicals, the Religious Right and their tactics are making headway each day, and in each denomination's leadership elections. D. Michael Lindsay shows the wide chasm between the Religious Right and the more inclusive moderate or inclusive churches demonstrated in the numbers. Call to Renewal, part of Sojourners ministries, is an evangelical left-leaning advocacy group lead by Jim Wallis, that in spite of its being in existence since 1975, only has a two hundred thousand email list, versus Focus on the Family's over two million on their email list. This is evidence that all those tactics are effective.

"Pray with us that God will guide our nation's policy makers and that conservative Christians from all walks of life will come together and lead the way with the biblically based solutions our country – and indeed the world – has been waiting for." Tony Perkins and Harry R Jackson Jr. *Personal Faith Public Policy,* Frontline, 2008.

Here we see *conservative Christians* called upon to pray, not *all* Christians. This is another example of how the Religious Right is exclusive in their view of who should be shaping the country. This point is critical, and let it serve as a warning to all moderate and liberal-leaning or progressive churches, the Religious Right does not include you in their company. Tony Perkins, Religious Right heavy-hitter, even singles out Former President Jimmy Carter, the first openly evangelical president, with obvious disdain.

"[President Jimmy] Carter has been sparring with the Religious Right ever since. His 2006 book, Our Endangered Values: America's Moral Crisis, repeated his long-standing argument in favor of his conception of 'separation of church and state' in a manner that was perhaps more strident than any of his previous

statements throughout the years." Tony Perkins and Harry R Jackson Jr. *Personal Faith Public Policy*, Frontline, 2008.

No live and let live

It is naive to think we can live together in peace and harmony because that would require all parties involved to desire such unity. Unfortunately, the Religious Right considers such a live-and-let-live premise to be compromise, and compromise is tantamount to surrendering to Satan, and makes anyone involved worse than any turn-coat Judas. The Religious Right does not even pretend to tolerate the moderate or liberal Christians, as the following quotes from Tony Perkins of the Family Research Council spotlight.

> *"Lately, we see a new level of cooperation between various members of the press and liberal Christians, who are allies of convenience against the religious Right. Liberal Christians are stepping up efforts to crack the unity of evangelicals, and becoming increasingly harsh and public in their criticism of the various views and tactics of the religious Right....*
>
> *Why is the Christian Left so quick to attack the religious Right? Probably because as a movement, the Christian Left has yet to build any lasting political or policy influence. The only power they have at the moment is in their shared goal with liberal non-Christians of reducing the influence of Bible-believing, conservative Christians in American politics and policy."* Tony Perkins and Harry R Jackson Jr. *Personal Faith Public Policy*, Frontline, 2008.

Liberal Christians are trying to crack the unity of evangelicals! We have three books mentioned in this section exposing the Religious Right's taking over moderate and liberal churches, but the Religious Right yet again cries that they are the victims and demonize everyone else. The book from evangelical Randall Balmer shouting that the Religious Right hijacking and ruining the Christian faith is somehow an attempt to split *the true believers* apart. Yet again the Right uses the tactic of blaming their critics of doing what they themselves excel at. To heap condemnation onto any liberals within the church, the Right claims they are in cahoots with the corporate press and non-Christians.

<u>Take With You From This Chapter</u>

➢ The Mountain of religion is to transform more moderate or inclusive churches into Religious Right churches, using underhanded tactics.

➢ More evangelicals are coming forward and speaking out about the dangers of the Religious Right.

➢ The Religious Right is not a friend of those who are not part of them.

Chapter 15
The Mountain of Business

What to Expect From this Chapter

➢   How businesses are themselves a mission field to their employees and associates.

➢   How there is a network that assists putting kingdom-minded into influential business positions.

➢   How business is needed to fund the culture war.

> *"In the world of business, evangelical executives have focused their energies on building corporate cultures amenable to people of faith. Executives now feel more comfortable incorporating prayer into business activities, such as offering an invocation before a board meeting ... They want young people with faith-shaped vocations not just at First Baptist Church but also at Goldman Sachs, the State Department, and the University of Chicago...Evangelicals populate elite centers like New York and Los Angeles now more than ever. They can be found at the top of nearly every social institution in America, and their influence can be seen in public policy, commerce, and the media."* D. Michael Lindsay, *Faith In The Halls of Power: How Evangelicals Joined the American Elite*, Oxford University Press, 2007.

Religious Right claims corporate Mountain

America has a large number of self-identified evangelicals, and those people are in the work force. That is not an issue in-and-of-itself. The Seven Mountains Strategy wants to see more kingdom-minded Christians in influential positions throughout corporate America. Utilizing evangelical networks they have a unique brand of nepotism whereby they nurture, mentor, and assist others of like-mind that serves to bolster their ranks in influential business positions.

> *"Almost all of this activity has begun within elite networks, within webs of*

interpersonal relations at the highest levels. Evangelicals would not be nearly as influential as they are today without these powerful networks. ... However, evangelicalism – as a salient, totalizing religious identity – provides a particularly strong bond for networks across sectors. Also, being an evangelical can have an empowering advantage: Fellow believers help each other rise in power." D. Michael Lindsay, *Faith in the Halls of Power: How Evangelicals Joined the American Elite*, Oxford University Press, 2007.

Funding the culture war

Having more Religious Right in influential corporate positions serves their end-goal in a few ways. Primarily, the more highly paid executives donating to Religious Right coffers aids in funding the continuing war.

One example is Tom Monaghan, founder of Dominos Pizza, who openly gives large donations to the radical Operation Rescue, Right to Life, and the Word of God fundamentalist group. From his Dominos Pizza wealth he created: the organization Legatus for Catholic business executives; Ave Maria Catholic Radio; Ave Maria University; Ave Maria School of Law; Ave Maria Florida, founded in 2005 as a planned township around the university that follows strict Catholic morals as civic law; The Thomas Moore Law Center; Ave Maria Mutual Funds; Ave Maria List with over five hundred advocacy groups of like-mind; and the Ave Maria Political Action Committee to influence politics. Tom Monaghan is a great poster-child for the Business Mountain Strategy.

Hobby Lobby is active in financially supporting and spreading the kingdom. Not only are they closed on Sundays and play Christian music in the stores, but they run newspaper ads with overt Christian messages, thus using their business to proclaim the Good News. The Green family gives to Oral Roberts University and other Christian causes regularly. The *New York Times* reported on June 12, 2010, that the evangelical Green family that owns Hobby Lobby, along with the company's president, have been spending millions collecting rare antiquities, manuscripts, and books, to open a Bible

Museum. As of May 16, 2011, the Green Collection is a traveling exhibit looking for a permanent home for 40,000 items. Only a small fraction of the total is featured in the worldwide traveling exhibits. Witness your crafting dollars at work.

Chick-fil-a is another example of an openly Christian organization that pumps profits into the Religious Right agenda. They co-sponsored The Art of Marriage: Getting to the Heart of God's Design Conference February 11, 2011, with the non-profit research and education group Pennsylvania Family Institute. Chick-fil-a has financial ties to California's Proposition 8 effort and the anti-gay National Organization for Marriage. Eat a chicken sandwich and fund the anti-gay frenzy?

Carl Karcher, the deceased founder of Carl's Jr. fast food chain, had been very public about his support of pro-life groups, as well as opening all of his board-meetings with the prayer of St. Francis of Assisi. Additionally, there is The Timothy Plan, a large group of mutual funds that reportedly only invests in companies that it feels run Christian pro-life, pro-family, and "traditional American values" businesses. This is definitely one of the reasons that the Religious Right has targeted business as an area to influence. A war effort costs money, and corporate profits help to finance the ongoing battles.

The workplace as a mission field

Beyond the financing of the Religious Right agenda is the fact that Americans spend much of their time at work, which makes the workplace a highly influential part of most American's lives. Research has shown that during an average workday, more time is spent at work than sleeping, or any other single activity.

Religious Right executives and managers have a captive audience to influence. The workplace can easily become a place where an employee's personal beliefs are used in promotion decisions, or they are simply made uncomfortable by an atmosphere to conform to a given faith. This seems impossibly alarmist to the average person, until you hear of instances where it happens. When the business world is viewed as a mission field, rather than a means of financial support for a person and his or her family, there is a setup for widespread manipulation, discrimination, and violation of rights.

"As most of you are probably aware, an American Airlines captain faces disciplinary action after evangelizing to passengers on a flight between Los Angeles and New York on Feb. 6. Roger Findiesen, pilot of American's Flight 34, who had recently returned from a missionary trip to Central America, asked Christian fliers to identify themselves by raising their hands, then urged them to engage their non-Christian seatmates, whom some witnesses say he referred to as 'crazy,' in a discussion about faith.... The mood was apparently so tense that when the captain asked non-Christians to identify themselves, very few souls (sorry) raised their hands." Patrick Smith, "Ask the Pilot", *Salon.com*, February 20, 2004

A correction to the article the following week explained that the pilot may not have actually called non-Christians "crazy." But the fact remains that the pilot did put passengers in a peer-pressure situation, and used his job as a continuation of his missionary work. Alaska Airlines provides a full color photo card complete with a Bible verse above their logo with meals, but not with the snacks. This will actually become more common in the workplace, the more the Religious Right gains the business sphere of influence.

"They also spoke of their calling as unique. Rick Tompane, a Silicon Valley executive, said, 'I can be involved in the lives of my employees at levels most ministers cannot.' Tom Morgan, the president and CEO of Hughes Supply, a Fortune 500 company, agreed: 'The opportunities I have for ministry in the business world are very different from the opportunity that my pastor has.' Morgan and other business leaders believe they can bear witness to their faith and be of greater assistance, both directly and indirectly, to the evangelical community as business executives than they could as ministers.' " D. Michael Lindsay, *Faith in the Halls of Power: How Evangelicals Joined the American*

Elite, Oxford University Press, 2007.

Everything from the Affordable Care Act law, estate tax, and closing corporate tax loopholes all become entangled in the Religious Right's strategic plan for the business sphere of influence. When you depend upon wealthy heads of corporations to fund your efforts, you don't want them taxed thereby losing some donations.

Take With You From This Chapter

➢   The Religious Right taking the Mountain of business provides funds to the culture war, and turns work places into missionary fields.

Chapter 16
The Mountain of Media

What to Expect From this Chapter

➢   How even news outlets are used to further God's kingdom, and what progress has already been made in taking the Mountain.

Media's influence

> "*For our purposes, media refers to the news outlets that report and establish news. Therein lies the power of the media – they can actually create the news. They can turn a non-story into the big story and turn what should be huge stories into non-stories.. Media outlets include television stations and networks, web sites, newspapers, radio stations, and magazines. ...*
>
> *News has the power to affect the psyche of individuals and even a whole nation. As believers rise in prominence on this mountain of media, we are to understand the godly philosophy of news and not collaborate in poisoning the psyche of a nation.*
>
> *One of the new creative ways that the Lord is going to release His evangelists onto this mountain is by imparting the wisdom to transform reporting a news story into preaching 'good tidings.' Any journalist who can tell a story of heroism that incidentally portrays the heroic act as the outcome of a relationship with God is in fact preaching the good news. We need an army of evangelists who are 'wise as serpents and harmless as doves' (Matt 10:16), lying low and blending in, while having a kingdom agenda.*" Johnny Enlow, *The Seven Mountain Prophecy: Unveiling the Coming Elijah Revolution*, Creation House, 2008.

Media, or news outlets are indeed influential, and the Religious Right understands that. Reporting news once meant the relaying of events. Journalism used to emphasize reporting facts and remaining unbiased while connecting a few dots for readers/viewers. Investigative journalists, once called muckrakers, would dig to find corruption and report the facts to bring wrongs to light and effect change. But that is not the news, or journalism, that the Religious Right have in mind; they would have a biased reporting of stories that promote, highlight, encourage, and favor their slant on news. Their definition of news is to share the story with a Christian aspect, showing biblical themes etc.

An example of just how persuasive media can indeed be, is found in the Tea Party. The Tea Party would not have gained its numbers if not for the amount of media coverage that a particular "news" channel continually afforded the movement.

As the hard-hitting investigative journalists are fighting to survive with more online news, bloggers, and the cable twenty-four hour sensationalized commentary, the opportunities are abundant for gaining influence on the media Mountain.

Religious Right's advances in media

> *"Over the last thirty years, they have built an impressive infrastructure. In particular, evangelicals have underwritten think tanks and programs for the movement's next generation of leadership, which bodes well for their long-term political success. In addition, it has given them tremendous access to cable news programs, which rely heavily on Washington think tanks for guests."* D. Michael Lindsay, *Faith in the Halls of Power: How Evangelicals Joined the American Elite*, Oxford University Press, 2007.

The Religious Right jumped on radio and television to reach followers but, it soon became a tool of influence. Take the case of "The John Ankerberg Show," started in 1980, which is a harsh diatribe in the form of an Evangelical talk show. The show has been criticized for deceptive tactics while receiving awards and praise. Ankerberg is aggressive, and employs standard fear tactics in topics such as "What Will Happen if America Legalizes Same Sex Marriage?" as well as multitudes of information on creationism-as-science and how modern Wicca is evil, and he offers help for debating how the Harry Potter books are against the Bible. The show is a mainstay and extremely influential, and has even won Christian awards. In my Religious Right days

I faithfully watched.

Of course there is the 700 Club presenting their brand of journalism with a Christian slant. The National Religious Broadcasters Association holds annual conventions, and in 2005 renowned and respected journalist Chris Hedges attended and shared his experience.

> *"...the National Religious Broadcasters association – brings together some 1,600 Christian radio and television broadcasters, who claim to reach up to 141 million listeners and viewers – is holding its annual convention.... MacDonald leaves little doubt that the convention is meant to serve as a rallying cry for a new and particularly militant movement in Christian politics, one that is sometimes mistaken for another outbreak of mere revivalism. In fact, this movement is a curious hybrid of fundamentalists, Pentecostals, Southern Baptists, conservative Catholics, Charismatics, and other evangelicals, all of whom are at war doctrinally but who nonetheless share a belief that America is destined to become a Christian nation, led by Christian men who are in turn directed by God."* Chris Hedges "Feeling the hate with the National Religious Broadcasters" *Harper's Magazine*, May 2005.

Those are impressive numbers of media channels and their subsequent audiences. It is a testimony to just how mainstream Dominionist ideology has become whether or not the audience knows the Dominionist term, or identifies as followers. Christian broadcasting has been dutifully presenting this worldview to the 141 million listeners.

Religious Right hits the big time

But what about a major cable show such as Fox? When you tune into the 700 Club you expect to have a particular brand of Christian worldview on any event they report on. You know what you are getting. The Religious Right is now regularly seen on news shows, like Fox, in which their side is presented favorably. Glen Beck and Mike Huckabee both featured Dominionist and Religious Right celebrity David Barton, promoting his alternate history of America unchallenged on their shows. Barton was praised and encouraged, but not once challenged in his debunked faux-history. Bill O'Reilly regularly presents and defends the Religious Right worldview in his commentaries. This is a huge media coop and signals that the Seven Mountains strategy for the Media Mountain has been very successful.

Consider the impacts of a major cable "news" network that presents a Religious Right slant on events in such a way that multitudes are convinced by their presentation without any disclaimer of a religious slant. The Religious Right has gone primetime and big time. It is important to see how this mainstream cable network that is nowhere identified as Religious Right, is able to present a Religious Right spin on issues without a disclaimer.

> *"Many Christians work in mainstream media, in fact, but they are compelled to work under current philosophical constraints of those media. A few may expose the hypocrisies of media – Sean Hannity operates in this role, for example …*
>
> *One [strategy] is having a prayer covering and blessing over anyone <u>currently on the mountain of media</u> who is neutralizing the dark side. FOX news is well below the standard the Lord will raise, but by forcing a level of accountability on other news outlets, it's neutralizing an even greater darkness released from some of them."* Johnny Enlow, *The Seven Mountain Prophecy: Unveiling the Coming Elijah Revolution,* Creation House, 2008. (underline added.)

The preceding quote was from a Seven Mountains proponent lifting up Fox news as currently influencing the Mountain of media for the Religious Right. This must be clearly understood, that Fox is recognized by the extremists as being a Religious Right organization that is conquering the Media sphere of influence for furthering God's kingdom in this nation, although they aren't the perfect model of what the Godly media should be, yet. They recognize their fellow soldiers in the war to take the nation.

Fox cable channel went ballistic over President Obama's 2011 YouTube Thanksgiving address because he did not mention God. Fox covered this manufactured issue in three of its shows throughout one day. That President Obama included a mention to God in his written address did not soften the coverage. This prompted Jon Stewart on November 28, 2011's, The Daily Show to ask, "When did Fox become the 700 club?" Yes, Virginia, the Religious Right media is stealthy, mainstream, and influential.

Take With You From This Chapter

➢ The Mountain of Media has succumbed to the Religious Right with a vast radio network, major cable news network, and Washington think tanks.

Chapter 17
The Mountain of Arts and Entertainment

<u>What to Expect From this Chapter</u>

➢ How artwork, music, fashion, sports, and all forms of entertainment are targeted to glorify God.

➢ How even entertainment channels are used to reinforce Religious Right approved values.

The Mountain of Arts and Entertainment is referred to as "celebration," since the A&E term is just so, well, secular. For the Religious Right, every aspect has been mapped out and the battle plans drafted.

"The mountain of celebration includes the arts, music, sports, fashion, entertainment, and every other way we celebrate and enjoy life. ...

A specific and primary target of the Elijah Revolution is to take the mountain that is presently releasing a dark and decadent pop culture. God will release the Elijah Revolution tsunami onto this mountain, and when it is taken, every form of entertainment and celebration will prophesy of God. Music, art, poetry, fashion, and film are all meant to prophesy to a culture.

The goal will not just be having Christian fare on television or at the theater: that's a weak and flimsy compromise, not a revolution. It's not enough just to portray Sunday school on the big screens and expect that to displace Hollywood's products. In the heart of our Creator are the most exciting stories and adventures in the world – and they aren't fiction, though they can be portrayed as such.

If you are a Christian of influence who is involved in sports, know that you are raised up and blessed by God to be a prophetic voice in and to your generation. ... This is your ministry, your platform, your pulpit – not your secular life."

Fashion is another prophetic tool, and if we don't engage this part of the mountain, the world will continue to prophesy with fashion.... The point is not for us to wear conservative clothing but to come up with radical styles that release the kingdom of God on Earth. To this point, WWJD bracelets are the closest thing we've seen of a Christian fashion trend. Even multitudes of non-believers thought it was cool to wear the bracelets. But we're going further than that. ...

Some cities are known for forms of entertainment that shouldn't even be saved. Las Vegas gambling, for example, has no redemptive value. There is not a Christian gambling alternative, just as there are no Christian prostitution alternatives or Christian strip clubs. Some entertainment is fit only for elimination....

Hollywood is clearly at the top of the mountain. New York, Seattle, Las Vegas, San Francisco, and New Orleans also have altars close to the top of the mountain....There are cities to be strategically targeted. There are institutions to be targeted. There are individuals to be targeted. There are altars to overthrow and many things to displace. But we must always remember to come in with a replacement for what was formerly there....

The Hollywood ratings board is a very important target, as are Disney and Motown. The critics who write reviews and committees that give awards like the Oscars and Grammys are also extremely important – their seal of approval can jumpstart movies and musicians who have no business being jumpstarted." Johnny Enlow, *The Seven Mountain Prophecy: Unveiling the Coming Elijah Revolution,* Creation House, 2008.

On the arts and entertainment Mountain, it is about targeting cities, specific industries, and individuals such as ratings boards and critics. Everything from music, art, fashion, sports, amusement parks, perhaps even board games, Facebook games, Wii, and video games (like the violent Left Behind game), shall be guided by the Religious Right to bring glory to the Kingdom as well. Even the beauty pageants that reach a broad televised audience are now spreading the Religious Right message, such as Carrie Prejean during the 2009 Miss USA pageant.

In sports there are many examples, including legendary Dallas Cowboys coach Tom Landry, Tim Tebow, Reggie White, Mike Singletary, and golfer Payne Stewar, to name a few. Tim Tebow is an interesting case, and his public displays of getting down on bended knee to pray is his right, but ironically is something that Jesus spoke against, not that it appears to matter. *"When you pray, you are not to be like the hypocrites; for they love to stand and pray in the synagogues and on the street corners so that they may be seen by men. Truly I say to you, they have their reward in full. But you, when you pray, go into your inner room, close your door and pray to your Father who is in secret, and your Father who sees what is done in secret will reward you."* Matthew 6:5-6, New American Standard Bible. Which puts much of the in-your-face-religion in question overall.

Books

Perhaps the best example of the Arts and Entertainment Mountain of influence being impacted is the *Left Behind* book series. This series of books crossed over to mainstream audiences rather than strictly Christian bookstore patrons. The massive success created a media empire built upon the *Left Behind* series of 12 books (55 million sold so far); based upon these sales numbers, its success rivals Stephen King and John Grisham. The *Left Behind* phenomenon has spread beyond just books, and includes videotapes, audio books, graphic novels, children's books, study guides, weekly email detailing how current events are fulfilling the book's view of prophecy, calendars, gift cards, apparel, and a violent video game.

> *"That is because among the best-selling fiction books of our times – right up there with Tom Clancy and Stephen King – is a series about the End Times, written by Tim F. LaHaye and Jerry B. Jenkins, based on the Book of Revelation. ... Only about half of Left Behind readers are Evangelicals, which suggests there is a broader audience of people who are having this conversation. ...*

The series has sold some 32 million copies – 50 million if you count the graphic novels and children's versions – and sales jumped 60% after Sept. 11. Book 9, published in October, was the best-selling novel of 2001....

Now the 10th book, The Remnant, is arriving in stores, a breathtaking 2.75 million hard-cover copies, and its impact may be felt far beyond the book clubs and Bible classes." Nancy Gibbs, "Apocalypse Now", *Time*, June 23 2002.

True to the Seven Mountains Strategy of business providing the money to further more Christian enterprise, Tim LaHaye reportedly gave 4.5 million dollars to Liberty University (founded by Jerry Falwell) for a new student center, a School of Prophesy, and additional funds for a campus ice rink. Tim LaHaye was involved in the founding of the Institute for Creation Research, and co-founded the Moral Majority long before he began writing books.

But the *Left Behind* series isn't the only example of fulfilling this mandate. Frank Peretti has long been writing fiction books (*This Present Darkness* has reportedly sold 2.7 million copies) with a Religious Right worldview and themes. The book market has an onslaught of such Religious Right-fueled fiction thrillers, currently including *Church and State* by Skip Coryell that uses the tactic of Christianity being persecuted for the plot. He envisions a nation that has outlawed any public expression of religion and the resulting dilemma of a Christian president. These books are getting attention outside the Christian stores and blogs, such as *Omnimystery News*, a newsletter for mystery fans, featuring skip Coryell's *Church and State*. These are examples of replacing the secular book industry with a proper Religious Right version, but also of propagating their worldview as well.

Film

The big budget movies of the Chronicles of Narnia triology are one example for the Entertainment Mountain. There were also movies such as Mel Gibson's *The Passion of Christ* that raked in blockbuster profits; *Facing the Giants*, produced by Sherwood Baptist Church of Georgia, that grossed over five million; *One Night With the King*, based on the story of Esther in the Bible, that made a over four million its opening weekend in spite of mediocre reviews; and the *Grace Card*, which grossed over one million its opening weekend.

To further develop and encourage this cultural influence, there is the Christian Film and Television Commission founded by Ted Baehr that provides help to evangelicals in every aspect of getting your script or movie done right and made a success. An example is the "Making, Distributing and Promoting Spiritually Uplifting Family Movies and Television Programs," panel discussion and networking event Ted Baehr held in Burbank, California in the summer of 2011. Part of the same organization is the Movieguide that has its own Christian awards in categories of Faith and Freedom Awards, Grace Awards, Kairos Prize, Epiphany Prize, and the Special Faith and Values Crystal Teddy Bear Awards. Additionally the Christian Film and Television Commission annually compiles *The Report to the Entertainment Industry*, where it gives its analysis and insights on all major films released in the last year, and is delivered to industry executives. Ted Baehr has won multiple awards for his work, including an Eagle Award bestowed by the Western National Religious Broadcasters acknowledging and validating his influence on the secular entertainment industry.

The plan is to replace the culture with the superior Christian form. The San Antonio Independent Christian Film Festival is the big shindig of the Christian Filmmaker's Academy, and gives us just one proof of cultural alternatives advanced to replace the existing terrible, horrible, *very* bad culture. This Film Festival makes it clear what the vision of the Religious Right America looks like.

"The goal of a rival film industry to replace Hollywood, though, is merely an interim goal. Reconstructionists' long-term goal is to produce a rival culture based in 'Biblical Law,' and through what they call 'multi-generational faithfulness' to the dominion mandate, to ultimately replace every aspect of our existing culture." Julie Ingersoll, "Replacing Godless Hollywood with Bible-Based "Cultural Dominion," *Religion Dispatches*, October 25, 2010.

But when a movie is presented that the Religious Right finds offensive, then an uproar is heard. Martin Scorsese's 1988 movie, *The Last Temptation of Christ,* received widespread condemnation. *"In the end, more than twenty-five thousand people protested outside Universal Studios in Hollywood, and opposition was so strong that Blockbuster Video refused to carry The Last Temptation of Christ in its stores, making it the most protested film in the history of cinema."* D. Michael Lindsay, *Faith in the Halls of Power: How Evangelicals Joined the American Elite*, Oxford University Press, 2007.

The movie the *Golden Compass,* starring Nicole Kidmann, was based on a children's trilogy by author Philip Pullman, who claims to be an atheist. The books won many prestigious awards, but that was not important. Before the movie was even released there was a tremendous uproar because of a perceived slight against Catholicism specifically, and Christianity in general. But, others felt the movie's symbolism made viewers question any group advocating a specific belief system and blind obedience to it. In Alamosa Colorado, the Ortega Middle School library pulled the books from its shelves, although reportedly returned them after the initial fury died down. Lubbock Texas' Shallowater Middle School came under some heat for carrying *The Golden Compass* book in its library. These are only a few examples. Many who do not even identify as Christians did not see the movie because of the bad press. There are many examples that demonstrate how they are capturing this mountain of influence. *The DaVinci Code* and *Harry Potter* were able to break the curse of Conservative Christian outrage with both the books and the movies, but that is proving to be the exceptions and not the rule.

Proof of their growing influence is the 2009 movie *Creation,* that many in the U.S. have never heard of because the "liberal" media and entertainment industry wouldn't distribute the film. It is based on Darwin's intense personal struggle over the death of his child and his inner turmoil over the triangle of his work, and how his deeply religious wife and their relationship would be affected.

"The film has no distributor in America. It has got a deal everywhere else in

the world but in the US, and it's because of what the film is about. People have been saying this is the best film they've seen all year, yet nobody in the US has picked it up.

'It is unbelievable to us that this is still a really hot potato in America. There's still a great belief that He made the world in six days. It's quite difficult for we in the UK to imagine religion in America. We live in a country which is no longer so religious. But in the US, outside of New York and LA, religion rules.

'Charles Darwin is, I suppose, the hero of the film. But we tried to make the film in a very even-handed way. Darwin wasn't saying 'kill all religion', he never said such a thing, but he is a totem for people." Anita Singh, "Charles Darwin film 'too controversial for religious America,'" *The Telegraph*, Sept 11, 2009.

The film eventually did get shown in the underwhelming amount of twenty-nine theaters (according to the movie's American website) out of the roughly eighteen thousand theaters in the U.S. This is an example of the Religious Right's influence on even our entertainment.

Television

Television has been influenced with shows like *Seventh Heaven, Touched by an Angel, Highway to Heaven,* and the TLC channel's reality show *19 Kids and Counting* that promotes no birth control, large families, and home-schooling. More overt shows like *Nothing Sacred* and *Revelations* have not been as well received by television audiences as *19 Kids and Counting* has. The cable channel TLC had done several specials titled *16 Children and Moving In* featuring the Duggars, showing them with only the sixteenth child due, trying to build a house big enough for them all. TLC seems particularly favorable of Religious Right themed shows. Jim Bob and Michelle Duggar of *19 Kids* fame have had celebrity guests appear on their show, such as Dolly Parton and Meredith Vieira of the *Today* Show. They have appeared on mainstream media shows, including *The Early Show,* multiple times on the *Today Show,* CNN's *American Morning,* and even *Larry King Live.* Besides the Duggars, television and film celebrity

Chuck Norris displayed his support for Religious Right candidate Mike Huckabee during the 2008 presidential primaries, and Norris' website has a Christian section.

Artwork

Besides the movie and television industries, consider the visual arts. Thomas Kinkade is a very well known painter with claims that one-in-every-twenty American homes contain a piece of his artwork. Mr. Kinkade is admittedly a Christian, and his work is openly Christian in its vision and outlook. This is a very comforting art style that many find soothing.

On the other end of the spectrum you have artist Jon McNaughton and his painting *One Nation Under God* that depicts Jesus holding the original U.S. Constitution, while behind him are the Founding Fathers and persons from the nation's history. McNaughton was very deliberate in portraying Jesus holding the Constitution. He has explained the symbolism of the painting, and he feels that the original U.S. Constitution was a God-inspired document. On his website, he explains every single person in the crowd, from the ashamed Supreme Court Justice, a school teacher, a liberal news reporter, to the pregnant woman, etc. He also painted *The Forgotten Man*, representing a haughty President Obama standing on the discarded Constitution. His description of the painting is filled with Religious Right Tea Party rhetoric. His artwork clearly presents the political religious end of the spectrum.

In the middle of the pack are artists such as Danny Hahlbohm and Donna Gelsinger, who paint obvious Bible themes that range from sweet to inspirational. Except McNaughton, these artists appeal to a wider audience and, in Kinkade and Gelsinger's cases, are not overtly Christian in their topics. Their mass appeal is the idea behind the Mountain strategy to replace art not inspired by Bible themes with appealing art that is promoting what they consider wholesome ideals.

Themeparks etc.

There are now evangelical amusement parks and similar entertainment, to ultimately replace the secular versions. Heritage USA was the first to capitalize on such an idea, but the Jim Baker scandal left it bankrupt and Hurricane Hugo in 1989 devastated the efforts to bring it out of bankruptcy. The Holy Land Experience in Orlando Florida is a recreation of ancient Jerusalem, complete with a replica of Jesus' tomb. The controversial Noah's Ark Theme Park being developed in Kentucky, wants to be a testimony to the historicity of the Bible, and made headlines because of the forty million dollars in state tax breaks that were given the endeavor (violation of separation of church and state, yet again.)

You can visit the wax museum in Mansfield Ohio, known as BibleWalk, that features seventy scenes and three hundred wax figures portraying Christian martyrs, the miracles of the Old Testament, and the life of Christ, and important Christians in history. BibleWalk also offers a dinner theater titled "Dinner With Grace," with subjects such as in ten years, will you still have the freedom to celebrate Christmas in "Christmas Revelation 2021." There is the Creation museum in Petersburg Kentucky, promoting creationism and a "total Bible experience." Additionally, there is the Museum of Biblical Art in Dallas, Texas. These serve as examples of the Religious Right replacements that are becoming more and more common.

It is important to remember that many of these are intended to ultimately be replacements for what exists today, not simply catering to a specific demographic.

Take With You From This Chapter

➢   The arts, music, sports, fashion, books, film, television, and any other form of entertainment, are targeted for replacement with Bible and God-centered versions.

➢   The Religious Right have already made great progress in these areas, and although they have not reached their goals of replacement, their influence is increasing.

Chapter 18
The Mountain of Education

<u>What to Expect From this Chapter</u>

➢ Why the Religious Right hates public schools.

➢ How they are using home schooling and private schools to destroy public school funding.

➢ How schools are ultimately to be used in the Dominionist plan to propagate extremist Christian ideology, primarily.

There are serious issues regarding the quality of education in our school system. But, the Religious Right has fabricated some sort of conspiracy out of the educational system. During the 2012 Republican primaries, presidential hopeful Rick Santorum expressed this view when he stated, "...that aren't taught by some liberal college professor, and try to indoctrinate them.' The public school system has supposedly stripped God out of our society and are actively brainwashing the youth of the nation.

"Harvard is at a very significant intersection between that mountain [of Government] and the mountain of education. ...

Education is knowledge or a skill obtained or developed by a learning process. In many ways in the West, it has been hijacked from its original objectives. This mountain has been infiltrated and taken over by forces opposed to those things originally intended to be there. Most American educational institutions, for example, were meant to serve as places of training and admonition in the fear of God. Their instruction was given in the context of a worldview that put God in the center of life as the One around whom we all orbit. God was the foundation of all areas of learning.

In securing the mountain of education, the gift of teaching is very important. These must be Holy Spirit-empowered teachers, as opposed to secularly confirmed teachers. The biblical role of a teacher is to instruct in the ways of the Lord.

As the church we are in much greater need of having these teachers in the education system than we are of having them in church. And having spiritually gifted teachers throughout the system isn't enough; the certification system and the curriculum itself must be overhauled...

As I've stated, targeting top-of-the-mountain institutions such as Harvard, Princeton, and Yale is central to this action strategy. We need intentional group of Elijah revolutionaries to band together and penetrate into these schools by attending them as their mission from God. Little sparks in these schools will create great fires. There will be significant and revolutionary revivals in all of these institutions, and when they take place, they will need to bring about wholesale infrastructural changes. There will eventually be professors at these institutions ... and will become transformers for the kingdom of God, as they realize they were created for such a time as this." Johnny Enlow, *The Seven Mountain Prophecy: Unveiling the coming Elijah Revolution*, Creation House, 2008.

Public schools must go

The Religious Right wants public education in its current form to go away. It isn't about some teachers not being quality educators, or that the quality of education is lacking, but rather that they teach the nation's children not from the position that all learning begins with God. They are angry because all public schools aren't seminaries for the nation's youth. They are quick to point out that many of our prestigious colleges and universities, such as Harvard and Princeton, began as training grounds for ministers, and they have never accepted the changes in education. In the Religious Right's mind, if you aren't teaching the God of the Bible, then you are teaching another god. There is no other option. It is not about critical thinking skills or any other lessons. It is a matter of what god you are teaching children to follow.

"I learned ... to send them to public school is to turn a child over to the government and the secular humanists. I was taught that children must be

trained up in the way they should go every minute of every day." Libby Anne, "My Life as a Daughter of Christian Patriarchy," *Butterflies and Wheels Blog Article,* September 3, 2011.

The Religious Right taking over the education system would ensure more of a captive and impressionable audience being taught the *correct* way. There are several approaches to this attack on public schools, that includes home-schooling, Christian schools, and vouchers to funnel tax money away from public schools; this impacts elementary through high school, in addition to colleges and universities. Attacking teachers' unions is just one more aspect of the picking apart of public schools by removing a teacher's voice.

"According to the film's [IndoctriNation: Public Schools and the Decline of Christianity in America] *promotional materials, through his travels [Colin] Gunn discovers a 'master-plan designed to replace God's recipe for education with a man-centered program that has fragmented the family, destroyed the social systems of our nation and undermined the influence of the church.'*

Indeed, dominionism is most powerfully evident in the Reconstructionists' approach to education, which in turn produces the 'biblical' filmmakers of the future. Whether through homeschooling or Christian schools, the goal is to 'replace' public education, which, as Gunn's film made clear, is considered unbiblical. According to Reconstructionism, the Bible gives authority for education to families – not the state – and the Bible does not give the state the authority to tax people to pay for the education of other peoples' children. Reconstructionists are therefore opposed to public education, not only for their own children, but at all. They long have been proponents of dismantling the federal Department of Education (a view echoed by [Sharron] Angle during the campaign) and reducing funding for public education at every opportunity." Julie Ingersoll, "Replacing Godless Hollywood with Bible-Based 'Cultural Dominion,'" *Religion Dispatches,* October 25, 2010.

Many will remember right after the tragic shooting at Columbine High School, how the story or poem went viral placing the blame for the shooting at a removal of God and prayer from schools. That email and similar ones went around the U.S. a few times at least, and made a complex situation appear black-and-white, thus not addressing the increasing problem of bullying or other factors that contributed to that May, 1999 shooting.

> *"If they succeed, several million families could take to home-schooling over the next several years, Moore* [Exodus Mandate Director] *says. 'If we could get up to 30 per cent of public-school students into home-schooling and private schools, the system would start to unravel and at some point implode and collapse,' he says. 'The government would be forced to get the states out of the education business altogether. It would go back to the churches and the families. It's a strategy for the renewal of society.'"* Amanda Gefter, "Home-schooling special: Preach Your Children Well", *New Scientist Magazine*, November 11, 2006.

What the *Exodus Mandate* director E. Ray Moore, Jr., a retired Army Reserve Chaplain, and political Campaign Consultant,k was saying regarding being able to bring the public school system to it knees, and for education to revert to churches and families is in referernce to how public schools are funded. Public schools are given our tax dollars at a per student fee based on census numbers. As fewer and fewer students are enrolled in public schools because of private schools or home schooling, the less the public school receives in funds until there comes a point where you can't pay teachers or administrative costs to keep a school going; the system starts to collapse.

So anytime you hear about educational vouchers, this is another way to funnel your taxes into supporting faith-based education and simultaneously weaken the public school system. The tax money that would have gone to public schools equally for all children in that district will be diverted to church-run schools, and will weaken the already struggling public school system. What ails the public school system is not going to be remedied by sabotaging the system and handing the nation's children to the churches to be educated.

This isn't a new idea, either. We see in church history in the 1400s how a Dominican priest named Girolamo Savonarola, known for his book-burning and destruction of what he considered immoral Renaissance artwork, promoted a similar idea. He campaigned that education should return to being church-run to keep God front-and-center in all education, in response to secular schools that had sprung up everywhere.

> *"I hope I will live to see the day when, as in the early days of our country, we won't have any public schools. The churches will have taken them over again and Christians will be running them. What a happy day that will be!"* Jerry Falwell, *America Can Be Saved*, Sword of the Lord Publishers, 1979, p. 52-53.

This following quote is from a popular Religious Right book dated 1996. It may sound familiar if you have heard or read much Tea Party views. Here is the precursor to the attacks on public schools, teachers' unions and public employees, such as the legislation Governor Scott Walker of Wisconsin rammed through.

"So as parents, we have to ask the question: Do we want character education that teaches moral absolutes, or do we want character education that teaches situation ethics and universal values?

> *...we're still in the traditional paradigm. We're still teaching our children biblical principles of right and wrong. So who do you think the education elite are going to go after? It's the people with the strongest belief system. It is us. It is the Christian community....*

> *In the past, you may not have understood that when you send your kids to public school, and even many private schools, you are sending them to war without even realizing it. Your children are challenged daily. And these teachers have the most influential hours of the day with children....Basically what we are talking about is pure socialist surveillance systems that monitor everyone in the system."* Anita Hoge, "Public Education: Don't Be Deceived!", *Steeling the Mind*

of America II, Edited by Bill Perkins, New Leaf Press, 1996.

When I went to school, and I have attended both public and private schools, teachers were to teach me how to read, do math, how to write coherently, develop critical thinking skills, have some knowledge of history, and yes, even understand basic science in the world around me. Parents were to impart their spiritual traditions, not the school. This provides a democratic system that doesn't enforce a particular belief system, but rather allows each parent to handle that personal area within their family. But there is the rub, and the problem.

Indoctrination

The next quote starkly exposes how every child is to be indoctrinated, which is why the current school system is on the wrong side of the Religious Right. The Religious Right are often heralded as the champion for children, speaking out against the evil influence of the culture on impressionable young minds. It works both ways though, and the Religious Right is counting on that working in their favor, too. But, what if a parent doesn't like how the message is being forced on his or her child? Most people are all for healthy and happy childhood experiences, but parents may not appreciate education being presented as only available through a specific faith, belief system, or dogmatic structure.

> *"Children are the prize to the winners in the second great civil war. Those who control what young people are taught and what they experience – what they see, hear, think, and believe – will determine the future course for the nation."* James Dobson, *Children At Risk: The Battle for the Hearts and Minds of Our Kids*, Thomas Nelson 1991, page 35.

Let's hear from a person who was home schooled about what the proper curriculum and worldview really is that dominated her instruction. Alisa Harris was raised Religious Right, and has written the book *Raised Right: How I Untangled My Faith from Politics*. The following is a special article she wrote.

> *"I attended Summit Ministries' Student Worldview Conference as a 15-year-*

old. ...

They gave us a handy worldview chart that had a vertical column for every area of life – economics, politics, pyschology, law – and a horizontal column that showed how Muslims, humanists, Marxists and New-Agers were wrong on every count. ...

I emerged from Summit finding that my fervor to stop abortion had grown from a disagreeable duty to an outright passion. I bought pro-life t-shirts. When I came back filled with worldview fervor, I read a book co-authored by David Noebel, the Summit Ministries leader whose writings Bachmann recommended.

It rumbled apocalyptic warnings that humanists, from the NAACP to the Rockefeller Foundation to the National Council of Churches, were conspiring to build a one-world socialist order. I began to secretly find Noebel a little bit kooky.

Still, my family purchased his curriculum and submitted our homeschool speech and debate class to a rigorous worldview training. I took worldview quizzes that graded my ability to reflexively respond to all questions with answers about the Christian worldview of limited government and free enterprise. I aced the quizzes. I had memorized it all and could spit it back." Alisa Harris, "I could have become Michele Bachmann," CNN Religion Blog, August 14th, 2011."

This is the truth of how they want children indoctrinated, that goes along with Dobson's view of children as spoils in the culture war. This one-dimensional mode of education does not develop critical thinking skills, and the idea that there may be some truth on either side of an issue. Businesses need people who can think creatively, and who can question and approach problems from different angles. This requires teaching that challenges children to think through issues for themselves, and not teaching them there is only one correct answer to any given problem. This does a dis-service to our nation as a whole in facing business or environmental challenges, and even personal problems.

The Religious Right claims that it is the humanists who are trying to take over the minds of our children, not them. James Dobson in his book *Children At Risk* paints "the family agenda of the left" as socialism itself, with the government indoctrinating children via child development professionals removing parental influences, driving a wedge between children and their parents, recruiting children into gay lifestyles, and the occult.

Dobson's *Children At Risk* is a blueprint for creating a fearful atmosphere of watching everybody around you as the enemy out to destroy you and your family. Within this book, written in 1991, is the political watch list for all Religious Right adherents to fight against. A litany of the Left's "anti-family" agenda that covers everything from sex-education, to gay pride parades, gay rights, and feminism, that are presented as a vast conspiracy against the family.

"These [Religious Right] organizations have led their followers to believe that public schools are moral wastelands where all manner of perversions take place. Many of those who follow the Religious Right really believe that all public schools are handing out condoms to fourth graders on a daily basis and that a truly voluntary prayer can get a student expelled. Kids read textbooks written by Satan himself and receive all their classroom instruction from members of ACLU, NOW, and the Gay/Lesbian Caucus.

Having built up a tower of lies, the Religious Right must then keep the myth alive with more and more outrageous tales of debauchery from the public school system. The quest for funds and new members leads them to send out hysterical fundraising appeals that have little connection to reality. As a result, millions of Americans who have had no contact with the public school system for decades believe they know exactly what goes on behind schoolhouse doors, and they don't like it one bit." Robert Boston, *Why the Religious Right is Wrong about Separation of Church and State*, Prometheus Books, 1993.

This battle over the minds of the children can be seen in the education controversy. In the 2008 presidential debates, the topic of school vouchers was brought up, and many Americans watching the telecast may not have considered it such a hot button issue. But vouchers, home-schooling, and private schools getting federal funds, are all a big issue and high on the Religious Right agenda. That is also a significant reason why funding is continually being cut for public schools by the Religious Right politicians in the Republican and Tea Parties.

The John Ankerberg show dedicated an episode to how evil public schools are, and presented the teachers' union as trying to socially engineer the nation's children. The show was titled, "Are the Public Schools Teaching Our Children New Age Religious Views?" It was hugely popular. Thus, we now have repeated attacks on the Teacher's union. Ankerberg also wrote the book *Public Schools: The Sorcerer's New Apprentice?* in 1999, continuing the attack he began with the 1993 book *Thieves of Innocence*. The Religious Right is creating the controversies, and then controlling how the topic is even addressed.

Tax-payer funded Religion in Schools

They are also working on the immediate issue of indoctrinating the children right now, rather than waiting until the public school system is dismantled. In the book *Standing on the Premises of God: the Christian Fight to Redefine America's Public Schools,* the author Fritz Detwiller paints a picture of Focus on the Family's *Teachers in Focus* magazine aiding teachers to counter non-Christian or non-Bible based curricula that they are given to teach in tax-payer funded public schools.

> *"To further assist teachers and school administrators who wish to use the schools to promote biblical Christian viewpoints, FoF [Focus on the Family] provides a number of movies and videotapes edited for public school use...Dobson also endorses Eric Buehrer's Gateways to Better Education, an organization that helps teachers transform their classrooms into arenas for Christian instruction. In one such promotion, Focus on the Family magazine featured a pamphlet titled A Gift for Teacher. The pamphlet implies that public school teachers can use their discussion of Christmas as an opportunity to teach religious dogmas to their*

students. They are further encouraged to use Christmas carols instead of secular songs in their classroom activities...

In the introduction to NACE's [National Association of Christian Educators] 1983 edition of Communicating a Christian World View in the Classroom, *Simonds wrote:*

'There is a great war being waged in America...This is a battle for the heart, mind, and even the very soul of every man, women, and especially every child in America...it is America's Last Great War...The combatants are 'secular humanism' and 'Christianity'...The Christian is the key to God's victory over Satan and the atheism of secular humanism. We can change the world in this generation! Our job is to evangelize, while time remains. Our schools are the battleground.'" Fritz Detwiller *Standing on the Premises of God: the Christian Right's Fight to Redefine America's Public Schools,* New York University Press, 1999.

On November 16, 2009, the ACLU filed a lawsuit on behalf of four students against the Cheatham County School Board of Tennessee. The lawsuit claims that the school board repeatedly promoted their own religious beliefs in the form of planned prayer at graduations; that the Gideons International (the organization that distributes Bibles to hotel rooms, to the military in various countries, hospitals, nursing homes, and prisons) were allowed to speak to classes and distribute Bibles; that a foot tall cross hangs in a classroom; a history teacher taught that the United States is a "Christian nation," condemned the separation of church and state; and another teacher required students to read and write about the biblical creation stories as an assignment for English class.

This is getting to be more common every day. Americans United for the Separation of Church and State brought a lawsuit against South Iron R-1 School District in Missouri for allowing Gideon's International to distribute Bibles to fifth graders during class-time. There are many more such cases from all across the nation as public schools are breaking separation of church and state by attempting to promote one specific faith for all, utilizing tax payer funds.

We also have many organizations that offer stealth evangelizing in schools under the guise of motivational messages. "Commandos! USA" offering school assembly programs that slip in Christian testimonies around feats of human strength and the military commando theme. Another utilizing the feats of strength, but dressed more like wrestlers, is "The Power Team" school assembly team imparting their message. "The Strength Team" is another featuring athletic prowess in school assemblies, who then invite students to their evening crusade. There is the Christian band, "You Can Run But You Cannot Hide" international ministry which also utilizes school assemblies only with rock music by Junkyard Prophets to present their Christian message to school children of all ages.   Yet another example is the Todd Becker Foundation, which targets high schools with the message of Todd Becker, who was killed by a drunk driver. The program is presented by Todd's surviving older brother and invites the kids to the evening Christian meeting.

While public schools do exist, they are continually being utilized as a mission field to the nation's youth. Parents need to be aware of these tactics towards their impressionable children.

The Good News Club

Additionally, while public schools and the Department of Education still exist, there is yet another way to use them for the Religious Right's purposes. In 2001, the Supreme Court ruled in *Good News Club vs. Milford Central School* to allow the use of tax-payer funded public schools by churches as their facilities, free, or for minimal custodian fees. Not only is this yet another violation of the separation of church and state, but it provides the illusion to students that their school sanctions that church, and that church and school are joined together. Katherine Stewart has written the book *The Good News Club: The Christian Right's Stealth Assault on America's Children,* which exposes this practice.

"I attended services all over Manhattan, in Brooklyn, Queens, and the Bronx. I watched as congregants prayed over pictures of children from diverse families that lined the school's hallways. In public school classrooms, I learned about creationism and was taught that all children who do not believe in Jesus will go to hell, along with their parents. At a public school in Greenwich Village, I heard a congregant describe the anti-gay ministry that is affiliated with the church planted at that school. From my seat in a public school library, I was instructed to pray for the glorious day that America's system of government, finance, media, and education would be overtaken by Christian control.

I even went to services at my own children's public school, and observed a youth ministry operating in what would soon become my son's kindergarten classroom. The churches I attended enjoyed, after school hours and on weekends, ample space and furniture, newly painted walls, renovated bathrooms, and prime neighborhood real estate. And not one of them paid rent.

I attended these churches while researching my forthcoming book on religion in public schools. Church-planting in public schools is just one of the dozens of religiously-driven initiatives made possible largely through judicial activism on the right: a combination of a surge in self-identified Christian law firms, along with a Supreme Court increasingly hostile to church-state separation....

The Good News Club decision created a new legal theory for opponents of church-state separation. The Court held that religion is nothing but speech from a certain point of view, and therefore all religious activities are protected by the Free Speech clause of the First Amendment. 'When Milford denied the Good News Club access... on the grounds that the club was religious in nature,' Clarence Thomas concluded in his majority opinion, 'it discriminated against the Club because of its religious viewpoint.'

Rather than examining whether the activity violated the Establishment

Clause, which prevents the endorsement or appearance of endorsement of a particular religion by the government, the case opened the door for church planters to claim they were being discriminated against by being denied the use of public space....

To the consternation of New York City's Board of Education, many of these new churches raised controversies in the communities where they were located. They irked parents and administrators by distributing free hot chocolate and candy to school children, and provoked concerns that New York City's public school system had been coopted into a taxpayer-financed source of real estate for houses of worship – almost all of them evangelical Christian." Katherine Stewart, "Rent-Free Religion in New York's Public Schools", *Religion Dispatches*, December 5, 2011.

So not only are churches tax-exempt, but now the Religious Right has influenced Supreme Court to open the way for tax-payers to fund churches facilities, while simultaneously giving them access to their children.

The issue of charter schools and vouchers

Charter schools figure into this scenario as well. More and more charter schools spring up every day. A charter school is still a public school and receives money from the same system that public schools do, but they are not subject to many of the same rules, regulations, and statutes that apply to their cousin public schools. But in exchange for having different rules, they are accountable to produce pre-determined results that are defined in the school's charter. Thus they are called Charter Schools. Charter schools figure into this Religious Right mix since Charter Schools can be founded by activists, Religious Right activists who don't agree with secular public schools. There are state-authorized charter schools that are increasingly established by non-profit groups (look at the list of Religious Right organizations in the Naming Names section for organizations who are mostly non-profits) or private Religious Right universities.

There is a lie being spread that charter schools (an intermediate step to full church-run schools) are beneficial for the underprivileged, a sort of great equalizer. Evangelical Randal Balmer shares how this is smoke and mirrors.

"Out of the twenty-seven students in [Dolly] Goodwin's classroom, only one was Anglo, and another African American: everyone else was Hispanic. When I remarked on the contrast between the eight student, overwhelmingly white classroom at West Park Lutheran School and the twenty-seven students in her charge, Goodwin noted that public money for education was going increasingly to religious schools and to charter schools. The voucher system, she said, was bleeding the Cleveland Municipal School District, but 'the charter schools are the real problem' because they divert education funds and siphon off the best students to privately run institutions. The charter schools and the voucher schools can choose which students they want to educate, whereas public schools must accept all students, including those from less-affluent households and those with physical, mental, or emotional disabilities.

Goodwin sought to dispel the notion that students learned about values only in religious schools. 'I have to teach them what is morally right, no matter what the system,' she said. Goodwin believes that it is incumbent upon her to reinforce each student's faith, regardless of his particular religious tradition. 'I tell the parents at the beginning of every year,' she said, 'that I will teach your child what is morally right until I am dead.'...

Because Ohio's voucher and charter school program directed taxpayer money to religious schools, the program faced a series of court challenges. ... As the case moved toward the U.S. Supreme Court, it pitted Susan Tave Zelman, Ohio's superintendent of public instruction, who argued for the constitutionality of the vouchers, against Doris Simmons-Harris, the parent of a public school student. Several conservative and Religious Right organizations, including the Becket Fund for Religious Liberty and Pat Robertson's American Center for Law and Justice, filed amicus briefs in defense of school vouchers for religious schools." Randal Balmer, *Thy Kingdom Come, An Evangelical's Lament: How the Religious Right Distorts the Faith and Threatens America*, Basic Books, 2006.

On June 27, 2002, the U.S. Supreme Court voted five-to-four in favor of taxpayers paying for private religious schools, with Religious Right justices Antonin Scalia and Clarence Thomas, joined by William Rehnquist, Anthony Kennedy, and Sandra Day O'Connor, voting for it.

"The only hope for the inner city is vouchers, so that all the churches can go in and plant Christian schools in the inner cities and capture these fatherless young people for Christ and teach them biblical discipline and so forth." Jerry Falwell, The 700 Club, CBN, Sept. 3, 1996.

This is what your tax dollars are paying for with vouchers. You have rights in this, so don't let your tax dollars go to pay for schooling that defies the separation of church and state that our constitution secured, thus instructing impressionable youth in an agenda that is threatening the democratic fabric of the nation itself, and promoting theocracy. This is the crux of the school voucher system that is being aggressively pushed. The more money that goes to Christian Schools via vouchers, the more we will see the quality of public school education go down, as qualified teachers seek better pay. Remember, any given public school is allocated funds according to how many students it has registered, so the more students taken out of the public school system, the greater chance of weakening the entire public school system.

"Religious schools across the nation are receiving public funds through voucher and corporate tax credit programs. Many hundreds, if not thousands, of these schools use Protestant fundamentalist textbooks that teach not only creationism, but also a religious supremacist worldview. They offer a shocking spin on politics, history and human rights. ...

In 12 states and the District of Columbia, almost 200,000 students attend private schools with at least part of their tuition paid with public funds. The money is taken from public school budgets to fund vouchers or by diverting state tax revenues to tuition grants through corporate tax credit programs. An interconnected group of non-profits and political action committees, led by the wealthy right-wing school privatization advocate Betsy DeVos and heavily funded by a few mega-donors, is working to expand these programs across the nation. The DeVos-led American Federation for Children hosted Pennsylvania Gov. Tom Corbett, Wisconsin Gov. Scott Walker, and Michelle Rhee at a national policy summit earlier in May....

Unsurprisingly, the textbooks are fiercely anti-abortion and virulently anti-gay, similar to the ideology of Religious Right organizations (heavily funded by Betsy DeVos and family) that have been labeled hate groups by the Southern Poverty Law Center....

They also teach a radical laissez-faire capitalism. Government safety nets, regulation, minimum wage and progressive taxes are described as contrary to the Bible. Many of these textbooks were first published in the 1980s, evidence that the merging of Religious Right ideology with extreme free-market economics predates the Tea Party movement by many years.

The textbooks exhibit hostility toward other religions, including Islam, Hinduism, Buddhism, Shintoism, and traditional African and Native American religions, and other Christians are also targeted, including non-evangelical Protestants and Roman Catholics." Rachel Tabachnick, "The 'Christian' Dogma Pushed by Religious Schools That Are Supported by Your Tax Dollars," *Alternet*, May 23, 2011.

Dr. Frances Paterson published *Democracy and Intolerance: Christian School Curricula, School Choice, and Public Policy*, in 2003. She conducted a study of the textbooks used in those schools receiving tax-payer funds via voucher, and provided the analysis in the quote above. The faulty supposition that private schools are better, and vouchers would make these "superior" schools more accessible to minorities is rubbish.

221

Vouchers are for private schools; those schools, since they are private, can legally reject anybody, for any reason, from attending.

"Make no mistake about it: What lies behind most of the rhetoric about school vouchers is the desire to garner taxpayer support for sectarian education. According to a 2001 study by Policy Matters Ohio, a nonprofit research institute, 99.4 percent of Cleveland's voucher students were enrolled in religious schools, most of them Catholic, but also places like West Park Lutheran School.

But still another constituency wants to divert tax money from public schools, namely, the affluent, many of whom already send their children to private schools and would welcome a subsidy from public funds. The confluence of interest between economically prosperous citizens and the supporters of religious education has the makings of a powerful coalition. The 'school choice' movement represents the alignment of the nation's wealthy with religious constituencies; although they may disagree on other issues, they have a mutual interest in seeing the vouchers succeed.

The results in Ohio bear this out. One-third of the students who use the school-voucher program in Ohio had parents who were wealthy enough to afford private education for their children before the voucher plan was implemented. According to Policy Matters Ohio, the nonprofit research institute, 33 percent of the students accepting vouchers five years into the 'school choice' experiment were already enrolled in private schools. 'The numbers suggest that vouchers in Cleveland are serving more as a subsidy for students already attending private schools,' the report concluded, 'than as an 'escape hatch' for students eager to leave the public schools.' " Randall Balmer, *Thy Kingdom Come, An Evangelical's Lament: How the Religious Right Distorts the Faith and Threatens America*, Basic Books, 2006.

The Badger Herald (published by the University of Wisconsin/Madison) ran an OpEd titled "Racism lies at the heart of School Vouchers," on February 24, 2005, that states: 1) *"When considering income levels and race...publicly educated students perform at the same level as those privately educated."* 2) *"More than 60 percent of Milwaukee's public school attendees are black, yet fewer than 5 percent of the students at Milwaukee's top three Catholic schools are black. Only 38 percent of the private schools in Milwaukee provide bussing, putting the poor and black at a further disadvantage."* So the Voucher system has the potential of alienating children from education in those schools that could be the only game in town, say for instance, those children who may have a single parent, or gay parents.

Ultimately public schools have become a battleground because the Religious Right has disagreed with nearly everything teachers and administrators do, once the God of the Bible wasn't the center of all teaching endeavors. They have done more to tear them down than find solutions to help fix the problems. Administrators that have never spent a day teaching carry a share of the fault in what ails public schools as well, but this does not excuse the actions of the Religious Right to dismantle quality education, without indoctrination, for every child.

Home schooling

Home-schooling has become more prevalent among Religious Right families over the last twenty years. Rushdoony was adamantly against public schools and first made a name for himself in fighting for home schooling, before sparking Christian Reconstruction/Dominionism with his writings.

"My parents were originally fairly ordinary evangelicals. Like so many others (it's a very common story), it was homeschooling that brought them to Christian Patriarchy and Quiverfull. They began homeschooling for secular reasons, and then, through homeschool friends, homeschool conferences, and homeschool publications, they were drawn into the world of Christian Patriarchy and Quiverfull. It starts slowly, one belief here, a book there. For those who are already fundamentalists or evangelicals, like my parents, the transition is smooth and almost natural. Suddenly, almost without realizing it, they are birthing their

eight or ninth child and pushing their daughters toward homemaking and away from any thought of a career.

Why are these movements so enticing to evangelical and fundamentalist homeschoolers? Simple. Christian Patriarchy and Quiverfull offer the enticing image of the perfect family and the promise that you can make a difference and change the world, raising up an army for Christ, without ever leaving your home. Organizations like Vision Forum and No Greater Joy promise parents perfect families in very explicit terms. If you follow the formula, you, too, can be like that pretty picture or happy face in the catalogue. They are the huckster traveling salesmen of the homeschool world, but this time they sell dreams.

By now, you may be wondering, how is this possible? How can parents indoctrinate their children in this way? The answer, I would argue, is simple: homeschooling. By homeschooling, these parents can control every interaction their children have and every piece of information their children come upon. My parents called it 'sheltering.' The result was that I knew nothing of popular culture or the lives of normal teens, besides that they were 'worldly' and miserable while I was godly and content." Libby Anne, "My Life as a Daughter of Christian Patriarchy," *Butterflies and Wheels Blog Article,* September 3, 2011.

Public schools are at a disadvantage financially against home schooling because of several factors, beginning with the fact that all the teachers must have a college education and be certified (there may be some exceptions, but this is the general rule), which indicates they should get paid accordingly, but a high school drop-out can home-school his or her children. Public schools have to pay for textbooks, while churches and home-school networks often help parents with those costs. Public schools have buildings, libraries, and gyms to maintain, not to mention desks, musical instruments, computers, and other equipment or teaching aids and tools.

In home schooling the woman typically stays home and teaches the children herself, rather than through the public school system. That is the very picture of the traditional family, a stay-at-home mother home schooling the children. Home-schooling is big business now, and there are support groups to do field trips together, and other activities.

"The idea was taken up in the 1970s by evangelical Christians, and today anywhere from 1.9 to 2.4 million children are home-schooled, up from just 300,000 in 1990... According to the US government's National Center for Education Statistics (NCES), 72 per cent of home-schooling parents interviewed said that they were motivated by the desire to provide religious and moral instruction.

He [Brian Alters of McGill University] is appalled by some home-schooling textbooks, especially those on biology that claim they have scientific reasons for rejecting evolution. 'They have gross scientific inaccuracies in them,' he says. 'They would not be allowed in any public school in the US, and yet these are the books primarily featured in home-schooling bookstores.'

In the 1970s and early 1980s, the practice was largely illegal across the US. 'The mechanism that was causing home-schooling to be illegal was teacher certification,' says Ian Slatter, director of media relations for the [Home School Legal Defense Assoc.] HSLDA. In 1983 two evangelical attorneys, Michael Farris and Mike Smith, founded the organization to defend the rights of home-school parents. They fought to remove requirements that parents be certified to teach their own children. Through an impressive run of legal battles and political lobbying, they managed to make home-schooling legal in all 50 states within 10 years. 'We rolled back the state laws,' says Slatter.

Exodus Mandate, based in Columbia, South Carolina, is an organization that urges Christian parents to pull their children out of public schools. Exodus Mandate has spent the past few years trying to win over the Southern Baptist Convention (SBC), a Christian denomination with more than 16 million members. Exodus Mandate is urging each home-schooling family to bring one new family into the movement. ...

The home-school movement is often described as a grassroots effort, scattered among a dispersed group of quiet, rural families. <u>The reality is</u> *that the movement is well organized from the top down, led by groups with strong political ties. Taken together, organizations like the Discovery Institute, Exodus Mandate, HSLDA, Generation Joshua and Patrick Henry College are working to sculpt a new generation of students armed with the skills and the motivation to fight for their religious beliefs and their version of science."* Amanda Gefter, *"Home-schooling special: Preach Your Children Well", New Scientist Magazine,* 11 November, 2006.

This clearly shows how the Religious Right want the system to come crashing down and become nothing but indoctrination centers for the children of this nation. How does that keep this country competitive in the world? It *doesn't.* It is yet one more area where the Religious Right can bring down this democracy by controlling what the people think and how they perceive the world around them.

The 'biblical' alternatives of homeschooling and Christian schooling constitute what Doug Phillips describes as 'Deuteronomy 6:6-8 applied – the daily discipleship of children by their parents (encompassing) not only the traditional academic instruction... but also worldview training, practical life preparation, and family vision–casting as well.' Every year Vision Forum invites homeschoolers from across the country to attend the Academy to learn to make 'culture-transforming films.'" Julie Ingersoll, "Replacing Godless Hollywood with Bible-Based 'Cultural Dominion'," *Religion Dispatches,* October 25, 2010

The Religious Right is very good at the multi-pronged attack. While they are fervently working to break down the funding for public schools, they work towards their long-term goal of creating a tax-dollar funded church-run school system.

Generation Joshua

"'There are two worldviews that are very much in conflict right now,

especially in Washington, D.C.,' [Ned] Ryun explained. The first, he said, is Judeo-Christian. 'It starts with God as the creator, but then it also protects life, it's about traditional marriage, one man, one woman,' he said. 'On the other side, you have secular humanism, which starts with man as the center of all things. There are no absolute standards, its all morally relative, anything goes as long as it has to do with sex,' he said.

According to Ryun, everything the government does derives from one of these systems, social security, the life issue, the marriage issue, all these various laws and policy, you can trace them back to one of these two world views.

Thus every political issue – indeed, every disputed aspect of our national life – is a struggle between good and evil." Michelle Goldberg, *Kingdom Coming: The Rise of Christian Nationalism*, W.W. Norton & Company, 2007.

Ned Ryun quoted just prior is the director of Generation Joshua. Generation Joshua is a privately funded outreach to Christian home-schoolers. Their mission is to provide resources and opportunities to mold children into Christian political activists and leaders. Resources include online communities, but also week-long camps to hone their political skills, book club online chats on Conservative Right political books, online classes on political subjects such as, "successful campaigning," all with a revisionist-history taught. Their mission is ultimately to fashion a political army. From home-schools, they can go to Patrick Henry College that actually creates Religious Right politicians and has provided more Washington D.C. interns than any other college in the US. This topic is covered more in the education section.

We should be very clear on the fact that an army is being raised to seize the leadership of local and national governing bodies, who see everything in life – from economics to international affairs, from social security to health care, from education to our national deficit – as a matter of a war between good and evil. As a taxpayer, is that who you want representing you locally or nationally? Do your children receive anywhere near such funding and attention to help them achieve in life?

"According to Generation Joshua's philosophy, Christianity holds the answer to every public and private dispute. But because the American people do not yet accept this, Christian ideas need to be rationalized in secular terms. Ryun teaches thousands of protégés this rhetorical two-step through online seminars, chats and book clubs." Michelle Goldberg, *Kingdom Coming: The Rise of Christian Nationalism,* W.W. Norton & Company, 2007.

<u>Private Christian schools</u>

The other growing trend is private Christian schools, where they can openly have prayer and Bible studies and teach/preach their own vision of history, science, and civics. Thus you will see the issue of school vouchers becoming more prevalent. They want to have their cake and eat it too. The Religious Right wants the federal government to assist or pay for Christian-based education (via your tax dollars), even though they chose to take their children out of the public schools, where the federal funds are supposed to go. Again, this weakens the wider public school system and becomes elitist.

But interestingly, private and religious schools do not have the same accrediting organizations. Private schools have different rules than legitimate publics schools in order to be recognized as legitimate, and through completely separate agencies. National Accrediting Agencies for private schools are the Association of Christian Schools International; the American Association of Christian Schools; the International Christian Accrediting Association; the National Christian School Association; and the National Independent Private Schools Association. Again, public schools are not on a level playing-field if compared.

"Are your state's tax dollars funding the teaching of religious supremacism and bigotry? What about creationism? The answer is undoubtedly yes, if you live in a state with a voucher or corporate tax credit program funding 'school choice.'

In 2003, Dr. Frances Paterson, a specialist in education law, published Democracy and Intolerance: Christian School Curricula, School Choice, and

Public Policy, summarizing her extensive study of the curricula of the three most widely used Protestant fundamentalist textbook publishers in the nation: A Beka Book, Pensacola, Florida; Bob Jones University Publishing, Greenville South Carolina; and Accelerated Christian Education, Lewisville, Texas.

Religious schools across the nation are receiving public funds through voucher and corporate tax credit programs. Many hundreds, if not thousands, of these schools use Protestant fundamentalist textbooks that teach not only creationism, but also a religious supremacist worldview. They offer a shocking spin on politics, history and human rights.

Unsurprisingly, the textbooks are fiercely anti-abortion and virulently anti-gay, similar to the ideology of Religious Right organizations (heavily funded by Betsy DeVos and family) that have been labeled hate groups by the Southern Poverty Law Center. A Bob Jones current events text argues against legal protection for gays, stating, 'These people have no more claims to special rights than child molesters or rapists.' The text uses an often-repeated phrase that homosexuals and abortion-rights supporters are 'simply calling evil good.'

They also teach a radical laissez-faire capitalism. Government safety nets, regulation, minimum wage and progressive taxes are described as contrary to the Bible. Many of these textbooks were first published in the 1980s, evidence that the merging of Religious Right ideology with extreme free-market economics predates the Tea Party movement by many years.

The A Beka civics text states, 'God's original purpose for government was to punish the evil and reward the good.' The same text describes the ideal form of government. 'All governments are ordained by God, but none compare to government by God, theocracy.'" Rachel Tabachnick, "The 'Christian' Dogma Pushed by Religious Schools That are Supported by Your Tax Dollars," *Alternet*, May 23, 2011.

Colleges and universities

Religious Right: The Greatest Threat to Democracy

The Religious Right provide their own colleges so that youth will continue in the sheltered and indoctrinated culture their parents and church expect. Liberty University, founded by Jerry Falwell and Biola University, are just a few examples of the 240+ Christian higher education establishments in forty-one out of our fifty states.

How about Patrick Henry College, that offers majors in government and boasts about its mission "to prepare Christian men and women who *will lead our nation and shape our culture* with timeless biblical values and fidelity to the spirit of the American founding?" Channel 4 of UK television ran "God's next Army" in June, 2006, reporting, "*Its mission is to train young fundamentalist Christians to become the next generation of America's cultural and political leaders. Though the separation of church and state is enshrined in the US Constitution, with financial backing from the evangelical community the college aims to 'rechristianise' America; to 'preserve the world from the sinfulness of man.'*" Patrick Henry College has very influential Religious Right backing and supporters, from Tim LaHaye's media empire money to Focus on the Family's prior president, and apparently every conservative Republican courting them. This affords them privileges and access that most colleges only dream of.

"*Now about a million and a half children, as many as two-thirds of whom are thought to be evangelicals, are taught at home. Farris bought the land for the Patrick Henry campus with four hundred thousand dollars from the Home School Legal Defense Association's reserves; he raised the rest of the money for the college, nine million dollars, from parents and donors such as Tim LaHaye, the author of the best-selling 'Left Behind' series. LaHaye's portrait hangs in the main hall.*" Hanna Rosin , "God and Country," *The New Yorker*, June 27, 2005.

Patrick Henry College has highly visible Moot Court Teams that compete nationally in a debate competition designed to "simulate appellate arguments before the U.S. Supreme Court." Patrick Henry College is truly churning out Soldiers for the Right to shape America's government.

Bear in mind that there is a separate accrediting organization for these schools, the Transnational Association of Christian Colleges and Schools. These schools are growing each year, and are increasingly turning out staunch Christian Soldiers to shape this country and its future without even realizing they are employing the Seven Mountain Strategy and fulfilling Rushdoony's dominionist utopia.

"Helped by the institution's friends-in-high-places, PHC has already provided the current White House administration with more interns than any other college in the USA." Amanda Gefter, "Home-schooling special: Preach Your Children Well," *New Scientist Magazine*, November 11, 2006.

~ ~ ~ ~ ~ ~ ~ ~

"By 2004, PHC students held seven out of 100 internships in the White House, a number even more striking when one considers that only 240 students were enrolled in the entire college. Last year, two PHC graduates worked in the White House, six worked for members of Congress and eight for federal agencies, including two for the FBI. 'Patrick Henry is something to worry about because these kids end up in the administration,' says Glenn Branch, deputy director of the National Center for Science Education in Oakland, California, which campaigns against the teaching of creationism as science.

Home-schoolers are drawn to PHC partly because of its political connections and partly because, unlike most Christian colleges, it boasts high academic standards. Besides the focus on creationism, much of the curriculum is dedicated to rhetoric and debate, preparing students to fight political and legal battles on issues such as abortion, stem cell research and evolution. The technique is effective. For the past two years, the college has won the moot court national championship, in which students prepare legal briefs and deliver oral arguments to a hypothetical court, and has twice defeated the UK's University of Oxford in debating competitions." "God's next Army," *Channel 4 of UK television*, June, 2006.

Evangelical networks are also utilized to increase influence at secular universities. One of the tenets of the education Mountain is not only to have replacements ready in the wings but also to influence existing colleges and universities. The following quote shows how the concept of having wealthy donors from the influence gained in business helps to fund the education war.

> *"Two private foundations have played particularly significant roles as patrons of evangelical academic activity over the last three decades: the Pew Charitable Trusts, founded by evangelical oil magnate J. Howard Pew, and the Lilly Endowment, established by the family behind the Eli Lilly pharmaceutical company."* D. Michael Lindsay, *Faith in the Halls of Power: How Evangelicals Joined the American Elite*, Oxford University Press, 2007.

Ultimately public schools have become a battleground because the Religious Right have disagreed with nearly everything teachers and administrators do, once the God of the Bible wasn't the center of all teaching endeavors. They have done more to tear them down than find solutions to help fix the problems. Administrators that have never spent a day teaching carry a share of the fault in what ails public schools as well, but this does not excuse the actions of the Religious Right in trying to dismantle quality education, for every child.

<u>Take With You From This Chapter</u>

➢ The Religious Right wants public schools to end, and for education to be provided by Christian organizations, or at home.

➢ The Religious Right views children as spoils in the war.

➢ While working towards eliminating public schools, they are bringing religion into the classrooms.

➢ Charter schools and vouchers are part of the plan against public schools.

Chapter 19
Rewriting History

<u>What to Expect From this Chapter</u>

➢ How the Religious Right is rewriting U.S. History to force a Christian nation myth in order to legitimize their Dominion.

➢ How the U.S. had many influences, not just Christian.

➢ How the Fourteenth amendment is despised and provides the real reason behind the current Constitution focus and rebirth of the states rights fervor.

➢ David Barton – again!

We follow the agenda to eliminate public schools with the fervent attempts to rewrite our nation's history. The nation's history is its identity, and our school system is charged with teaching our history to preserve that identity. It is not surprising that when one comes under attack, the other does.

In a previous chapter we looked at how religion became interwoven into patriotism so that to be a good American you somehow need to be a Christian. This was the precursor to the claim that "Christians founded the nation on Christian principles," so it is accepted without question, when *in fact* it is false.

With the new American Patriot's Bible, we see combined the "good patriot is a Christian" idea with a rewriting of our history within a translation of the Bible. *"Americans looking to combine love of God with love of country this July 4th can quote the new American Patriot's Bible, which says God has influenced America through godly Founding Fathers, presidents and soldiers. 'This Bible is designed for the decent, hardworking core of America, the ordinary man or woman who loves this nation and believes it springs from godly roots,' says Richard G. Lee, a Southern Baptist pastor from Georgia who served as the Bible's general editor."* Steve Rabey, "New 'American Patriot's Bible' sees USA's 'godly roots,'" *USA Today*, July 2, 2009.

Many influences

The United States was founded upon many philosophies, including the ideas of a "social contract" in which the authority of the government must be derived from the consent of the governed. A mixture of John Locke (English Philosopher) and Jean-Jacques Rousseau (French Philosopher), and even Voltaire, lead the way in the Social Contract influence on our Founding Fathers. Such Enlightenment philosophers greatly influenced the American revolutionaries and leaders of the day. Greek and Roman government ideas and structure influenced America's Founding Fathers and our founding documents, as well as ideas of how the British system should have worked with the division of powers. Lastly, The Iroquois Confederacy had an influence, but historians debate the extent of that influence. There is a vast difference between the existence of Christian founders and all the founders intentionally setting up a Christian nation based upon the Bible. Don't confuse the two.

Have we forgotten that this country was founded, populated, homesteaded, and farmed long before one single European Christian ever set foot on this continent? Is it ethically right to forget the Native American peoples who settled this land first? This land was theirs long before any white European muscled their way in, Christian or not. Secondly, has it been conveniently forgotten that this country was colonized by Britain and then we rebelled against the British? This country was founded on aggression against native peoples and rebellion against the colonizing *mother* country. That is the truth of how this country began, and hopefully we have grown and are better than our shaky beginnings.

Democracy in the Bible?

If the United States was supposedly based upon Christianity then we should be able to find examples of a Democratic society in the Bible. The Bible has no real governmental structures except rule by priests, judges, and then monarchs, there is no democracy, anywhere. How is the democratic United States based on those principles of a priest, judge, or a king from the Bible?

The Bible gives us the account of Israel that had priests, with judges leading them in matters of war. In the first book of Samuel, chapter 8, we are told that the people of Israel didn't like Samuel's sons who would take over when Samuel died, so they wanted a king. God related that He didn't like it. But at absolutely no point did God say that a king was not his *favorite*, or how about a democracy? A government run by the people and for the people, will be just the thing for you? No. Rather, God has Samuel relay back to the people what a bad idea a king is, and let's just leave things status quo with the High Priest ruling. The people rejected status quo, and Israel gets their first king, Saul.

As an example of this lack of democracy in the Bible, my Religious Right pastor said once from the pulpit that people in America had a hard time really understanding God's absolute authority over our lives, because we don't live under a king, a monarch. That people of biblical times had no problem understanding God's total control of their lives because they lived under such rulers, rather than in a democracy.

Bible promises not to United States

A key feature of the Religious Right's agenda is convincing the masses that the U.S. began as a Christian nation and was intended to be a Christian nation, only and forever, and thus we must get back to the strict biblical stance of our Christian roots. The Religious Right purport that a covenant was entered into with God at the founding of this nation, and that if we don't remain a Bible-based-nation, we are going to cease to be a powerful nation, for God's favor will be taken away.

"Now it shall be, if you will diligently obey the Lord your God, being careful to do all His commandments which I command you today, the Lord your God will set you high above all nations of the earth. And all these blessings shall come upon you and overtake you, if you will obey the Lord your God." Deuteronomy 28:1-2 NASB.

"For if you are careful to keep all this commandment which I am commanding you to do, to love the Lord your God, to walk in all His ways and

235

hold fast to Him; then the Lord will drive out all these nations from before you."
Deuteronomy 11:22-23 NASB.

The preceding Bible promises *were not made to the United States*; they were made to the Jewish people, as an ethnic heritage. That does not stop Religious Right leaders from applying those and other similar quotes to America when no such promise has been made, in the Bible to the U.S. The argument becomes that the *intention or principle* is held as a truth and that God will honor that principle with the U.S., but we have to give dominion with a capital D to the radical conservative Christian faction to ensure this. Promises to a chosen ethnic people, Hebrews, were expanded to include individuals who personally accepted Christ's salvation, via a spiritual grafting. It does not apply to another nation at all.

What is the covenant with God, then?

I have yet to see in any museum a display of the actual documented covenant that our Founding Fathers supposedly entered into with God that we would be a Christian nation, and in return God would bless this country and make it a great and powerful nation. For surely it should be on display next to our Constitution, if such a covenant existed? It *doesn't* exist, except for arguable conjecture about our Founding Fathers and the subjective interpretations of a few writings, and in taking biblical quotes out of context and forcing them to apply to the United States.

The myth that America was established as a Christian nation is sometimes attributed to the early Puritans, who traveled from England to America in 1630. Apparently the Massachusetts Bay Colony, while on board the *Arbella,* listened to a sermon by John Winthrop where he uses the phrase "A City Upon a Hill" to describe their intentions in settling in the new country. This phrase is referencing a Bible passage from Matthew 5:14 and the Sermon on the Mount, imploring Jesus' listeners that, "You are the light of the world. A city that is set on a hill cannot be hidden." Thus John Winthrop's sermon to the Puritans was that the new community they intended to build when the ship landed in the new world would be an example of

Christian charity that could be observed by the world. Somehow, this constitutes in the Religious Right's mind a covenant with God that America was to be a Christian nation solely and only. This shining city upon a hill is brought up in some political speeches today, but not many understand its significance.

A few things should be noted here. The Massachusetts Bay Puritans were not the first Europeans to settle in the new world, so it is not only presumptuous, but wrong, to claim that the Puritans spoke for the intentions of every settler, before and after them. Many early settlers where highly religious or were escaping religious persecution for their *out-of-favor* brand of worship, but there were a great many settlers who were looking for financial rewards and business opportunities, solely. Further, the Massachusetts Bay Colony was a Charter Colony, which means the King of England granted a charter to the colonial government establishing what rules the colony was to live by. How is this the beginning of a Democracy? Lastly, when it came to the difficult work of revolution and defining a new country that could stand on its own, there was no such pact with God that was the rallying cry.

Another claim to the Christian founding of America is the Mayflower compact, which was a document written by Pilgrims while onboard the Mayflower ship. The document was not a covenant with God; it was an agreement providing for a temporary government when they were blown off course from Virginia, that their original English charters were intended for. It is considered significant that they provided even temporary self-governance until their new colony in Cape Cod could be sorted out back in England, and their new charter or status could be defined. The specific signers of the Mayflower compact were Christians. But not everybody on the Mayflower signed the document. The short wording of the compact follows:

> *"In the name of God, Amen. We, whose names are underwritten, the Loyal Subjects of our dread Sovereign Lord, King James, by the Grace of God, of England, France and Ireland, King, Defender of the Faith, e&. Having undertaken for the Glory of God, and Advancement of the Christian Faith, and*

the Honour of our King and Country, a voyage to plant the first colony in the northern parts of Virginia; do by these present, solemnly and mutually in the Presence of God and of one another, covenant and combine ourselves together into a civil Body Politick, for our better Ordering and Preservation, and Furtherance of the Ends aforesaid; And by Virtue hereof to enact, constitute, and frame, such just and equal Laws, Ordinances, Acts, Constitutions and Offices, from time to time, as shall be thought most meet and convenient for the General good of the Colony; unto which we promise all due submission and obedience. In Witness whereof we have hereunto subscribed our names at Cape Cod the eleventh of November, in the Reign of our Sovereign Lord, King James of England, France and Ireland, the eighteenth, and of Scotland the fifty-fourth. Anno Domini, 1620."

It is important to note the key phrasing that Religious Right adherents believe makes America founded on Christianity: "…for the Glory of God, and Advancement of the Christian Faith, and the Honour of our King and Country…" For the Glory of God and the advancement of the Christian Faith is written large and referenced widely, while they leave off "and the Honour of our King and Country." This was not intended for a democracy, either.

The Founding Fathers all recognized that the Mayflower Compact was special for the idea of mutually agreed upon self-governance. But, neither the Pilgrims nor the Puritans were the sole founding members of this country. The Mayflower compact bound those specific passengers who signed the compact to a temporary government, in roughly 196 words. The Plymouth Colony was an English colonial venture, which means it was England colonizing or expanding into another continent. Ultimately, they answered to their King – King James of England, as they clearly state in the compact. How is this the intentional founding of our representative Democracy?

Why rewrite our history?

Thus, part of the education agenda for the Religious Right is to rewrite the history of the United States to force it to read that Christians came to this continent and with the primary thought of creating an entire new nation founded on Christian dogma. This way, it is easier to convince people to do away with separation of church and state, and the Religious Right's extremism becomes the national religion.

Does that seem too outlandish? Well, Chris Rodda thought it was at first, when she stumbled upon Internet message boards full of Religious Right members setting forth an entirely different history than most of us were taught, and respected historians maintain. They are rewriting information about America's Founding Fathers and founding intentions, and publishing them in Christian Revisionist history books. They have nullified the contributions of the Native Indigenous peoples or their significance (specifically the Iroquois tribe), as well as the French writers Voltaire and Jean-Jacques Rousseau's tremendous impact on our Founding Fathers ideals for this nation.

Chris Rodda shares in the introduction to volume 1 of her projected 3 volume set *Liars for Jesus: The Religious Right's Alternate Version of American History,* how she would do research and post documented replies in the message boards that were inundated by Christian Reconstructionists presenting a different history. It became a battle, and before long others in the message forums were encouraging Chris to write all this in a book, since she would give details from primary sources, leaving no room for the Right to lie or twist the information. And thus, a massive defense of America's true founding began for Chris Rodda. The title, *Liars for Jesus,* unabashedly proclaims what Chris was experiencing – a rewriting of our true history to accommodate the Religious Right's goal of claiming dominion over the United States government.

"James Madison, in his 1785 'Memorial and Remonstrance' against a bill by fellow Virginian Patrick Henry, argued that taxpayer funding of any church 'will be a dangerous abuse of power. ... Faithful members of a free state (are bound) to remonstrate against it.'

Religious freedom, Madison continued, is 'one of the noblest characteristics of our late Revolution. ... Who does not see that the same authority which can establish Christianity in exclusion of all other religions may establish with the same ease any particular sect of Christians. ... That the same authority which can force a citizen to contribute three pence only of his property to the support of any one establishment may force him to conform to any other establishment in all cases whatsoever?'

State religion, he added, has been used 'to erect a spiritual tyranny on the ruins of Civil Society,' and has fomented 'pride and indolence in the clergy, ignorance and servility in the laity ... superstition, bigotry, and persecution.'" Tim Wheeler "Bush, Religious Right Target Churches", *People's Weekly World*, July 3, 2004

Faith of our Fathers

A good number of our Founding Fathers would not be considered Christians by today's standards, and some were apparently Deists. That doesn't mean much anymore to people, since the label is old. Let's look at what our Deist Founding Fathers believed and how that matches the current Religious Right litmus test. Deists believe that a supreme being created the universe, but they don't necessarily believe in the God of the Bible. Many of our Deist founding fathers would refer to God as divine providence etc., but they weren't invoking the same God as the Religious Right has in mind. Deists believed in reason and observation to understand the natural world around them and tended to not believe in miracles or revelation. Deism is labeled humanism by the Religious Right of today and is seen as an enemy.

Thomas Jefferson, true to his Deist beliefs, edited the Bible down to what he felt was rational. Deists don't generally believe in sacred texts nor the inerrancy of the Bible or that Jesus was God incarnate, but they typically held Jesus' moral teachings in high regard. *The Jefferson Bible*, also known as *The Life and Morals of Jesus of Nazareth*, is New Testament only (minus Paul's writings, Revelation and the letters of Peter, James, John and Jude), and had all supernatural aspects removed including anything miraculous about Jesus' birth, all mention of miracles; the Last Supper is stripped out, and nothing about Jesus' resurrection. In the Library of Congress' Rare

Book and Special Collections Division, you will find on display Jefferson's personal copy of George Sale's 1734 translation of the Koran, showing that he acquainted himself with other world religions as well in his personal education. Remember that Jefferson authored our Declaration of Independence, served in the Continental Congress, was the first Secretary of State under Washington, was the third president, and was a respected Founding Father.

"Whereas, for Deists, the principal revelation for Christianity – the Bible – bore every sign of human counterfeiting or alteration, they saw the magnificent design of nature as revealing a Creator, or what Thomas Jefferson termed 'a superattending power.'" David Holmes *The Faiths of the Founding Fathers,* Oxford University Press, 2006.

~ ~ ~ ~ ~ ~ ~

"If anyone in 1831 knew the difference between appearance and reality in the religious beliefs of the founding fathers, it would have been Bird Wilson. In his sermon delivered in Albany, New York, in October of that year, Wilson attacked the current stories that were circulating about the admirable religious piety of such founders as George Washington. Washington, he said in the sermon, had not been an orthodox Christian; in reality he had really been an eighteenth-century Deist. Wilson cited support on this point from clergy who had known Washington and whom he himself knew. Then – in significant words – went on to state that 'among all our presidents downward, not one was a professor of religion, at least not of more than Unitarianism.' ...The Episcopal cleric [Bird Wilson] wrote to the most reliable source of information he knew – the man who had been chaplain of the Continental Congress and Washington's pastor when the national capital was in Philadelphia. On December 1, 1832, [Bishop] White replied in words as significant as those of Wilson: 'I do not believe that any degree of recollection will bring to my mind any fact which would prove General Washington to have been a believer in the Christian revelation.'

...Deism influenced, in one way or another most, of the political leaders who designed the new American government. Since the founding fathers did not hold identical views on religion, they should not be lumped together. But if census takers trained in Christian theology had set up broad categories in 1790 labeled 'Atheism,' 'Deism and Unitarianism,' 'Orthodox Protestantism,' 'Orthodox Roman Catholicism,' and 'Other,' and if they had interviewed Franklin, Washington, Adams, Jefferson, Madison, and Monroe, they would undoubtedly have placed every one of these six founding fathers in some way under the category of 'Deism and Unitarianism.'" David Holmes, *The Faiths of the Founding Fathers*, Oxford University Press, 2006.

The Founding Fathers, Thomas Jefferson, James Madison later in his life, Thomas Paine, Benjamin Franklin and even George Washington, are reportedly all *Deists* and would not pass the Religious Right's litmus test for a Supreme Court judge, let alone as major players in shaping the nation today. Those Founding Fathers who were Christians were on good working terms generally with the Deists in the political arena, or they never could have worked out the Constitution. They worked together better than our current politicians who can't agree on much of anything in taking moral stands on a variety of social issues. Most importantly, the founders of the nation were thinking men who took great pains to set up a framework for a new country that would allow it to grow and develop with religious liberty for all.

The Treaty of Tripoli

"As the Government of the United States of America is not, in any sense, founded on the Christian religion;..." The Treaty of Tripoli Article 11, signed by President John Adams and ratified by the U.S. Senate on June, 10 1797 and publicly published in The Philadelphia Gazette on June, 17 1797.

The Treaty of Tripoli passed the Senate with that very clear declaration boldly standing. The Religious Right claims that particular wording is just a translation, and that the senate did not agree to such wording in their translation. That is not true. *As the Government of the United States of America is not, in any sense, founded on the Christian religion;..."* is the exact translation that the senate approved and ratified and that President John Adams signed. To say anything else is a boldfaced lie.

David Barton's view of history

There exists an organization called WallBuilders, founded by David Barton, that is dedicated to "presenting America's forgotten history and heroes with an emphasis on our moral, religious and constitutional heritage." Wall Builders is active in the war on separation of church and state. On the WallBuilders website (as of March, 2012) the stated goal is *"to exert a direct and positive influence in government, education, and the family by 1) educating the nation concerning the Godly foundation of our country; 2) providing information to federal, state, and local officials as they develop public policy which reflect Biblical values; and 3) encouraging Christians to be involved in the civic arena."*

David Barton and WallBuilders are significant because they are successful in their efforts to rewrite our nation's history. They have been instrumental in getting a 2007 law (authored by Republican Representative Warren Chisum and signed by Governor Rick Perry) passed in Texas mandating that all Texas public school districts must offer the literature and history of the Bible, beginning with the fall, 2009 school session. This broke down the wall of separation for federally funded schools, and many Jewish organizations complain that the curriculum is more devotional than it is academic.

> *"Most of the courses promote one faith perspective over all others and push an ideological agenda that is hostile to religious freedom, science and public education, according to the 76-page report, "Reading, Writing and Religion," released yesterday* [September 13, 2006].
>
> *The Texas Freedom Network surveyed the more than 1,000 school districts in the state to learn which offered Bible electives. Mark Chancey, a biblical studies professor at Southern Methodist University, then analyzed the curricula,*

going back five years, from 25 districts, about 3% of the total, that offered them as electives in 2005-2006.

The report was a joint effort by Chancey and the Education Fund of the Texas Freedom Network, a liberal watchdog group.

The study found the vast majority of the electives to be explicitly devotional, with an almost exclusively Christian, usually Protestant, perspective. It also found most of the Bible courses were taught by teachers with no academic training in biblical, religious or theological studies and who were not very familiar with the issues of separation of church and state.

'We stand with parents who believe that the Bible is a great way to teach students about the importance of religion in history and literature. But we think pressure groups have hijacked a good idea and the end result is that these courses can betray families' faith in our public schools by teaching courses with a narrow religious perspective above all others,' said TFN President Kathy Miller." "Most Bible courses in Texas schools not academic, study finds," *First Amendment Center*, Nashville, Tenn., Thursday, September 14, 2006

In other words, a narrow Protestant Christianity was taught, and not an academic look at the Bible. By academic treatment we mean such topics as: literary devices used in the Bible (allegory, metaphor etc.); the similarities of Bible stories to other cultures' traditions (such as the Bible's flood to the Sumerian Epic of Gilgamesh's flood, or the Egyptian god Osiris as one of the earliest examples of a resurrected god); the Abrahamic faiths consist of Judaism, Islam, and Christianity since they all claim Abraham as the patriarch of their faith and contain other similarities; Roman Emperor Constantine declared a specific flavor of Christianity as the official religion, and that other expressions were illegal, and the impact this had on the church's development; the Council of Laodicea in 363 CE decided what books would be included in the *New Testament*, while chapter divisions were not added until 1205 CE and verse numbering was done later and only for convenience; the first five books of the *Old Testament* are traditionally said to be written by Moses and are called the Torah, but seventeenth century German textual criticism of the Bible's first five books resulted in the "Documentary Hypothesis" that theorizes there were actually four authors referred to as J writer, E writer, D writer, and P writer, rather than only Moses. This would be a more academic teaching on the Bible, but it was found to be Sunday School lessons in tax payer provided public schools. This is not an unbiased teaching of the Bible as literature or in history, but indoctrination. This was only one factor, as the history books were revised to downplay separation of church and state and emphasize Religious Right champions.

Remember, that the Mountain of education is to replace the existing structure with home-schooling or church-run schools. The children and what they are taught is crucial to the future of the nation. Changing school curriculum to incorporate the Bible is intended to undermine that separation of church and state. But, it reinforces the deliberate rewriting of the nation's history as a Christian nation. David Barton has taken Rousas Rushdoony's revisionist history and has been peddling it as truth.

David Barton was introduced earlier as the new conductor of the Religious Right, effectively stepping in as James Dobson's power diminished. Barton got a Bachelor's degree in Christian education from Oral Roberts University and then taught at a fundamentalist Christian school, but is now critiquing Texas public school social studies and history standards. He was the vice chairman for the Texas Republican Party from 1998 to 2006. A sign of just how successful Barton has been was the April 2007 Time magazine cover story by David Van Biema supporting the idea of teaching the Bible in federally funded schools.

> *"In 1998, a conservative member of the California Academic Standards Commission appointed Barton to an advisory position, asking the Texan to critique proposed social studies/history standards. From that perch, Barton attacked the portion of the standards that discussed the development of religious freedom, trying to remove every reference to separation of church and state....*

He is active in the National Council on Bible Curriculum in Public Schools, a North Carolina group that works to persuade public schools to adopt a fundamentalist-oriented Bible curriculum under the guise of teaching 'about' religion. Barton serves on the organization's advisory board, alongside several other Religious Right figures....Barton spearheaded an effort to add a plank to the [Republican] party's platform attacking church-state separation as a 'myth.'" Rob Boston, "Texas Tall Tale," *Church & State*, July/August, 2009.

David Barton and the curriculum in Texas impacts every state since, as Texas Freedom Now's President Kathy Miller explains *"Texas is the second largest purchaser of school textbooks in the country...so to avoid spending money on multiple editions, publishers often write their textbooks to meet Texas curriculum standards and then sell those textbooks in other states."* Rob Boston, "Texas Tall Tale," *Church & State*, July/August, 2009.

David Barton is the front man, but you will hear Pat Robertson repeatedly hammer a revisionist view of America's beginning and founding to his massive audience. James Dobson and pastors of mega churches (like Coral Ridge Presbyterian Church with a radio and television empire) all over Religious Right's kingdom are doing the same thing. Do you have any doubts as to how dangerous this is? This is the stuff of cults who brainwash their members in terms of a different reality. It is all too real, and happening right now. This tactic of rewriting history isn't new. The old Roman Catholic Church was known for doing the same thing during the Dark Ages. It is commonly accepted that a victor in a war will write the history for that country to favor the victor, but they usually have waited until they have conquered the land.

"History was rewritten to become a verification of Christian beliefs. Orthodox Christians thought history necessary only in order to place the events into Biblical context...Blind faith replaced the spirit of historical investigation... Although the Church restricted historical inquiry more severely, it carried on a process of rewriting history that had started much earlier. Twentieth century

archeology is beginning to reveal a very different picture of human history than may have been told even in pre-Christian Rome...Distorting and rewriting history gave the impression that Christianity had not only lifted society from harsher, more barbaric times, but that a social structure of hierarchy and domination had always existed and was therefore inevitable." Helen Ellerbe, *The Dark Side of Christian History*, Morningstar Books, July 1995.

How effective has this rewriting of our history been? The Pennsylvania state House unanimously passed H.R. 535 in January of 2012. H.R. 535 is a resolution declaring 2012 to be the year of the Bible. The resolution enshrines a Religious Right history in its declaration that *"WHEREAS, The Bible, the word of God, has made a unique contribution in shaping the United States as a distinctive and blessed nation and people; and WHEREAS, Deeply held religious convictions springing from the holy scriptures led to the early settlement of our country; and WHEREAS, Biblical teachings inspired concepts of civil government that are contained in our Declaration of Independence and the Constitution of the United States; and... RESOLVED, That the House of Representatives declare 2012 as the "Year of the Bible" in Pennsylvania in recognition of both the formative influence of the Bible on our Commonwealth and nation and our national need to study and apply the teachings of the holy scriptures."* I would say they have been exceedingly successful. Pennsylvania State Representative Jerry Stern gave an interview with the Christian Post reporter Michael Gryboski, and defended the resolution. He felt that the first amendment establishment clause was only for the federal government and doesn't impact Pennsylvania at all.

In August, 2008 Americans witnessed true history, when a pastor grilled the presidential candidates over religion, in a Christian church, televised. Did you feel indignant? This is one result of rewriting our history and loudly proclaiming again and again that we were intended to be a Christian nation. Did you question what an insult to a candidate this would have been if (s)he had been Jewish, agnostic, Native American or worst of all, an atheist or Pagan? This act set a precedent that

Christianity is indeed part of the presidential selection process, and that there was very little focus on how well suited candidates are to serve and lead the country. This was in direct violation of our U.S. Constitution, but there was no outrage – not really. The pundits argued over who *won*, rather than grieving over the death of one of our country's founding ideals.

> "*The Senators and Representatives before mentioned, and the Members of the several State Legislatures, and all executive and judicial Officers, both of the United States and of the several States, shall be bound by Oath or Affirmation, to support this Constitution;* **but no religious Test shall ever be required as a Qualification to any Office or public Trust under the United States.**" U.S. Constitution Article VI – Debts, Supremacy, Oaths. (emphasis added.)

~ ~ ~ ~ ~ ~ ~

> "*I never will, by any word or act, bow to the shrine of intolerance or admit a right of inquiry into the religious opinions of others...In every country and every age, the priest had been hostile to Liberty.*" Thomas Jefferson. This quote is displayed in the Jefferson memorial in Washington, D.C.

This straying from our nation's true history of religious liberty for all, not just Christians, is staggering. But that it is being done with barely any outrage is the saddest testament to how far they have actually succeeded in the Seven Mountains of influence.

Take With You From This Chapter

➢   The Religious Right is rewriting history to smooth the way for Christian Reconstruction and Dominion.

➢   John Lock, Jean-Jacques Rousseau, Voltaire, and The Iroquois Confederacy all had influence on our Founding Fathers.

➢   There is no example of democracy in the Bible as a government structure.

➢   John Winthrop's sermon "A City Upon a Hill" with Massachusetts Bay Colony and the Mayflower Compact are not examples of a democracy and do not speak for all settlers before or after them.

➢ Many of the Founding Father's faith would not pass the Christian test today.

➢ The translation of Treaty of Tripoli that passed clearly says, "America is not, in any sense, founded on the Christian religion."

Chapter 20
The Church and Science – a long battle

<u>What to Expect From this Chapter</u>

➢ The problem the Religious Right has with science.

➢ The history of the church and science has been one of continuous battles.

➢ How the United States is suffering because of the continual battles against science in schools.

<u>American anti-science leaders?</u>

Encompassed within the Mountain of education is the rewriting of the nation's founding and history. This rewriting includes science, as well. We now move into a discussion of the comprehensive assault on science in America. This is one of those areas that has been progressive but largely unnoticed, except by the scientific community.

Chris Matthews MSNBC show "Hardball" on May 5, 2009 witnessed Matthews pointedly asking Indiana Representative Mike Pence if he believed in the scientific method. Why would this even be a question for a government official? The interview actually started with a question about Mike Pence's party, the Republican Party, and a perceived lack of passion for environmental issues and climate change, in particular. It quickly spun off into – did Representative Pence personally believe in the scientific method?

In the 2011 mob of candidates struggling for the Republican presidential nomination, Jon Huntsman stood tall and said he believed in evolution, which the following article surmised resulted in his loss of the nomination.

"...polls have shown that almost 70 percent of Republicans deny evolution.

By contrast, the Republican party's denial of evolution is much older and more grassroots in nature, dating at least to when the national parties traded places during the civil-rights era. The conservative South, in addition to its other charming qualities, has a long history of passing laws hostile to science, from Tennessee's Butler Act, the 1925 law prohibiting the teaching of evolution that led to the Scopes trial, to Louisiana's 1981 Balanced Treatment Act, which decreed that 'creation science' had to be given an equal share of classroom time.

But while fundamentalists have always been hostile to evolution, the modern creationist movement got its start in the 1960s, primarily due to the influence of an evangelical author named Henry Morris. Morris' 1964, book The Genesis Flood ...

The larger lesson to be drawn from this is that the religious right isn't just targeting the theory of evolution. By their own words, they can't be. They believe that a person's morality is completely determined by their factual beliefs -- that being a good person depends on believing the right things about the origin of the universe. And since they believe that all truths worth knowing have already been revealed in the Bible, it follows that science is at best unnecessary and at worst a fatal deception that leads people away from salvation. Why, then, do we need science at all?

To those who hold the creationist worldview, everything has been going downhill since the Enlightenment. The willingness of people to think for themselves, to question authority, to investigate the world for truth – they see all this as a disastrous trend, one that only takes us farther from their ideal vision of a medieval, theocratic state. They seek nothing less than to turn back the clock of progress by several centuries, abolish the rational, reality-based view of the world, and return to the superstitious mindset in which blind faith is the answer to every problem. And, again, these are the people who've completely captured one of America's two major parties. What kind of havoc will result if they gain political power again?" Adam Lee, "Why the Anti-Science Creationist Movement Is So Dangerous," *Alternet*, September 8, 2011.

This is a truly critical point to grasp. They actually believe that a person's moral compass depends on whether they believe in the account in Genesis or not. Thus we see science under a full-scale assault. This is Dominion thought, via the Seven Mountains of influence. They had enough cultural influence to make belief in science a bad thing; this is becoming a more pervasive trend in the nation.

<u>What is best for the nation?</u>

The United States fought to obtain a scientific prowess among the industrialized nations. But in the last few decades, that has been eroding. China is now investing in cutting-edge scientific research, while the U.S. cuts scientific research dollars and fewer children look to scientific career fields.

> *"In the years since man unlocked the power stored up within the atom, the world has made progress, halting, but effective, toward bringing that power under human control. The challenge may be our salvation. As we begin to master the destructive potentialities of modern science, we move toward a new era in which science can fulfill its creative promise and help bring into existence the happiest society the world has ever known. ...*
>
> *Science contributes to our culture in many ways, as a creative intellectual activity in its own right, as the light which has served to illuminate man's place in the universe, and as the source of understanding of man's own nature."*

President John F. Kennedy Address to the National Academy of Science, Washington D. C., October, 22 1963.

President John F. Kennedy brought science into modern households with the space program, and children grew up dreaming of scientific exploration. The technology advances from the space program have benefited the nation in many sectors. From advances in breast cancer detection, heart defibrillators, weather satellites tracking hurricanes, increases to crop yields, robotic surgery, increasing our life expectancy, and even common ATM transactions and pay-at-the-pump conveniences can all be traced back to scientific pioneering from the space program. All of these advances have also directly spurred our economic growth. But everywhere you turn in

America, science is the new taboo. Two books expose this phenomenon, *Unscientific America: How Scientific Illiteracy Threatens Our Future* by Chris Mooney and Sheril Kirshenbaum, and *Fool Me Twice: Fighting the Assault on Science in America,* by Shawn Lawrence Otto. There are others as well, but the point is clearly made that science is on the *out* list in the U.S.

Therefore, we have science being shunned, funding cut, and now, for many American citizens, truth is not found in facts, research, or objective testing, but the Bible, only. We are witnessing the modern version of Galileo's fight with the Holy Roman Catholic Church over whether the sun revolves around the Earth because the Bible tells us so, or the Earth revolves around the sun because science proves it. We are fighting for this nation's betterment and competitive edge in a global economy. It comes back to what is best for the nation and our democracy.

Science and politics

In the 2008 Presidential debates, our nation's scientific community rallied together in a truly historic move and created Science Debate 2008, that resulted in finally getting Obama and McCain to participate in written answers to fourteen questions on the looming science policy issues that must be faced. The candidates never agreed to the several attempts at televised debates that were arranged. A large majority of citizens did not even hear about this massive scientific community effort to get the people who aspire to leading the most powerful nation on the planet to answer fourteen questions on our biggest challenges facing us – that only science can address.

"Senator John McCain (R-AZ) ignored the invitation entirely. Instead, Clinton and Obama chose to debate religion at Messiah College's Harrisburg, Pennsylvania, campus – where, ironically, they answered questions about science.

How, it's reasonable to ask, has American political culture come to a point where science can be discussed only in a forum on religion? What little news coverage of this stunning development there was didn't seem to affect the campaigns at all. The candidates continued their policies of nonengagement.

...we recruited marine scientist and former AAAS president Jane Lubchenco to help organize a debate in Oregon in August. Obama and McCain refused this one too, opting instead to hold yet another faith forum, this time at Saddleback Church in Lake Forest, California.

... Science has been responsible for roughly half of all US economic growth since World War II, and it lies at the core of most major unsolved policy challenges.

In an age when most major public policy challenges revolve around science, less than 2 percent of congresspersons have professional backgrounds in it. The membership of the 112th Congress, which ran from January 2011 to January 2013, included one physicist, one chemist, six engineers, and one microbiologist.

In contrast, how many representatives and senators do you suppose have law degrees – and whom many suspect avoided college science classes like the plague? Two hundred twenty-two. It's little wonder we have more rhetoric than fact in our national policy making. ...

The ignorance of Congress also extends to the willful variety, with powerful members vocally and publicly rejecting science almost as a way of proving their bona fides. In April of 2002, then-House majority whip Tom DeLay (R-TX) quoted the evangelical Christian authors of a 1999 book when he told a Texas church group, 'Only Christianity offers a comprehensive worldview that covers all areas of life and thought, every aspect of creation.' DeLay, who would soon become House majority leader, said he wanted to promote 'a biblical worldview' in American politics." Shawn Lawrence Otto, *Fool Me Twice: Fighting the Assault of Science in America*, Rodale Books, October, 2011.

It would seem we need more politicians who have a solid grasp of science to make sound policy judgments. Instead, we have the reverse. A Republican presidential candidate for 2012, Jon Huntsman, killed his bid for the Republican nomination because he dared to say in a tweet, "To be clear, I believe in evolution and trust scientists on global warming. Call me crazy." He backed his position up on ABC's *This Week* and polled near rock bottom ever since.

Science is a competing god

"You shall have no other gods before me." Genesis 20:3

Science has been a thorn in organized religion's side for a very long time. Shortly after the great Roman Empire collapsed, Europe began several hundred years known popularly as the Dark Ages. The historical record shows what happens when the *church* is institutionalized into the government. History shows it didn't do the government much good, but more to the point – it didn't do the people nor the church much good, either. It slowed scientific advances (thereby hurting the people) and the church didn't step up to the changing knowledge-base about the universe around them, and they did not grow. Nobody won in those instances.

The Religious Right routinely warns against the *religion* of reason or humanism placed before faith. This is a common mindset. You can't worship God and appreciate reason or science at the same time. Does acknowledging the importance and value of science mean you automatically worship it? In the book *Fool Me Twice: Fighting the Assault of Science in America,* by Shawn Lawrence Otto, the author goes into how many of the puritans in America strongly held that God gave us natural laws and the capacity to reason that worked harmoniously with faith.

There is a book titled *The Politically Incorrect Guide to Science* that is found under "current events," *not science,* in the bookstores. This book seems to epitomize and widen the chasm between the devout of the Religious Right and others. The front cover has the bold statement "Liberals have hijacked science for long enough. It's time to set the record straight." Pure science is not liberal or conservative, but the Religious Right makes everything a religio-political issue. The Heritage Foundation sponsored an event to promote the book. There have been many scathing reviews of this book by those more qualified, particularly by Chris Mooney who is a contributing editor for

Science Progress and author of the book *Unscientific America*. Let me share the nuggets from this book that illustrate how wide the division is in scientific endeavors between the Religious Right and the mainstream scientific community and other Christians.

> *"The priesthood of science is undisturbed, and that is the way they like it...*
>
> *Evolutionists who insist that this doctrine is true must therefore also claim that religion is a delusion. ...*
>
> *Scientists are peddling hope as well as fear. There's a growing utopian inclination to believe that relief from the human condition – disease, aging, and perhaps even death itself – can be engineered with the latest technology."* Tom Bethell, *The Politically Incorrect Guide to Science*, Regnery Publishing, 2005.

Mr. Bethell drew conclusions that those who believe in evolution couldn't have a faith in God, and that the two are polar opposites and that evolution is a *religion*. This isn't new. It is just that now these ideas are being peddled to the masses. The book has been heavily criticized for its lack of much real substance. But that hasn't stopped the excitement by Heritage Foundation and those of like-mind to defend and promote it. You can almost see the chasm between science and Christians widening into the Grand Canyon, with each person who reads the book. This is an unfortunate situation, since there are many Christians who don't see a conflict between their faith and science, at least for now.

Fortunately, there are efforts such as the Clergy Letter Project, which is an international organization that brings together religious leaders and scientists to show how they can coexist. Perhaps they challenge one another to grow? A person of faith today does not believe that a sneeze is an evil spirit escaping and that you must say "bless you," to somehow protect that person. We know what causes sneezes from science, and thus the erroneous superstition was debunked. Science is based on observable, repeatable, verifiable evidence, and faith is a belief in spiritual matters that are often unseen and not verifiable. In spite of it being apples compared to oranges, the

Religious Right takes the Seven Mountains Strategy and has targeted science for destruction.

Back in time

All indications show that the Religious Right would have us all going back to the Middle Ages, back to a time where a literal interpretation of the Bible ruled over science, medicine, and the legal system, unchallenged. We are back to Nicolaus Copernicus in 1514, and Galileo in 1633, fighting with the church for their lives because they dared to say the earth circled the sun. Thus we see politicians being bluntly asked if they believe in the scientific method. Religious Right adherents believe that science is a direct challenge to the God of the Bible, and that science is a competing god. We should not look to a future where American scientific pursuit has been dropped, children no longer dream of growing up and making great discoveries, and politicians are proud they are science-ignorant.

"Today, science in the United States – once a world leader in virtually every research field – is under intense assault from the extreme religious right, ...

The United States now educates fewer scientists each year and now imports more high tech products than it exports. ...

Meanwhile, the administration sends anti-choice lobbyists as delegates to international meetings on women's health, and global conferences on AIDS to have Reverend Franklin–Graham lecture on 'faith-based solutions to AIDS.' The religious right's effect on Bush's opposition to stem-cell research is notorious, despite the majority of scientists – and U.S. citizens, including evangelicals – supporting research that potentially could have as massive an impact on health as antibiotics did, particularly affecting research on cancer, Parkinson's disease, other neurological disorders, diabetes, and paralysis." Robin Morgan, *Fighting Words, A Toolkit for Combating the Religious Right*, Nation Books, 2006.

~ ~ ~ ~ ~ ~ ~

"A great many leading lights of the scientific revolution and the

257

Enlightenment – Nicolaus Copernicus, Francis Bacon, Rene Descartes, Johannes Kepler, Galileo Galilei, Isaac Newton, Robert Boyle – were distinctly religious and viewed science as a better means of understanding God's creation and the laws governing it.

Granted, there have been many episodes of conflict between science and faith: The stories of sixteenth-century Copernican Giordano Bruno (burned at the stake by the Roman Inquisition for his unorthodox views, including the contention that the universe is infinite and there are many worlds) and Galileo (censored, forced to recant, and committed to house arrest by Pope Urban VIII. for defending Copernican heliocentrism) certainly come to mind...

Increasingly, science has offered explanations for aspects of existence or reality that were once described as miracles or the product of divine intervention. Over time, diseases have come to be understood as naturally caused, not due to be cured by exorcism or prayer but by medical treatments. Similarly, an awe-inspiring phenomenon like lightning – once assumed to be divinely impelled – was recognized to be a natural occurrence ...

The Darwinian revolution, and the considerable religious resistance it triggered, certainly upped the intensity level for conflicts between science and religion. But again, that does not mean acceptance of evolution and belief in God are incompatible. Even at the time, many religious thinkers, including major Anglican clergymen such as Charles Kingsley and Frederick Temple, had no problem adapting to Darwin's ideas....

We should instead adopt a stance of respect toward those who hold their faith dear, and a sense of humility based on the knowledge that although science can explain a great deal about the way our world functions, the question of God's existence lies outside its expertise." Chris Mooney and Sheril Kirshebaum, *Unscientific America: How Scientific Illiteracy Threatens Our Future,* 2009.

What common sense that quote exhibits, to respect each side for what they intrinsically bring to the human experience. Facts and science are necessary if we do not want to revert back to the superstitious mode of the Dark Ages, but an individual's personal belief system should be respected for what it brings to his or her life and communities. It is a fine balancing act, one that the Religious Right does not believe in nor support. Scientific inquiry promotes critical thinking, which is the linchpin to innovation and ingenuity, once considered a primary American characteristics, but not so much anymore.

Scientific method

Gone are the days when the Scopes Monkey Trial caused fundamentalists embarrassment. The Religious Right is worldly savvy and understands packaging and marketing very well. So now, we even have the Religious Right version of science, a replacement for secular science. In 1970, the Institute for Creation Research in California began, established by Henry Morris, Tim LaHaye (of the video game and *Left Behind* best-selling book empire) and Scott Memorial Baptist Church. Their stated mission from their website is, *"ICR equips believers with evidence of the Bible's accuracy and authority through scientific research, educational programs, and media presentations, all conducted within a thoroughly biblical framework...to prepare scientists, teachers, and professionals in the key issues of science, creationism, and apologetics to thoroughly understand and effectively communicate biblical truth in the field of science."*

That statement in and of itself is counter to basic scientific methods, and starts with bias and unproven hypothesis, that the Bible is accurate in scientific matters, whenever touched upon. The scientific method attempts to start from a blank-slate, not pre-existing suppositions and a worldview, such as the Bible being absolute truth. The Institute for Creation Research states nine "Tenets of Scientific Creationism" and seven "Tenets of Biblical Creationism" which are the foundation for their brand of science and their educational philosophy. How sound a science is it? Well, let's take a look at the unbiased scientific research (investigation) method.

The scientific method is a series of steps scientists take to acquire, test, and describe the natural world. The scientific method is an ongoing process that is revised as more data is discovered or understood. The following is a basic description and sequence that may not stay in this order as testing, revising and retesting take place: define and ask a question about a phenomenon; research the topic including any prior experiments or inquiry; formulate a theory (hypothesis) on what the seeming cause of the situation is; test the theory with controls on factors that can influence the results; and gather information; possibly adjust the theory per the information observed and collected; reformulate the theory, and test again.

Revisions to the hypothesis (beginning question or theory) take place quite often when the facts do not fit the working theory, and then the process is run through again. Results of the experiment are written up and documented. It is also common for the results of the experiment to provide an opportunity for more questions about the same phenomenon or related phenomena, which begins the process of developing a hypothesis over again with a new question. The scientific method is a long and tedious process and is full of frustration, as the process may not support the hypothesis you began with.

The Religious Right approaches the natural world around us with a 180–degree different view. They have the Bible that gives them an inside track. To them, if you truly believe that the Bible is absolute truth, then science has it all wrong. The scientific method is unnecessary at best, and easily used by Satan, at worst. It is a matter of knowing that you are starting with all the answers and a completed puzzle, rather than the scientist who is blundering around in the dark trying to piece things together. But with challenges coming from the scientific field, devout Religious Right advocates who are scientists are coming forward and have adopted a new and improved *method* for their inquiry. Start with the Bible as absolute truth, and prove it. Objectivity and unbiased observation are needless when you are starting with the answers provided. Right?

The Truth Project

Focus on the Family has "The Truth Project" (www.truthproject.org) that is a DVD-based instructional course with thirteen hours of instruction. Within the course, claims such as "But Darwinian theory transforms science from the honest investigation of nature into a vehicle for propagating a godless philosophy" are made. Showing again they don't simply disagree; they demonize those who may believe differently.

Sociology, the systematic study of the development, structure, interaction, and collective behavior of organized groups of human beings is also dismissed in "The Truth Project" as being actually limited to *only* "*the social systems God has established: family, church, community, state, labor, and the union between God and man.*" Anything else is taking the wrong stance, the wrong approach and is not to be listened to. Never mind that this thinking is limiting and doesn't encourage questions and inquiry.

This brings us back to the scene in the Garden of Eden. It is stressed that Eve's putting her own interests or reasoning before God and his commands is what lost paradise for mankind, and ushered in sin and death to the world. Thus, reason above faith is the crux of sin. Doesn't the creation story say God created the human race with reasoning capability "in His image," and yet that same reasoning capability exemplified in science is wrong?

Dangerous and damaging

With the assault on science we now have atheistic scientists pushing back, such as Richard Dawkins and his book *The God Delusion*, and the other side lining up with David Berlinski and his book *The Devil's Delusion: Atheism and its Scientific Pretensions*. This growing chasm isn't good for science, or for the people, yet again. Science is intended to dig for answers in a systematic manner, while faith – is faith, often taken on faith. The one does not have to be at odds with the other when that is kept in mind. But consider the scenario if we were living in a country where the Religious Right is truly integrated into our government and judicial system – would science be supported in the least? You may not agree with one or the other position, but they have a right to express it civilly and you have a right to read it, or not.

It is not a matter of whether you believe in evolution or not, but that a significant man (Darwin or another scientist) and event in history (theory of evolution, or a discovery) is completely taboo to some because of a growing Religious Right inlfuence over every aspect of life in America, that is the issue. The concern is that the fertile ground for expanding the mind with questions and challenges is being stripped away and further limiting the competitiveness of America. This is creating an isolationist mentality that anything outside of an extremist little box just isn't allowed to even be considered, or to exist.

How will America's global competitive edge fare if science is suppressed for supporting a Biblical view of the natural world? How will disease-control and medical advances be negatively impacted with a Bible-based science promoted in this country, as the Religious Right would institute? How scientifically sound is it to just relegate the spread of disease to God's judgment? Yet, that is what the Religious Right regularly does because that is their worldview. This impacts your health and the health of your children.

The Religious Right warns of evolution taught in public schools because it doesn't conform with the Genesis creation story. Since when are people tested in science about what they *personally* believe? You are asked to learn this lesson how certain theories or events build upon each other, and how we got to where we are today. Students in science class taking exams or writing essays are not asked what their personal beliefs are on origins of life. Yet, now we have schools teaching what a certain segment of society believes as if it is science. Such an approach is not education, but social engineering through brain washing, which is exactly what the Religious Right accuses public schools of doing.

Restating an earlier comment, the suppression of science doesn't do the government any good, but more importantly, it doesn't do the people nor the church any good. It slows scientific advances (thereby hurting the people) and the church doesn't step up to the changing knowledge-base about the universe around them, and grow. Nobody wins.

Climate change fury

How much money does our government spend on scientific research and endeavors that will be axed by Religious Right political agenda? According the book *Unscientific America: How Scientific Illiteracy Threatens Our Future,* by Chris Mooney and Sheril Kirshenbaum, the authors report, *"The United States features a massive infrastructure for science, supported by well over $100 billion annually in federal funding and sporting a vast network of government laboratories and agencies, the finest universities in the world and innovative corporations that conduct extensive research."* All of which are in jeopardy, the more the Religious Right takes over the U.S. government.

The government is supposed to work for the ongoing viability of the country and for its citizens to survive, thus any threat of a major climate change that could have disastrous impacts really is for the government to address and protect its citizens wherever possible. But the Religious Right feels that immorality and straying from the God of the Bible are the only true threats to the country's viability to thrive. It is critical to understand that the Religious Right has a completely alternative reality that determines what is relevant and important, than the rest of the U.S.

> *"Republicans, who take control of the House of Representatives in January [2011], plan to eliminate a global warming committee created by Democrats [non-Religious Right] to focus attention on the causes and effects of climate change."*
> "House Republicans ax global warming committee," *USA Today*, December 2, 2010.

The book *Unscientific America* continues with *"The nation itself has become politically divided over the nature of reality, such that college-educated Democrats are now more than twice as likely as college-educated Republicans to believe that global warming is real and is caused by human activities. Meanwhile the United States stands on the verge of falling behind other nations such as India and China in the race to lead the world in scientific endeavor in the twenty-first century."*

Global warming, or climate change, is a hotly contested issue currently. Most of the ranting contributes to downplaying science and scientists. Large corporations paying for studies with pre-determined conclusions have muddied the waters as to what really is factual in the climate change problem. But why is the Religious Right so worked up over this issue? When you know the end of the story you don't like somebody trying to rewrite it. Let's hear from the Religious Right themselves why they aren't concerned over global warming.

"In the New Testament, Jesus Himself actually has something to say about the changes in the weather and our environment. Although He does not mention global warming directly, He does help us perhaps understand the role disruptions in our weather patterns may play in the days leading up to His return....

We believe it is possible that Jesus is referring to dramatic, national weather changes in this passage [Luke 21:7-12]...Did you notice that what Jesus warned would occur in the last days are almost identical to what some global warming theorists are saying is going to happen?...

Jesus also said there will be an increase in spiritual deception that is intended to get Christians off our game and render us ineffective when we should be running our two-minute drill. Deceived people are, by definition, not in tune with the priorities of Christ's kingdom. They put their faith in something other than God. And this is exactly what environmental alarmists ask us to do. The language they use and the policies they promote are humanistic. How many times have you heard them appeal to others to 'help save the planet'? The whole premise of the statement presupposes that mankind is ultimately in charge of the fate of our planet. It springs from the same idea that we can save ourselves and that we don't need the atoning work of Christ on the cross...If undue focus on the environment is indeed a type of spiritual deception, then its proponents are conditioning people to look to government and to the powers of man – not God – to save them." Tony Perkins and Harry Jackson, *Personal Faith, Public Policy,* Frontline, 2008.

So if the environment is going down the drain, it is simply signs of Jesus' Second Coming and you should be about the business of preparing to meet your maker rather than saving the planet entrusted to you. You should not, whatever you do, look to fix the environmental disasters that might be avoided with decisive action. Dear reader, have you heard of the self-fulfilling prophesy? Do you want this sort of worldview and reasoning in charge of public policy, or even international affairs?

Replacement science

Christian Reconstructionists and Dominionists want to have replacements ready to take over every aspect of life in America; science is no different. Earlier the Discovery Institute was discussed and how they replaced the scientific method. You can find a replacement for most any scientific field of study.

Psychology has a Christian version as well, relying more on the Bible than on Freudian or Jungian theories. James Dobson is an example of a Christian psychologist. Christian counselors abound, but their methods are Bible based as opposed to psychology based.

"I did not know when I first became a Christian that the development of my understanding of the meaning and implications of my Christian faith would eventually led me to a crossroads where I would have to choose between two masters – between the mental health professions and Christianity, between the mental health religion and Jesus Christ...and to recognize the mental health system as a rival religion, a crude form of idolatry inimical to the dissemination of the Christian faith and to the realization of the Christian vision of the kingdom of God on earth...

Since the rise of modern psychology/psychiatry there has been yet a new compartmentalization: the spiritual versus the psychological. But there are no 'psychological' needs or capacities that are not spiritual…the church has severely compromised its authority and enabled the practitioners of the idolatrous religion of mental health to promulgate their faith system and thus to gain control over the hearts and minds (and pocketbooks) of millions of Americans." Seth Farber, *Unholy Madness: The Church's Surrender to Psychiatry,* InterVarsity Press, 1999.

The Christian version of almost everything in science, from medicine, archeology, economics, physics, biology, chemistry, to agriculture, is available so you never have to be subverted by the humanistic world of science again. It has been rather successful at standing up replacements.

"Other sciences are also being modified to suit the creationist perspective that God created Earth about 6000 years ago. Take for instance this advice on climate change in the book Science Order and Reality published by A Beka Book: 'Because most environmental scientists see the universe and even life itself as mere products of chance, it is easy for them to visualize potentially catastrophic changes occurring on the Earth. As Christians we must remember that God provided certain 'checks and balances' in creation to prevent many of the global upsets that have been predicted by environmentalists.' For those who still worry about global warming, another A Beka book, Science of the Physical Creation, flatly denies it is happening: 'All of the scientific evidence gathered indicates that there is no danger of a global warming disaster.'

Chemistry textbooks argue that radiometric dating is unreliable and therefore not a concern for those who believe in a 6000-year-old Earth. And geology books claim that the Grand Canyon in Arizona – a gorge carved by the Colorado river, exposing 2 billion years of Earth's history – was formed rapidly during the worldwide Biblical flood, and all the sedimentary strata visible in the canyon walls were deposited then.

Even astronomy is being rethought to address what many creationists consider their most difficult challenge: explaining how starlight from billions of light years away has reached the Earth in only a few thousand years. Books like Taking Back Astronomy by Jason Lisle suggest possible explanations: maybe God created the light already en route; or maybe the Milky Way sits in a large gravitational well where the time-stretching effects of general relativity can explain the anomaly; or – the creationists' favorite – maybe the speed of light was much, much greater in the past." Amanda Gefter, "Home-schooling special: Preach Your Children Well," *New Scientist Magazine,* November 11, 2006.

Each has its place

Science is necessary for survival. Without science we would not understand germs, viruses and disease, or how they spread, so we can prevent outbreaks, or how tornadoes form so that we can warn communities in advance; how the human body functions so it can be repaired, how the human mind works so it can be healed, such as treatments for post traumatic stress syndrome, and so much more. For many people, their personal spiritual path is equally important for their soul's enrichment. Science is not concerned with spiritual matters because, of necessity, it focuses on concrete observable, repeatable phenomena, and that very focus has benefited the entire planet greatly. Science needs to remain focused to continue to benefit the world.

The faithful are to have faith without proof. Hebrews 11:1 *"Now faith is the assurance of things hoped for, the conviction of things not seen."* NASB

Rather than fighting a presumed competing God and trying to return to the days when the ruling Church of the day approved science, would not the country be best served if the faithful remained focused on what the Bible says they are to be busy with? It seems that the world could use more good works and acts of kindness without political or spiritual strings attached, such as in the case of the Good Samaritan. If science focused on its concrete world and the faithful were busy with good works such as the Bible directs and exemplifies, there would be no conflict.

Take With You From This Chapter

➢ Science is under assault in America, and to many has become taboo.

➢ Scientific method and areas of discipline are being replaced by Religious Right versions.

➢ Science is routinely considered a competing religion in spite of the fact many Christians are scientists and don't see a conflict.

Section 5: The Family Mountain

In this section …

Behind all the hype about traditional family values, what does it really means in terms of women, and their role, and just how and why are gays viewed as a threat? It isn't what or how you may think, and this section will probably challenge you.

Chapter 21
Women's Role

<u>What to Expect From this Chapter</u>

➢ Behind the Religious Right's deceptive language we look at what a woman's role is really supposed to be.

➢ Why the feminist movement is despised.

➢ Timeline of America and women's rights.

<u>The modern Christian woman</u>

Either you reconcile the Bible and woman's changing role, or you are at odds between the two. The Bible teaches specifically and through examples how women are to be submissive, and how their status is far different than what most modern American women can honestly understand. Many Christians today have reconciled that women no longer are expected to stay home having and raising children; they recognize that women have God-given intelligence and talents that benefit the world outside the home. Some churches even have women as pastors leading and teaching. Thus, we see how many Christians have faced the challenge of the times and have found peace with it. Then there is the Religious Right that gets migraines over the changes to the traditional family structure.

"Within this patriarchal framework, women – daughters, wives, mothers, sisters – were subordinates, and like younger sons, are often not mentioned. Even when they have narrative significance, they are frequently unnamed; we are never told the names of Noah's wife, Lot's wife, Jephthah's daughter, Samson's mother, Job's wife, and many other notable women.

Not only were women subordinates in the family structure, they were also considered essentially inferior....

This patriarchal bias was also expressed socially. Husbands and fathers had virtually absolute control over their wives and daughters. Sarah refers to her husband as her 'lord,' and later Abraham is referred to as her 'master.' Both of these terms are indicative of the status of the wife: she was under her husband's rule, she was his property, like the donkey that knows its master's feeding trough; the word 'master' is frequently used for ownership in the laws concerning property." Michael Coogan, *God and Sex: What the Bible Really Says*, Twelve, 2010.

The Religious Right wants, when it is honest, to revert back to a traditional family blueprint. What is the traditional family that is bandied about so often? The Seven Mountains Mandate has the Family Mountain of influence listed alongside government and education, because we have strayed from the proper family definition. Key to the traditional family values that are flung about in speeches and fund-raising appeals is the role of the woman in the family.

American Women's Rights Timeline

It is vitally important to remember the sacrifices that were made to obtain basic rights for women, including control over their own reproduction.

In the United States women have made great advances, but they came at a cost. We tend to forget the beatings that women's rights activists suffered marching for the vote, or how many were jailed. We look at old black and white photos in dusty books that show women in long skirts demonstrating or marching, and we cannot see the red blood that flowed. We don't talk about the arrests and brutality that these activists endured just so twenty million modern women can choose not to vote in elections, but have the right to vote if they choose. Now is a good time to review the history of women's ongoing struggles for equality in the United States.

➤ May–September 1787: US Constitutional Convention places voting qualifications in the hands of the states. Women in all states loose the right to vote; New Jersey was the last hold out.

➤ 1868: Fourteenth Amendment passes Congress, defining citizens as "male;" this is the first use of the word male in the Constitution.

271

➢   1870 Julia Ward Howe conceives the Mother's Day Proclamation that was a call to women to be activists for peace in the wake of the Civil War atrocities. This was the original Mother's Day intention, for women to rise up.

"Arise, then, women of this day!

Arise all women who have hearts,

Whether your baptism be that of water or of tears

Say firmly:

'We will not have great questions decided by irrelevant agencies,

Our husbands shall not come to us reeking of carnage,

For caresses and applause.

Our sons shall not be taken from us to unlearn

All that we have been able to teach them of

charity, mercy and patience…."

➢   1873: Comstock Law passes, which places birth control in the same class as pornography, thus making it illegal to send contraceptives or even information about contraception through the mail.

➢   1878: Suffrage amendment reaches the US Senate floor; it is defeated two-to-one.

➢ 1907: The English suffragists' tactics of parades, street speakers, and pickets are introduced to the American movement.

➢ 1912: Teddy Roosevelt's Progressive Party includes woman suffrage in their platform.

➢ 1913: Women's Suffrage parade is attacked and many injuries are reported.

➢ 1917: National Women's Party posts silent "Sentinels of Liberty" at the White House. Reportedly close to five hundred women are arrested, 168 women served jail time, and their jailers brutalized many.

➢ 1918: Appellate court ruled all those arrests were illegal, but the physical and emotional damage had been done. President Wilson declares support for suffrage. Suffrage Amendment passes US House with exactly a two-thirds vote, but loses by two votes in the Senate.

➤ 1920: The Nineteenth Amendment, called the Susan B. Anthony Amendment, is ratified by Tennessee on August 18. It becomes law on August 26, and women can finally vote.

➤ 1963: Equal Pay Act signed by John F. Kennedy guaranteed equal pay to women for equal work (Comparable Work), but achieving that goal is still being realized. It took forty-three years after obtaining the right to vote to get this legislation.

➤ 1965: Griswold v. Connecticut ruled on a Connecticut law that criminalized the provision of counseling and medical treatment to married persons for the purpose of preventing pregnancy. The Supreme Court recognized the constitutional right of married couples to use contraceptives via marital privacy. This essentially legalized birth control that had been illegal or seriously restricted since the Comstock Law in

➤ 1873: Many women today don't even realize it was ever, illegal and take birth control for granted.

➤ 1967: President Johnson expanded affirmative action benefits to include women.

➤ 1968: It became illegal to place help-wanted advertisements that specified the gender of the employees sought.

➤ 1972–1982: Equal Rights Amendment supporters lobbied, marched, rallied, petitioned, picketed, went on hunger strikes, and committed acts of civil disobedience until it failed to get enough support to pass by the deadline. The Equal Rights Amendment was reintroduced in Congress on July 14, 1982 and has reportedly been introduced in every session of Congress since that time.

➤ 1974: The Equal Credit Opportunity Act was passed, and it became illegal to discriminate in credit opportunities based on gender or marital status. But, it took time for legislation to translate into common practice.

➤ 2009: Lilly Ledbetter Fair Pay Act: The bill amends the Civil Rights Act of 1964 stating that the 180-day statute of limitations for filing an equal–pay lawsuit regarding pay discrimination resets with each new discriminatory paycheck.

➤ 2011: Walmart class-action lawsuit involving 1.5 million women claiming sexual discrimination in pay and promotions was defeated. Justice Ruth Bader Ginsburg claimed that the other Supreme Court Justices had disqualified the case from the beginning.

➤ 2012: Republican presidential candidate, Rick Santorum, Catholic Bishops, and others make birth-control a social hot button issue again.

It is from this starting point that we enter into the rest of our examination of woman's role and the Religious Right. This timeline is only a few of the events that took place in American women's fight for equality, a fight that is ongoing and includes the issue of a woman's role in or out of the home. Never forget the struggles that gained the freedoms we enjoy today, or they could be taken away simply because they were taken for granted.

The traditional family blueprint

The traditional family blueprint and values come down to the roles of the man and woman. Woman's role and function is to have babies and tend the home-fires, with updated labels such as "home worker," while the man takes his *proper* leadership role in the family unit as a provider and decision-maker. This is not even a "Leave it to Beaver" plan, for you don't see Mrs. Cleaver working very much. For the vision of the proper family, it is best to look at the Puritans and Pilgrims whom the Religious Right elevate.

The following is from Libby Anne, who was raised by evangelical parents who then became Religious Right. Libby tells exactly what the traditional family of the Religious Right looks like and what the Seven Mountains Mandate is moving toward.

"I learned that women are to be homemakers while men are to be protectors and providers. I was taught that a woman should not have a career, but should rather keep the home and raise the children and submit to her husband, who was her god-given head and authority. I learned that homeschooling is the only godly way to raise children, because to send them to public school is to turn a child over

274

to the government and the secular humanists. I was taught that children must be trained up in the way they should go every minute of every day. I learned that a woman is always under male authority, first her father, then her husband, and perhaps, someday, her son. I was told that children are always a blessing, and that it was imperative to raise up quivers full of warriors for Christ, equipped to take back the culture and restore it to its Christian foundations." Libby Anne, "My Life as a Daughter of Christian Patriarchy," *Butterflies and Wheels Blog Article,* September 3, 2011.

Child Bearer

"...be fruitful and multiply, and fill the earth..." Genesis 1:28

The earth needs to be filled, so women are to have babies and lots of them, but what happens when the earth is filled?

"But women will be saved through childbearing." (1 Tim. 2:15) Bible scholar Charles Ryrie points out that this *saved* doesn't refer to salvation, but rather "that a woman's greatest achievement is found in her devotion to her divinely ordained role: to help her husband, to bear children, and to follow a faithful, chaste life." Charles Ryrie, *The Ryrie Study Bible,* Moody Bible Institute, 1995.

The protestant hero, Martin Luther, who nearly single-handedly began the Reformation, says childbearing is a woman's duty.

"This is also how to comfort and encourage a woman in the pangs of childbirth ... by speaking thus, 'Dear Grete, remember that you are a woman, and that this work of God in you is pleasing to him. Trust joyfully in his will, and let him have his way with you. Work with all your might to bring forth the child. Should it mean your death, then depart happily, for you will die in a noble deed and in subservience to God. If you were not a woman you should now wish to be one for the sake of this very work alone, that you might thus gloriously suffer and even die in the performance of God's work and will. For here you have the word of

God, who so created you and implanted within you this extremity.' Tell me, is not this indeed (as Solomon says [Prov. 18:22]) 'to obtain favour from the Lord," even in the midst of such extremity?' Martin Luther's 1522 sermon titled "The Estate of Marriage." (Emphasis added.)

This rather calloused view towards women's life being in peril during childbirth was revisited during the 2008 presidential race. "... 'Health' of the mother. You know, that's been stretched by the pro-abortion movement in America to mean almost anything. That's the extreme pro-abortion position; quote, 'health.'" (John McCain during third Presidential candidate debate on 15 October, 2008.) It certainly appears that the health of the woman is not a priority, making babies is. Some women want this role; others have talents and dreams, and thus desire to get a higher education and solidify a career before considering a family, but the Religious Right believe this is truly against the natural order and a woman's appointed role.

Child-bearing is the *woman's role, her mission, her purpose* along with tending the home. Work outside the home in this day-and-age rarely requires hard manual labor for a woman, and we have found that, in spite of even physical demands of a job, women are up to the task. But the Religious Right maintains the mentality, as witnessed by the True Woman Conference and Mary Pride's anti-feminist writing, that men are still to be the heads of their houses and women dutifully keep those houses and have babies. The role of child-bearer is staunchly maintained and defended by the Religious Right as being the way the country should be as a whole, and anything less is tearing the country to shreds. Abortion and birth control methods have been a battleground for ages concerning this exact dilemma – not just in the last few decades!

The role of women and the value of their lives are clearly on display with legislation such as Georgia's HB1, introduced by Georgia State Rep. Bobby Franklin. *"Under Rep. Franklin's bill, HB 1, women who miscarry could become felons if they cannot prove that there was 'no human involvement whatsoever in the causation' of their miscarriage.... Even more ridiculous, the bill holds women responsible for protecting their fetuses from 'the moment of conception,' despite the fact that pregnancy tests aren't accurate until at least 3 weeks after conception... In the bill's logic, a fertilized egg is the same as a person, and its destruction is murder. Sometimes even a fertilized egg will fail to adhere to the uterine lining, so would that make a uterus a murderer?"* Jen Quraishi, "Ga. Law Could Give Death Penalty for Miscarriages," *Mother Jones*, February 23, 2011.

We started with a timeline to remind us of how long it took just to get fair credit policies for women, fifty-four years after obtaining the right to vote. Birth control has been illegal or restricted for longer than it has been legal in this country. The rallying cry of traditional family values has been used before in national politics, though many wish to forget this infamous speech sounding so much like our modern Religious Right. *"The National Government will preserve and defend those basic principles on which our nation has been built up. They regard Christianity as the foundation of our national morality and the family as the basis of national life."* February 1, 1933 radio address, *The Speeches of Adolph Hitler, 1922-1939, Vol. 1*, Oxford University Press, 1969.

Put into perspective, the concept that a woman isn't fulfilling her God-ordained role of a "home working" wife or celibate daughter, then she is shaking her fist at God's sovereignty and at the divine order of the universe. The woman who goes against God's clear definition of her only role is out of God's favor. She is being selfish at best, and sinful at worst.

Promise Keepers involves the push to promote male headship and leadership by rallying men to take a stand, not only in their families, but communities as well. In October of 2008, Chicago hosted the first "True Woman Conference" with a turn-out of over 6,000 women who affirm "Biblical Womanhood" and "the Patriarchy Movement." Organizers happily proclaim that it is directly counter to the women's liberation movement of the nineteen sixties. The True Woman Conferences are the female version of Promise Keepers, and meet annually just as Promise Keepers continue to do. Here we see the idea that a true woman needs to submit to her pre-defined role for the only liberation needed.

> *"The 'countercultural' attitudes that signers* [of the 'True Woman Manifesto'] *support the idea that women are called to affirm and encourage godly masculinity, and honor the God-ordained male headship of their husbands and pastors; that wifely submission to male leadership in the home and church reflects Christ's submission to God, His Father; that 'selfish insistence on personal rights is contrary to the spirit of Christ;' and, in a pronatalist turn of phrase that recalls the rhetoric of the Quiverfull conviction, their willingness to 'receive children as a blessing from the Lord.'*
>
> *Finally, in a reference to the importance of woman-to-woman mentoring within the conservative church, they affirmed that 'mature Christian women' are obliged to disciple the next generation of Christian wives, training them in matters of submission and headship, in order to provide a legacy of 'fruitful femininity.'"* Kathryn Joyce, "Women's Liberation Through Submission: An Evangelical Anti-Feminism Is Born," *Religion Dispatches*, January 11, 2009.

How does this impact you? The Religious Right believes that women in the workforce, not at home raising children and tending the house, are the single most significant problem facing this country. The Religious Right view feminism as women not fulfilling their "home worker" role, and this weakens the country as a whole in every area. Thus, the Religious Right and their Republican politicians continually move towards women being in the home. It is hard to comprehend that in this day and age, we are seeing women's advances rolled back to the 1800s, but it is happening daily. The fight over abortion is actually about contraceptives across-the-board, and this fight is to relegate women back to the home.

Women are viewed by those supporting the "traditional family values" as mandated in the home to fulfill the role given them, not running companies and getting college educations. Which is why it is so very curious to see these Religious Right women getting into politics, as happened when the ERA debates started. Ruth Murray

Brown in her book *For A Christian America,* tells how Phyllis Schlafly's husband, because of the importance of what she was doing, *allowed* her to head up a grassroots anti-ERA movement.

Having a woman tell other women that you must be a housewife is better marketing and more palatable than a man saying it. Mary Pride, who is regarded as the queen of the home-school movement and wrote *The Way Home: Beyond Feminism,* the anti-feminism standard, is a multi-published author, editor of a home-schooling magazine (100,000 subscribers) and runs the world's most visited website on home-schooling. It is amazing how Mary Pride is benefiting from the years of feminist work that enables her to run such businesses, and yet she rabidly preaches against such feminism. The Religious Right is using marketing savvy by having women speak out against feminism. But in fact, these very women are profiting from the advances made by the feminist movement in their favor.

What if a woman wants to have children without the "headship" of the man in the house? At least the woman is fulfilling her role. This premise was put to the test when the controversial book *Knock Yourself Up: No Man? No Problem* by Louise Sloan was published. The Religious Right went ballistic over it. No, you cannot have just one side of the formula, it must include having children and tending the house, with the husband exerting his authority-headship over that family. The Religious Right feels that this is yet another modern travesty of the "traditional values" that should be held with reverence. Thus, no gay or lesbian couple should be allowed to have children either, not because they are bad parents (there is no scientific data to claim same sex-couples are bad parents).

"Whether by choice or circumstance, the evidence suggests that more and more women are considering single parenthood. Unwed births among 30 to 44-year-olds rose 20 percent from 1991 to 2006, and last year alone, four in ten U.S. babies were born outside of marriage even though teen pregnancies hit their lowest point in 65 years. Fairfax Cryobank, one of the biggest sperm banks in the

United States, says its single-female clientele jumped 20 percent in the last decade and now accounts for 60 percent of its customer base." Lorrain Ali , "Knocking Yourself Up", *Newsweek*, November 5, 2007.

Single parenthood is counter to the traditional family values blueprint, and is not to be encouraged. There is a new, slick, marketing term that the Religious Right is utilizing now, the *natural family*. This automatically labels everything where men don't have headship over women and where she is birthing their babies, as unnatural. The Natural Family Manifesto has been generated to wax poetic over the virtues of a specific family make-up.

"[Allan] Carlson is a compelling conservative historian who uses secular arguments to craft a social science rationale for the necessity of large patriarchal families, or the 'natural family,' as he calls it in his manifesto...aims to turn America and the Western world away from the perils of liberal modernity and back to the 'natural family' model, where fathers lead and women honor their highest domestic calling by becoming 'prolific mothers.' In this scheme, families are the fundamental unit that society and government should be concerned with promoting, and individual rights are valued insofar as they correspond with pronatalist aims. Thus Carlson and Mero qualify their 'wholehearted' support of women's rights: 'Above all, we believe in rights that recognize women's unique gifts of pregnancy, childbirth, and breastfeeding.'" Kathryn Joyce, "Missing: The 'Right' Babies," *The Nation*, February 14, 2008.

Feminism is demonized

Feminism is linked with the breakdown of the traditional family. The rise of "sex addiction" therapy for celebrity or famous men still does not get as extreme a response from the Religious Right as does any feminist activist.

The following quote is from Mary Pride, who wrote the influential book *The Way Home* in 1985, and became known as one of the pioneers of the Quiverfull movement, and queen of the home-school movement. The book is written for Christians, and thus we see what a *traditional family* is defined as, and the role expected of a woman.

"Titus 2:3-5

Likewise, teach the older women to be reverent in the way they live, not to be slanderers or addicted to much wine, but to teach what is good. Then they can train the younger women to love their husbands and children, to be self-controlled and pure, to be busy at home [literally, home-working], to be kind, and to be subject to their husbands, so that no one will malign the word of God.

...Christians have accepted feminists' 'moderate' demands for family planning and careers while rejecting the 'radical' side of feminism – meaning lesbianism and abortion. What most do not see is that one demand leads to the other. Feminism is a totally self-consistent system aimed at rejecting God's role for women. Those who adopt any part of its lifestyle can't help picking up its philosophy. And those who pick up its philosophy are buying themselves a one-way ticket to social anarchy.

...If women can't be women, by golly they will by men! All because two or more generations have grown up and married without ever hearing that the Bible teaches a distinct role for women which is different from that of a man and just as important.

Homeworking is the biblical lifestyle for Christian wives. Homeworking is not just staying at home either (that was the mistake of the fifties). We are not called by God to stay home, or to sit at home, but to work at home! Homeworking is the exact opposite of the modern careerist/institutional/Socialist movement. It is a way to take back control of education, health care, agriculture, social welfare, business, housing, morality, and evangelism from the faceless institutions to which we have surrendered them. More importantly, homeworking is the path of obedience to God. Homeworking is based on what the Scriptures say....

Homeworking, like feminism, is a total lifestyle. The difference is that homeworking produces stable homes, growing churches, and children who are

Christian leaders." Mary Pride, *The Way Home: Beyond Feminism, Back to Reality*, Crossway Books, 1985.

Where to start regarding the above quote? Feminism equals social anarchy? Every person who was raised by a single mother should be insulted. If you are a feminist, like male straight actor Alan Alda, then you are promoting a sexual orientation, socialism, or abortion? Feminism (ideals such as equal pay for equal work, access to quality higher education for females, equal opportunities for females, stopping domestic violence, halting sexual harassment and assault etc.) leads to social anarchy, really? The career-minded woman is a Socialist? Here we see how feminism is one of the great evils in the Religious Right Republican universe.

Could it be that feminism is evil because it allows a woman to be the master of her own future, rather than embracing what Mary Pride insists and the Religious Right feels is a woman's only calling? When you hear the Religious Right rant about the breakdown of the traditional family bringing this nation to ruin, this is how they come to that conclusion. Women not being mothers and homeworkers and the men not fulfilling their ordained role of leadership have led this country down the drain. They believe it, and this is what they really mean when they use the phrase *traditional family values.*

Similarly to the myth of Lilith that cast an independent woman as the snake in the garden tempting Eve, we have women being demonized by the Religious Right because they choose to follow a dream or career.

Dr. C.J. Pascoe with me: *"They* [Religious Right women] *don't see that they need liberation, because for them the liberation is not from male power, but from sin and Satan. So in their minds they have already been liberated. They see themselves as free, free from sin, and that is what is important...So the idea that feminism could liberate them simply doesn't resonate, since there is nothing to be liberated from."* Dr. C.J. Pascoe, email interview with author, 2008. Thus, feminism is focusing on the wrong things. They don't see that treating approximately half of the population with the same regard and consideration as the other half is part of the Christian life.

Women's rights that are acceptable are limited to those that reinforce pregnancy and childbirth, under the "headship" of a husband. There should be no single women having babies, and no same-sex couples having babies. Forever and only, the strict formula is women at home raising babies, and being content with fulfilling their duties. The following quote shows how control over having children, or not having children, has been a power struggle over the centuries.

> "*Trying to control reproduction has been a human activity from as far back as historians can trace it. Reproduction control efforts constitute part of the evidence that biology has never been destiny, that even those functions most often described as 'natural,' such as reproduction, have always been formed by cultural and social organizations.*
>
> *...birth control is inevitably about gender....The three political campaigns for reproductive freedom – in the 1870s, the 1910s, and the 1970s and 1980s – coincide with peaks of women's rights agitation....All three periods were marked by campaigns for sex education and against sexual obscurantism, particularly for women's sexual and reproductive self-knowledge as the basis for self-control.*"
> Linda Gordon, *The Moral Property of Women: A History of Birth Control Politics in America*, University of Illinois Press, 2002.

Women's rights come down to a woman's role in the world, and for the Religious Right that role is forever and always as working in the home and having babies under the headship of a man.

The breakdown of the family is largely blamed on women deciding their own destinies, from voting and higher education to delaying starting a family for a career. Feminism is demonized so that it is somehow taboo to want equal pay for equal work or equal opportunities.

How could modern women ever go back to the role the Religious Right insists is the only correct way for our nation as a whole? It seems inconceivable that once you have obtained something, it can be taken away. Yet we have examples of just that sort of forgetfulness occurring. On the twenty year anniversary of Tiananmen Square, some of the people of China do not even remember anything took place. I remember the image of one student standing in the path of a line of military tanks, but the people of China don't seem to remember. The students stopped fighting and became distracted; the media began to ignore it, the schools never mentioned it, and thus in twenty years it is as if it never happened. That is how women in America could give up everything they gained; they could stop fighting and take what they have for granted; home-schooling or private schools will teach women's proper role; media will reinforce that role; laws will restrict birth control and planned parenthood etc., that allowed any other role, and viola – women's rights could be gone.

This section covered how women's advances are *really* viewed by the Religious Right and their politicians as the core of the family breakdown. Traditional family values include restricting birth control and women returning to being housewives and having babies. Some women feel a desire for that life and it fulfills them, and others want a career and family down the road, etc. But the issue is whether a woman gets to choose. Next, we shall look at the Quiverfull movement that is the fulfillment of this traditional family. Then we will look at how the Religious Right is working hard to control women so that they have no other real options; and the first step is to limit access to birth control across-the-board, not just abortion.

Take With You From This Chapter

➢ The traditional family blueprint is for the woman to fulfill her role by having babies and working in the home, and the man exercises headship over the home.

➢ Feminism is demonized as being a large factor in the breakdown of the family, and thus wreaking havoc with the nation as a whole.

➢ It is important to remember the sacrifices made to obtain women's basic rights.

Chapter 22
The Quiverfull Movement

<u>What to Expect From this Chapter</u>

➢ What would the *Traditional Family* really look like?

➢ Quiverfull – no contraceptives allowed, and the man is the head of the family.

➢ Interview with former Quiverfull member, Vyckie Garrison.

The Family Mountain is important because in Christian Reconstruction and Dominionism they view the family as one of the God-ordained institutions to govern by. This makes a family unit far more than a couple in love who have children and prepare them to be the best they can be; this makes the family part of governance. If you have ever felt the hardship of being single in a world of families, you haven't seen anything yet.

> *"Reconstructionists criticize the 'conflation' of spheres of government. They draw clear distinctions between various forms of government they believe to be delegated by God. There is self-government, and then there are three forms of institutional government: family, church and state."* Julie Ingersoll, "Rand Paul and the Influence of Christian Reconstructionism", *Religion Dispatches*, May 225, 2010.

Practically speaking, the family concept has a huge impact on the next generation who will influence this nation's direction. The family is so important to the Religious Right that they try to legislate who can adopt children and who cannot, such as in the cases of Utah and Arkansas. Family, and what happens in a family, is very personal and private, but when women's role and what a proper family constitutes are specified, this easily moves into public territory. The *Quiverfull Movement* is the Religious Right's ideal of what the proper family is. They believe that how many children a *married* couple (a man and a woman, only) has should be left completely up to God. No family planning whatsoever is allowed and the idea of stewardship becomes a non-issue. Don't worry about having the personal finances to support a large family, that is not a consideration. No contraceptives are allowed because that is saying *no* to God's will concerning how many children He wants you to have. Not to over-think this, but how will this Bible-based idea impact the poor who can't afford the one or two children they already have?

The Duggar and Bates families

Jim Bob Duggar and his wife Michelle of Arkansas are Quiverfull believers and at last count they had 19 children, all home-schooled too! Jim Bob was an Arkansas Legislator from 1999 to 2002, and he was defeated in his run for US Senator in 2002, and again in 2006. Apparently, his biggest platform issue was rabid opposition to anything abortion related.

> "'Be fruitful and multiply' ... is a command of God, indeed the first command to a married couple. Birth control obviously involves disobedience to this command, for birth control attempts to prevent being fruitful and multiplying. Therefore birth control is wrong, because it involves disobedience to the Word of God. Nowhere is this command done away with in the entire Bible; therefore it still remains valid for us today." Charles D. Provan, The Bible and Birth Control, Zimmer, June 1989.

There are many books out there that sing high praises for the traditional family values in the form of Quiverfull, such as *Open Embrace: A Protestant Couple Rethinks Contraception*; *Do You Dare Trust God for Your Family Size?* and *The Duggars: 20 and Counting!* and also the longstanding favorite, *A Full Quive,r* by Rick and Jan Hess. A quick note on Jim Bob and Michelle Duggar, who now have nineteen children after a miscarriage of the twentieth December, 2011, a reality TV series on TLC network, and published books and DVDs that provide a lot of money to fund such a large family – money that the average person does not have. The Duggars are celebrated as the flag bearers of the *traditional Family*. Here is the actual definition of what traditional family values are for the Religious Right. The Duggars are friends with the Bates family, who have twenty children. They aren't the only ones with such super-sized families. The Jeub Family in Monument Colorado made local news with their sixteen children, and counting. There is probably a Quiverfull family near you.

"ABC's Primetime Nightline recently aired a segment featuring the Gil & Kelly Bates family – a conservative, Evangelical mega-family of twenty. The Bates, who are close friends of Jim Bob & Michelle Duggar of TLC's '19 and Counting' fame, hold to the extreme fundamentalist ideals of the growing 'Quiverfull movement.'

During the one-hour special, Gil, Kelly, and their children explained the family's lifestyle which, to all modern appearances, represents a throw back to the imaginary 60's-style 'Leave It to Beaver' family combined with strict, Victorian Era sexual mores and the atavistic gender roles of ancient goat-herders. The Bates eschew all forms of birth control and adhere to the marriage model of the biblical Patriarchs – with Gil as family leader and Kelly as submissive 'help meet.' Kelly and the girls adorn themselves in modest, hand-sewn dresses, while Gil and his clean-cut sons teach Bible study and participate in local Tea Party politics." Vyckie Garrison, "How I Escaped the 'Biblical Family Values' Nightmare That Drives Perry, Bachmann, and Tea Party Politics," *Alternet*, August 29, 2011.

Fine for them, but not for you? Well, that is the dilemma, because this could be the future of the American family. The Family Mountain means not just influencing evangelical families, but influencing laws on birth control as well. Both the Duggars and the Bates are active in politics. Jim Bob was elected Arkansas Legislator from 1999 to 2002, and Gil Bates is active in his local Tea Party politics. Being active in politics is a component of Quiverfull, and they are making an impact.

The Quiverfull movement of the Religious Right appears to be the face behind contraceptives falling out of favor, and the Religious Right's backing such legislation seeking to de-fund Planned Parenthood. The real reason behind the February 18,

2011's [Mike] Pence Amendment to the Republican spending bill halting all federal funding to Planned Parenthood and 102 affiliated organizations, is all about the Religious Right's Quiverfull movement, and has nothing to do with a concern for spending cuts. Their influence can be seen behind trying to slip a new definition of rape into a spending bill to restrict access to the *morning after pill* by rape victims in a hospital. The guise of a deficit and needing to cut spending to the bone was the excuse for the building vendetta against all contraceptives. They don't care that millions of women will lose access to Planned Parenthood-provided contraceptives and health care services, including STD/HIV testing and treatment, breast exams, and preventive cancer screenings.

The interview

Vyckie Garrison was a Quiverfull follower who home-schooled her children, and became known within the movement for the articles she wrote for Quiverfull publications. She wrote for *Christian Mommies* and *Unless the Lord* about the Quiverfull life, and even published her own conservative Christian newsletter. Vyckie eventually left the movement after having seven children, in spite of the serious risk to her life from the pregnancies. Vyckie has an insider's view and agreed to answer some very pointed questions for this book. Below is the full interview conducted via email.

"What is the primary or main role and purpose of women according to Quiverfull?

Quiverfull draws on a number of key Bible verses which address the woman's role, beginning with the creation account in Genesis in which Eve is referred to as Adam's 'help meet' or 'helper.' God's purpose in creating woman was to relieve Adam's loneliness and supply him with a 'corresponding' person to assist him in fulfilling the Dominion Mandate – that is, to fill the earth and take dominion over it.

The specific ways in which a woman enables her husband to accomplish the Lord's plan for his life are: 1) by producing children for him, and 2) by submitting to his leadership as he pursues whatever vision for ministry the Lord lays on his heart.

In the New Testament, women are commanded to submit to their husbands, to bear children, to dress modestly, to exhibit a meek and quiet spirit. From the book of Proverbs, Quiverfull women are taught that their role is to guide the household in order to enrich their husbands and bolster their position as community leaders. Wives are to be like fruitful vines, bearing many children in order that their husbands will prosper.

Naturally, these ideas do not sound terribly appealing when spelled out in black and white terms – but when a woman first hears the Quiverfull message from its devoted, charismatic leaders such as Nancy Campbell, Mary Pride, Debi Pearl, Nancy Leigh DeMoss, etc. – to finally know her true and very special purpose for which she was created is incredibly inspiring. The ideals are presented as a grand vision of godly womanhood, which resonates with a woman's natural inclination to nurture her family and sacrifice herself for their betterment.

Growing up in Quiverfull movement, did you feel like you had any control over your life (i.e. to go to college, choose a career, decide when to marry, decide when to have children?)

I did not grow up in the Quiverfull movement. I discovered the teachings through homeschooling materials which I encountered in my late 20s. I had already made many important life decisions – including marriage, divorce, remarriage, college, three children and sterilization for my husband due to extremely difficult pregnancies and deliveries which led to serious health concerns.

When I read and accepted the Quiverfull teachings, I made one choice which, at the time, felt incredibly empowering and freeing: I chose to give up my right to decide for myself. Instead, I turned control of my life over to the Lord and trusted Him to guide me in the right (most godly) direction. I believed that the Lord would use my husband to guide me.

I felt great relief in relinquishing all control over my reproductive choices and following my husband's lead regarding major life decisions. According to the patriarchal ideals of Quiverfull, because God has given the husband/father ultimate authority over his family, He [God]/he [husband] also bears the eternal responsibility for how things turn out. Believing that it was truly God making the choices for my life, through my husband, I felt assured that He would ensure everything in our lives was ultimately for our good.

<u>Do you feel that girls raised in Quiverfull have a healthy self image and self respect? What about women in Quiverfull?</u>

Quiverfull is all about instilling a deep, abiding tendency toward self-abnegation in women. It is the hallowing of martyrdom for females of every age. There is no 'self-image' or 'self'-anything because the central message for women is self-denial – they are conditioned not to think about themselves at all.

At the same time, the patriarchal teachings create a profound distrust of the female nature. Women, according to the fundamentalist interpretation of the Bible, are uniquely susceptible to deception. By their nature, women desire to usurp authority and exert power over men – power which their conniving hearts will unscrupulously use to the destruction of order and decency.

In my own mind, this distrust was so ingrained that I came to regard my intuition as a sort of anti-indicator of right and good. What I wanted, my desires, whatever seemed reasonable to me – all of my personal will was subject to selfishness and wickedness combined with the subtle manipulations of Satan – therefore, if an idea or decision appealed to me, it must not be God's will - and I would deliberately choose the opposite.

<u>Looking back, do you feel that females are respected and truly regarded as</u>

Sisters in the Lord within the movement?

This is a tricky subject – because the roles of wife and motherhood are so idealized that it would appear that women in the Quiverfull movement occupy a special place of supreme importance, but in truth, it is only the ideal of the godly woman which is venerated while actual, real, imperfect women are degraded, marginalized and subjugated.

Quiverfull is a bait-and-switch paradigm, which promises purpose and value for women, but ultimately fails to deliver. As a devoted Quiverfull wife and mother, I knocked myself out serving my husband and children. I worked harder than any other woman I knew, prayed more, gave of myself continually, even risked my life – and yet, I always felt inadequate – like I was never doing enough, never good enough.

The expectations that I had of myself and that my family had of me were unrealistic – the ideals set me up for failure and my family for disappointment.

Women are approximately half the citizenship of the United States. Do you feel that Quiverfull respects women as autonomous citizens with equal voting rights and a voice in the country's direction, policies and future?

Absolutely not. The Dominionist ideas, which undergird the Quiverfull movement, allow no place for women in any leadership capacity. Within that world, I frequently encountered individuals and groups who sought to deny women the right to vote, the right to own property – and even driving privileges.

It's ironic that Quiverfull believers fear the take over of America by Muslim extremists, yet the theocratic world which they envision eerily parallels the anti-woman proscriptions of Sharia law.

How mainstream do you feel Quiverfull ideology is becoming in the Christian community?

It is my contention that the Quiverfull movement is regular Christianity lived out to its logical conclusions.

When Christians teach 'the husband is the head of his wife' (Eph. 5:23), Quiverfull believers put that into practice – and nearly every time, the husband becomes a despot in his own home.

*The majority of Christians will have their excuses for why their wife has to work outside the home, or why they personally cannot have more than two children, or why it won't work for them to home-school. If you ask the average Evangelical what a truly godly, 'biblical' family looks like, they will **begin** to list Quiverfull ideals:*

· *Husband as head of the household and final authority (Eph. 5:23)*

· *Wives submit to their husbands (Colossians 3:18)*

· *Obedient children (Eph. 6:1)*

· *Trust the Lord with family planning (i.e., no birth control ~ Psalm 127)*

· *Stay-at-home-mothers (Titus 2:3)*

· *Home-school the children (Matthew 12:17 – 'render unto God that which is God's' - since children bear the image of God, parents ought not render them unto Caesar, i.e., government schools. See also, Deut. 6:7)*

· *Modest dress (1 Peter 3:3)*

· *Debt-free living (Romans 13:8)*

· *Political domination (Psalm 127 and The Dominion Mandate in Genesis 1:28)*

In my experience, the evangelical Christians believe most all of the principles of patriarchy taught in the Quiverfull movement; fortunately for Christian women, few actually put it into practice the way Quiverfull believers do.

<u>Do you see the Quiverfull influence on politics in regard to women's rights, particularly birth control, sex education in schools or even limiting access to abortions for rape/incest victims or mother life endangerment?</u>

I do. I've addressed this question in my response to the next one.

What do you feel is the end goal of the Quiverfull movement?

Political domination is a core principle of the Quiverfull worldview.

Quiverfull's proof-text, Psalm 127, promises that the man whose quiver is full of arrows 'will not be ashamed, but will speak with the enemies in the gate.' We were taught that in Bible times, the city gate was the place where male leaders made decisions regarding local government.

The whole point of having a quiver full of babies is to

1) out-populate the 'enemy,' that is, the godless, liberal, lesbian feminists, and;

2) launch those many arrows 'straight into the heart of the enemy.' And by that, we meant that our children would grow up to be leaders in all the major institutions of our society: Faith, Family, Education, Art, Business, Media, and Government – this is known as the "Seven Mountains doctrine."

I see the Quiverfull movement accelerating the implementation of patriarchal and Dominionist ideas and policies using an impressive marketing savvy which is proving frightfully effective among the Evangelical population.

Hierarchy. Tradition. Control. Privilege. Conformity. Intolerance. Hegemony. These are the values of right wing politics. Under the guise of 'family values,' the Quiverfull movement is bolstering the legitimacy of the Right's misogynistic agenda. Quiverfull is the break in the dam, which is building up to a flood of extremism.

Whether by an appeal to tradition and authority, an appeal to nature, or an appeal to fear, Quiverfull leaders are providing the moral justification for right-wing political battles, which have been raging in our country for decades. Because these are thoughtful people with well-defined and high-minded propositions, their influence is giving wings to a vestigial body politic which thus far has been rightly grounded by the weight of the Right's own discriminatory and inequitable baggage.

Let me give you just one example.

An uninitiated modern woman might think it's irresponsible and impractical to toss out her birth control pills and leave her reproductive life 'in the Lord's hands.' But, let that woman spend a weekend with Nancy Campbell at an Above Rubies retreat, and she very well could come away with a new understanding of the power of motherhood and God's vision for families. What higher purpose could there be – what better eternal use of her time, energy and talent – than to invest herself in the lives of her children? If she catches the vision, her entire life from that point forward will be consumed by her determination to conceive, birth, and raise as many of 'God's mighty warriors' as she is capable of producing.

In other words, Quiverfull teachers are masters at SPIN. They have the ability to convince a woman that she WANTS nothing more than to stay home, have lots of babies and serve her husband. In today's world of seemingly unlimited choices for women, making the best choice can be an overwhelming responsibility and it's extremely tempting for a woman to choose to have no choice.

How different would life for American women be if Quiverfull gains the political and social power it desires (i.e. women obtaining credit on their own, equality in workforce, free from sexual harassment in workplace, fair treatment of rape victims etc?)

If the Quiverfull ideals were ever enshrined in US law (and the possibility of such a scenario is not as far-fetched as it might seem), women would lose every political and social advantage. Women would be relegated to their bronze-age status in which wives were property and children were a commodity.

This is not an exaggeration by any means. As a Quiverfull believer, I read countless magazine and web articles, listened to sermons, and attended seminars in which the principles of patriarchal male-dominance were the express goals of the Dominionist agenda. Any and every instance of male/female interaction mentioned in the pages of scripture is considered 'biblical' – therefore, whatever women could expect in Old Testament society is exactly what would become the norm in the Quiverfull vision of a truly 'godly' America.

<u>How do you feel Quiverfull would impact Democracy (of the people, by the people, for the people) in this country if it gained more political power?</u>

Quiverfull believers have no interest in maintaining America's democratic political system. Their lives are centered on living 'biblically' and they are determined that all of America follow suit." Vyckie Garrison email interview with author, August, 2011.

Welcome to the real *traditional family values* that are being marketed in every corner of America. This is the truth behind the catchy little slogans used as propaganda. Is that the future you want for your daughter? Is this how you, as a tax-paying citizen want to be told how to live your life? The anti-birth control phenomenon is more than a presidential candidate suddenly standing on such ideals; it has been building for a few decades.

Not only is a woman's role and purpose to have children and be a home-worker, but your behind-closed-doors private life is clearly defined as well. The Quiverfull movement is the Religious Right's ideal for what the family should look like across the nation, and they are working diligently to make that a reality.

<u>Take With You From This Chapter</u>

➤ Quiverfull is the template for the Religious Right's idea of a proper family, and this is what they envision when they use the phrase *traditional family values*.

➤ Quiverfull is Dominionist and is politically active.

➤ Quiverfull uses savvy marketing to win over evangelicals, and home-schooling is an effective delivery system.

Religious Right: The Greatest Threat to Democracy

➤ Quiverfull has no interest in a democracy, or women's rights.

➤ Dominionism and Quiverfull family values are closer to being enacted in the nation than many people realize.

Chapter 23
Not Just About Abortion!

<u>What to Expect From this Chapter</u>

➤ The anti-abortion movement has all contraceptives in its sights.

➤ Contraceptives are seen as immoral and mini-abortions.

Women's role and purpose is to have babies and work in the home, and to be submissive to a husband (or father pre-marriage). Quiverfull gives the template for what that family life is supposed to look like to properly live the Bible's example. In order to achieve these ideals, women's independence must be eliminated to make living this lifestyle inevitable rather than a choice. The single most important factor in modern women's advances has been birth control and abortion. Birth control made it possible for women to enter the work force, to be focused on education and a career, and to have a say over when they want to raise a family, and how big that family will be.

Initial church support for abortion

The Religious Right have targeted abortion and have made it the banner they wave before them. This is one of their biggest tools to manipulate the emotions of well-meaning people. If we conducted a 'man on the street' interview of passersby asking, why did today's Religious Right form; what was the driving force that birthed them, you could safely bet that almost every person would answer that abortion is what created the Religious Right. In chapter two, we went over how it was the early ERA effort, not abortion, that started the trent that would evolve into what we have today. But the catalyst of the Religious Right is surprising.

"... the vast majority of evangelical leaders said virtually nothing about it [Roe vs. Wade decision]; many of those who did comment actually applauded the decision. W. Barry Garrett of Baptist Press wrote, 'Religious liberty, human equality and justice are advanced by the Supreme Court abortion decision.'

*Indeed, even before the Roe decision, the messengers (delegates) to the **1971** Southern Baptist Convention gathering in St. Louis, Missouri, adopted a resolution that stated, 'we call upon Southern Baptists to work for legislation that will allow the possibility of abortion under such conditions as rape, incest, clear evidence of severe fetal deformity, and carefully ascertained evidence of the likelihood of damage to the emotional, mental, and physical health of the mother.' W.A. Criswell, former president of the Southern Baptist Convention and pastor of First Baptist Church in Dallas, Texas, expressed his satisfaction with the Roe v. Wade ruling. 'I have always felt that it was only after a child was born and had a life separate from its mother that it became an individual person,' the redoubtable fundamentalist declared, 'and it has always, therefore, seemed to me that what is best for the mother and for the future should be allowed.'"* Randall Balmer, *Thy Kingdom Come, An Evangelical's Lament: How the Religious Right Distorts the Faith and Threatens America, Basic Books,* 2006.

What was the true catalyst for the Religious Right?

We have the grassroots organizing first done to prevent ERA from being ratified that was the initial inspiration, the germ of an idea of the potential at hand. Yet, it was still a very loose gathering of rag tag groups. As we have just read, the initial responses were positive towards the Supreme Court's ruling of Roe v. Wade. If it was not abortion that provided the ingredient to bind them together in purpose and vision, then what was it?

"... he [Paul Weyrich] said animatedly, that the Religious Right did not come together in response to the Roe decision. No Weyrich insisted, what got us going as a political movement was the attempt on the part of the Internal Revenue Service (IRS) to rescind the tax-exempt status of Bob Jones University because of its racially discriminatory policies.

'What caused the movement to surface,' Weyrich reiterated, 'was the federal government's moves against Christian schools.' The IRS threat against

segregated schools, he said, 'enraged the Christian community.' That, not abortion, according to Weyrich was what galvanized politically conservative evangelicals into the Religious Right and goaded them into action.

The abortion myth serves as a convenient fiction because it suggests noble and altruistic motives behind the formation of the Religious Right." Randall Balmer, *Thy Kingdom Come, An Evangelical's Lament: How the Religious Right Distorts the Faith and Threatens America*, Basic Books, 2006.

The question then becomes, why did they grab onto abortion as their big issue? Based on the Religious Right's tendency toward manipulating the common person with emotionally shocking pictures or imaginings, that began back with the fight against ERA, it seems as though abortion was their marketing bonanza to pull in massive donations, and to build upon. It was the convenient tool that could be easily utilized to tear at people's hearts, despite the fact the church was initially supportive of the Roe v. Wade decision.

Abortion: the marketing bonanza

The Religious Right continued to hone their marketing appeal messaging, and focused on what they perceived as the terrible state of the family, and those corrupting feminists. Abortion was something they could use to manipulate emotions, just like an episode of *Little House on the Prairie* or a Lifetime movie special. They reveled in splashing disturbing images to move you into the action they wanted. They learned how to utilize abortion for the greatest shock value possible and it has helped them raise significant volunteers and money.

"Although birth control is very old, the movement for the right to control reproduction is young. About two centuries ago, when the movement began, birth control had been morally and religiously stigmatized in many parts of the world, so illicit that information on the subject was whispered, or written and distributed surreptitiously. Birth control advocates in the United States served jail terms for violation of obscenity laws. Moreover, reproductive rights advocates

were often dissenters in other dimensions as well – trade unionists, socialists, feminists, for example. As a result, the modern birth control movement has at various times included campaigns for women's rights, economic justice, freedom of speech, freedom of the press, and the extension of democracy.

...People have tried to control reproduction in virtually all known societies, and not simply as private matters. These attempts were always acknowledged and socially regulated in some way....Systems of sexual control change as women's status changes; they both reflect and affect each other. There has been an especially strong connection between the subjection of women and the prohibitions on birth control: the latter has been a means of enforcing the former. Inversely, there has been a strong connection between women's emancipation and their ability to control reproduction." Linda Gordon, *The Moral Property of Women: A History of Birth Control Politics in America*, University of Illinois Press, 2002.

Women's status is tied to birth control as per the above quote. The Catholic Church chose birth control as an issue to contest with the federal government. The Catholic Church does not allow any form of birth control, even a vasectomy, in their hospitals, which is imposing their beliefs on everybody else. In some cases a Catholic hospital is the only choice in smaller towns and thereby they can dictate their stance on the captive population.

Several states (Colorado, Georgia, Iowa, Montana, New Hampshire, Vermont, Washington, and Wisconsin) already had laws requiring birth control to be covered one hundred percent by health insurance companies, with no exceptions for religious groups. Those laws were never challenged. Two thousand twelve dawned with the Catholic Church suddenly angry that the church would have to pay for birth control when they, as an institution, feel it is immoral. Polls varied and arguments followed over just how many Catholic women used birth control, regardless of the Church's stance. Amazingly, many women defended the Catholic Church for dictating their lives by dutifully repeating the ingrained response that the church was being persecuted. This situation is serious, and needs to be put in perspective:

1) The church is insisting that they must be above or exempt from the law. This is staggering and destroys the republic the nation claims to be. A republic is a government where every one is equally under the same laws. The Catholic Church is attempting to shred that foundational ideal.

2) Exempting the church would set a precedent that a church can claim a moral objection to a law and be above the law. The ramifications that will follow could easily include: the Mormon church can have multiple wives again, child abuse under "spare the rod and spoil the child" sects is acceptable again; it can be argued that child brides are acceptable, since Mary was around twelve when she was married; interracial couples can be refused marriage licenses, and so on.

3) This controversy quickly inspired the "Blunt Amendment," attached to a transportation bill, that would have allowed any employer or health insurer (not just a church) to opt out of any essential benefit or preventive service coverage under the excuse of a conscience or religious objection.

4) To exempt the church from a law is the true violation of the Establishment clause, because it is unequal treatment. You would have to open it up for all individuals to personally decide if they morally believe in a law and if they want to obey the law. Otherwise, you are showing favoritism to religious organizations, providing them with a different set of rules than others.

5) This controversy covers the many people who are employed by businesses that the Catholic Church runs. Many of the women employees may not be Catholic, yet have a moral view dictated to them by their employer without any voice. There is no concern shown for their religious freedom, or for violations of their rights.

6) Catholic women are seen as objects to be told what their role is, with no voice, no choice, and no dignity. The male Catholic hierarchy is using this as a political maneuver in an election year, violating the religious freedom of each woman to decide

her moral position on birth control. What about each woman's religious freedom that the Catholic Church attempts to trample? They don't care how many women may leave the church in the wake of this, either. The women are completely a non-issue to them. Yet, many women blindly mouth the standard tactic that the church is being persecuted.

Thus, we see how bold the Religious Right has grown in challenging birth control. We have additionally seen how many women are already so desensitized that they don't see the insult and disregard for their well-being, their religious liberty as individuals, nor their rights. Many have advanced this anti-birth control view by pushing the idea that birth control is really abortion. This ensures they can further manipulate the abortion outrage and direct it towards birth control in general.

The Religious Right likes to perpetuate the belief that they formed over the abortion issue. They continue to put forth that valiantly standing up for unborn children is the foundation of their work. But as we mentioned before, it was actually the Equal Rights Amendment that brought various groups a semblance of unity. Abortion was long considered a Catholic Church issue, and Protestants were not engaged in the debate. It was not until Francis Schaeffer and his son Frank got involved that abortion became *the* issue of the Religious Right. Frank Schaeffer has since apologized for his part in creating the monster.

What is a sincere Christian to believe about abortion then? Consider Frank Schaeffer's view of abortion:

> *"I am still pro-life and I also believe that abortion should be legal. But... we ought to find ways to help women, help children, give contraceptives, sex education to lessen the number of abortions. I think abortion is a tragedy..."*
> Frank Schaeffer "Rachel Maddow Show", <u>MSNBC</u>, June 1 2009.

Strategy against abortion and the pill

When it comes to the all-out war against reproductive rights (a woman's right over her own reproductive system) the radical right has a four-pronged political plan. This approach works against contraceptives as well as abortion.

"...abortion foes soon turned to the more piecemeal strategy we know today, what Gandy referred to as the effort to overturn Roe 'one step at a time.' The first major victory in this strategy was the Hyde Amendment, legislation that excluded abortion coverage from Medicaid, which Congress passed in 1976 and the Supreme Court upheld in 1980.

This strategy of death-by-a-thousand-cuts has four major elements: The first, in the spirit of the Hyde Amendment, is to chip away at actual access, through restricting public funds, threatening clinics, and throwing up roadblocks such as parental consent requirements. The second would remake the nonprofit sector by taking away funds from organizations that support and provide abortions, while increasing the cash flow to pro-life organizations such as crisis pregnancy centers. The third, a purely ideological battle, aims to establish the precedent that life – and thus human rights protections – begins at conception, a project that plays itself out in countless congressional amendments and scientific regulations. The final strategy trumps all the others: to remake the courts through pro-life judicial nominees who will eventually have the power to overturn Roe.

...By the end of 2002, these efforts had triumphed: thirty states now mandate counseling prior to an abortion, following a strict script that, in many cases, includes frightening and scientifically inaccurate claims. Three-quarters of all states require minors to receive parental consent – or judicial bypass – before getting an abortion; more than half of all states prohibit state funds from being used to cover the cost of abortions. What's more, thirty-five states have passed laws that single out abortion providers for often-absurd regulatory oversight (like a law in South Carolina mandating that abortion clinic lawns be kept free of grass that could harbor insects)." Esther Kaplan, *With God on Their Side*, New Press, 2004.

They have been incredibly successful in this piecemeal approach and a legal medical procedure has become harder and harder to obtain in this country. But, we still have higher abortion rates than countries that have free and easy access to abortions, which is a counter-productive situation. An additional tactic has been added, to traumatize or abuse the woman. This is the mentality behind states proposing legislation requiring trans-vaginal ultrasound before having an abortion.

Of course, there is the classic propaganda move combined with misdirection in the claim that abortion is detrimental to the black community. This has been put forth many times, and some people actually believe it. The Women of Color Reproductive Health Collective stepped in and made it clear that was absurd.

"*Ross* [the National Coordinator of SisterSong: Women of Color Reproductive Health Collective (www.sistersong.net)] *also stressed that abortion needs to be seen as a human rights issue and points to the 1948 Universal Declaration of Human Rights, which declares the right of every person to live free of slavery. And being forced to bear children is most certainly a form of slavery as Ross is quick to point out.*" Lucinda Marshall, "The Abortion Conversation We Should Be Having", <u>AlterNet</u>, April 27, 2008.

Not just abortion, but all birth control

Abortion became the hot issue that is utilized to shock the average person and build the war chest of the Religious Right. The abortion issue has been ideal for this purpose. Hysteria has been encouraged at every turn, with a specific end goal in mind, to get rid of birth control methods. This sounds ludicrous, because a few generations have now grown up taking the convenient pills for granted. But, it was a battle to even get birth control pills tested, safe, and ultimately accepted and legally accessible. That a Catholic hospital won't perform a simple vasectomy is evidence that control of women's reproductive rights is about *all* birth control methods. But, the Religious Right has taken it to new heights.

Roe vs. Wade and the legalizing of abortion was a further level of control over a woman's own life. Birth control pills may not be available to some women (mostly poor), and accidents or rapes resulting in pregnancy do unfortunately occur. To have control over their own lives led many women to obtain risky abortions that could even kill them, before the procedure became legal.

The Religious Right is working systematically and diligently to reverse the historic Roe vs. Wade decision. It is an obsession among them, and it is about women turning away from the *traditional* family role and, and children being raised up in the *correct and proper way*, than anything else.

The fight is not over abortion solely, but over birth control across the board, and the Religious Right sees birth control as perhaps the biggest single factor in the destruction of the *traditional family values* that envisions the woman having children and tending the house. The high emotions surrounding abortion are being shifted to the pill, by saying that in reality birth control pills are just miniature abortions. Sadly, it is working and there is growing moral outrage towards the pill now.

How do you reverse the women's rights movement and the gains they have made? Simply get rid of what aided their liberation in the first place; eliminate the availability of the pill by a sweeping "conscientious objection" to these mini abortions. We are back to the mentality that spawned the poem equating the pill with a mining disaster taking multiple lives. Since approximately the 1870s women in America have been fighting for birth control freedom, and won it in 1965.

We now have entire generations of women who have no concept of a world without readily accessible birth control, until now. This impacts men too. The modern man, for the most part, believes in birth control until ready to settle down and have a family and not until then – and even then may only want to have the children that can be financially supported. But, the Religious Right's view is set in stone and completely the opposite. Federal and state legislative bills abound with the intention to limit women's rights and move the clock back to a time when women had only one future. How do you feel about a woman's destiny being pre-ordained and the courts and elected officials making that mandatory, piece by piece?

"Trying to control reproduction has been a human activity from as far back as historians can trace it. Reproduction control efforts constitute part of the evidence that biology has never been destiny, that even those functions most often described as 'natural,' such as reproduction, have always been formed by cultural and social organizations. In the twentieth century there was rapid, if intermittent, progress in birth control but also some disappointment. Methods became safer and more efficient, and their use became more wide-spread. But many people have been excluded from this progress. Women continue to suffer, even die, from birth control efforts, especially abortion – causalities that are due more to prohibitions and criminalization than to necessary risks.

...the most influential, mainstream pro-birth control organizations relied primarily on individual rights as the ground for the ethics of birth control and seemed, at least to social conservatives, to be undermining the communitarian and selfless values of family. The abortion conflict not only intensified but spilled over into conflicts about policing pregnant women's behavior, stem cell research, and welfare. In this process the distinction between contraceptives and abortion lost some of its precision, and it became obvious that the conflict was now about fundamental sex, family, and gender values.

...birth control is inevitably about gender....The three political campaigns for reproductive freedom – in the 1870s, the 1910s, and the 1970s and 1980s – coincide with peaks of women's rights agitation....All three periods were marked by campaigns for sex education and against sexual obscurantism, particularly for women's sexual and reproductive self-knowledge as the basis for self-control." Linda Gordon, *The Moral Property of Women: A History of Birth Control Politics in America*, University of Illinois Press, 2002.

Linda Gordon is a professor of history at New York University, and she clearly states that controlling reproduction and birth control methods is strongly connected with the subjection of women. We see Republicans and Tea Partiers rapid pursuit of Planned Parenthood's destruction; whether it serves a vital role or not is negated.

This explains why Republicans were outraged when insurance companies were to cover birth control free under the U.S. Department of Health and Human Services new guidelines that went into effect August 1, 2011. Birth Control, *all* birth control is against the Bible and God's plan so *all* birth control must be stopped. Women are not to have any control over this, only God. If you don't want children, then you must be single and celibate! There is no other option for you according to the Religious Right. They are making headway politically with this agenda.

Birth Control was liberating

This is important to keep in mind because women gained a degree of control over their lives when birth control was finally freely accessible. In 1965, the Supreme Court in "Griswold v. Connecticut, 381 U.S. 479" overturned a Connecticut law that prohibited the use of contraceptives. After the Supreme Court's ruling, more and more women incorporated birth control pills into their lives. They had control over their destinies.

When birth control was going through its struggles to be accepted and mainstreamed there was a very controversial song that a country music legend recorded. Loretta Lynn had to wait a few years before her record label would even allow this song to be included in a record release. When it was released, many radio stations refused to play it and it easily became known as her most controversial song. The song is a reflection of just how liberating birth control was for women and it hints that women could now enjoy sex because the considerable anxiety of pregnancy had been removed. It is important enough to include the 1975 song, *The Pill*, lyrics written by T.D. Bayless and recorded by Loretta Lynn that shows the cultural revolution for women that birth control represented and how it wasn't that long ago.

"You wined me and dined me

When I was your girl

Promised if I'd be your wife

You'd show me the world

But all I've seen of this old world

Is a bed and a doctor bill

I'm tearin' down your brooder house

'Cause now I've got the pill

All these years I've stayed at home

While you had all your fun

And every year that's gone by

Another baby's come

There's a gonna be some changes made

Right here on nursery hill

You've set this chicken your last time

'Cause now I've got the pill

This old maternity dress I've got

Is goin' in the garbage

The Clothes I'm wearin' from now on

Won't take up so much yardage

Miniskirts, hot pants and a few little fancy frills

Yeah I'm makin' up for all those years

Since I've got the pill

I'm tired of all your crowin'

How you and your hens play

While holdin' a couple in my arms

Another's on the way

This chicken's done tore up her nest

and I'm ready to make a deal

And ya can't afford to turn it down

'Cause you know I've got the pill

This incubator is overused

Because you've kept filled

The feelin' good comes easy now

Since I've got the pill

It's gettin' dark it's roostin' time

Tonight's too good to be real

Oh but daddy don't you worry none

'Cause mama's got the pill

Oh daddy don't you worry none

'Cause mama's got the pill"

A few generations have grown up now with birth control as an expected part of their lives. The decades of struggle have been long forgotten and it seems inconceivable that it could be taken away. But that is what the Religious Right intends if they have their way.

Birth control was also viewed as immoral

William Sanger, husband to feminist activist Margaret Sanger, was arrested in 1915 for distributing a birth control pamphlet. The judge's words below are coming back into fashion.

> "*The judge convicted Sanger, declaring the pamphlet 'immoral and indecent,' and scolded, 'Such persons as you who circulate such pamphlets are a menace to society. There are too many who believe it is a crime to have children. If some of the women who are going around and advocating equal suffrage would go around and advocate having children they would do a greater service.'*" Elaine Tyler May, *America and the Pill*, Basic Books, 2010.

Women's fight for equal rights, voting and control over their own futures was intimately tied to having autonomy and control of having children or not.

Not everybody saw birth control pills as a good thing. Birth control had long been considered immoral, a travesty, and an outrage. The Religious Right leaders still thank that. In 1968, Richard Brautigan wrote a poem comparing birth control pills to a mining disaster in Nova Scotia that took many lives.

"The Pill Versus the Springhill Mine Disaster

When you take your pill

it's like a mine disaster.

I think of all the people

lost inside of you."

This growing attitude against birth control was seen on June 16, 1999 when Texas Republican Representative Tom Delay speaking on the House floor related the horrific shooting at Columbine High School to being about contraceptives. As the nation was in shock, contraceptives (and lack of prayer in schools) were the quick fall-guys to a more complex problem.

> *"It couldn't have been because we have sterilized and contracepted our families down to sizes so small that the children we do have are so spoiled...*
>
> *It couldn't have been because our children, historically have been seen as a blessing from God, are now being viewed as either a mistake created when contraception fails or inconveniences...Nah, it must have been the guns."*

Congressional Record – House, H4366, June 16, 1999.

In North Dakota, on February 19, 2009, the state legislative house passed a bill stating that a fertilized egg is a person, but failed to get it through the state senate. Mississippi in 2011 had a *personhood* bill introduced in 2011, with the expectation that the Bible-Belt would be the charm to get it passed. However, it was defeated by voters. The ramifications of such personhood amendments are beyond just setting a precedent to challenge Roe v. Wade, but will make any endangerment, even unintentional harm, of a fetus a crime like manslaughter or premeditated. Bills such as these are most certainly meant to be nails in the coffins for contraceptives. This initiative has the same attitude towards pregnancy in common with some Muslims. Iranian law holds that anyone who brings about a miscarriage must pay a monetary fee; the Religious Right is attempting to make it more of a crime. The Religious Right is more radical on this point than even Iran!

"I would, however, just like to add that the language of this bill is also a direct challenge to contraception as well as abortion, since non-barrier methods of contraception are believed to maybe cause fertilized eggs to fail in attaching themselves the uterine wall. I'd also like to add that since that attachment to the uterine wall is the only real way that we are currently able to identify pregnancy, and therefore how we define it, this bill would also give these fertilized eggs rights from before the moment at which we are currently able to scientifically prove that they even exist. Just wrap your head around that one." "North Dakota Takes a Sh*t on Women's Rights," *Alternet* February 19, 2009.

Yes, contraceptives themselves are under attack now, it isn't just abortion. Abortion is just the shock-value item, the wedge issue the Religious Right vulgarly shoves in our faces to repulse and horrify as best they can as an entry – a foothold. Their ultimate goal is for all women to accept their duty as a blessing, an honor and not be selfish in wanting to fulfill individual dreams or goals outside of being housewives. Apparently the attack on contraceptives, particularly on those most affordable and easily available, is working. On February 24, 2009 the Guttmacher Institute released a comprehensive study that found low income and minority women are using fewer contraceptives, which is a reversal of the prior trend data. That directly equates to more unwanted children that the taxpayers get the bill, for either in welfare costs or social services and juvenile crimes.

Birth control politics have been a battle since the 1870s in America, and are heating up again. Unfortunately, not many have understood the intent nor how widespread these attacks against birth control have been. The political force against all birth control is only beginning. You now know what the intention really is, and the purpose of these attacks. The power is in your hands to take a stand.

Job one of Religious Right Republicans

When the new Republican majority House of Representatives began their session in January, 2011, the nation was clear that jobs were priority number one. So, the Republican representatives made lots of promises that they were listening and that was their focus, and promptly drafted H.R.3 titled "No Taxpayer Funding for Abortion Act." This bill initially went so far as to redefine rape on the wild premise that a woman may cry rape just to get a free abortion. Due to public outcry, they had to drop the redefining of rape. Across the nation there was a tsunami of anti-abortion bills, rather than jobs initiatives; often they were slipped into *budget* measures.

Here we see the Religious Republican Right's work. Tell the people we will focus on jobs and immediately crank out legislative bills that are a slap in the face to approximately fifty percent of citizens. The sting of redefining rape for those citizens whose worst nightmare is to be raped (no matter how violent), and then have to live with it the rest of their lives, is still felt. Oh, and you must prove it was violent before that morning-after-pill or any other procedure. You may have been held at knifepoint, but there is no evidence? That doesn't seem to matter. Or, you may have been drugged with a date rape drug, or coerced by vicious threats? An argument in defense of the proposed rape redefinition was that women are so cunning that they would lie to get an abortion or the morning-after pill. Other than further limiting any poor-to-middleclass woman from getting an abortion, the biggest accomplishment of this bill was to stop the use of the *morning-after"* pill, emergency contraceptives for rape victims! The language was pulled from the bill, but added in again right before the House vote and the Religious Right Republicans passed it.

There are other measures in other states to prevent women from circumventing restrictions and forcing them to have babies. Consider the Georgia H1 legislation drafted by State Republican Representative Bobby Franklin (degree in biblical studies) that would require proof that a miscarriage occurred naturally, not via a hanger or even unintentional neglect, or face a possible felony charge. Consider the Utah legislation allowing the state to charge a woman with criminal homicide for inducing a miscarriage, all with an eye to eliminating home abortions. The trend is sweeping the nation. Women are to have the babies; not birth control nor *induced* miscarriages nor abortions are acceptable.

Women have been slapped with criminal charges for miscarriages too. Rennie Gibbs of Mississippi was fifteen years old when she had a stillbirth at thirty-six weeks and received a murder charge because she had cocaine abuse in her history. Bei Bei Shuai was charged with murder and jailed because her premature baby died; it may have been related to Shuai's failed suicide attempt. Amanda Kimbrough's premature baby died after only nineteen minutes alive. Kingrough, a mother of three, was charged with chemical endangerment of her child with claims that Kingrough took drugs, a claim Kingrough vehemently denies. She is facing prison time on top of the emotional toll of her child's death. Charges are brought against women using supposed alcohol or drug use as a reason for prosecution; soon it will be exposure to cigarette smoke, or maybe insufficient prenatal care that the impoverished can't afford etc? This trend is in line with the repressive Islamic Sharia law that has prosecuted women for miscarriages too. Religious extremism under any name often takes similar form.

Faith and conscientious objections

It is dangerous to deny that their agenda includes all contraceptives across the board. The Department of Health and Human Services in July of 2008 released a proposal that was easily identified as Religious Right initiated, which paves the way for anyone who receives federal grant money to obstruct women's access to contraceptives, within their purview, on *faith* grounds. The proposal defines any abortion as the termination of a pregnancy, which includes the Religious Right's definition of 40% of the commonly used contraceptives (hormonal contraceptives) as preventing the fertilized egg from attaching to the uterine wall to grow, and are therefore considered abortions! But where is the evidence that those contraceptives actually work that way? Who needs evidence, facts, proof? The proposal says "*...the conscience* of the individual or institution should be paramount in determining what constitutes abortion." In other words, I think IUDs are a form of abortion and against my faith so I (as a doctor or pharmacist worker) don't have to allow you to have them. The definition of abortion is open to anybody's interpretation under this ruling.

> *"That is, committed to neo-orthodox pro-family doctrines condemning contraception as an 'abortifacient' and a rejection of God's greatest blessing, children: a theology gaining ground among all branches of Christianity. It's a point [Allan] Carlson makes frequently, supplementing his 'airtight' social science case for traditional values with praise for religious orthodoxy as the 'yeast' that will make the family movement rise: compelling people to sacrifice their individual goals to raise large families."* Kathryn Joyce, "Missing: The 'Right' Babies", *The Nation*, February 14 2008.

It is becoming more and more clear that the ultimate goal is that a female's only protection against pregnancy should be abstinence or the infamous rhythm-method, even if she is married. Many states have laws that a pharmacist can refuse to fill a prescription on reason of faith or *conscience*. Married women, even with their spouses by their sides, have still been turned down at pharmacies for birth control. It is hard to believe, but it really is about being at home and raising kids; this is baffling to so many people. Again, it is about women's role in life.

> *"This is a struggle often masquerading as a moral controversy. At its roots, however, it's about sex and power; whether women will be allowed to keep striving for an equal place in society or confined, as much as possible, to the nursery... those who, underneath it all, oppose the increased social power women attain from expanded equality and justice. Proof of this?*
>
> *James Leon Holmes, nominated by President Bush and confirmed by the Senate to the U.S. District Court in the Eastern District of Arkansas, says it straight out in an article: 'It is not coincidental that the feminist movement brought with it artificial contraception ... To the extent we adopt the feminist*

principle that the distinction between the sexes is of no consequence and should be disregarded in the organization of society and the Church, we are contributing to the culture of death.' His stated solution is that '... the wife is to subordinate herself to her husband." Gloria Feldt, "The Right's War on Contraception", *Women's eNews*, July 3, 2006.

"If you think children's welfare is really what's at issue, consider, finally, that a recent study published by the Washington Post showed how the states with the strictest abortion laws also had the poorest services for indigent women and their children. As for South Dakota [fighting anti-abortion legislation for the second time], the New York Times recently noted that it has the highest child poverty rate in the country...Legislatures that pass laws without a meaningful 'health-of-the-mother' exception, or who pair anti-abortion laws with anti-contraception laws, do not see women as equal, either." Elaine Cassel "The Battle over Abortion and Contraception, Part One: How It's Playing Out in the States and in the Supreme Court," *FindLaw*, March 14 2006.

It is critical to remember that the Religious Right's vision is that all children should be born and raised in exactly the *correct* way.

"In an awakened America...[B]abies would not be aborted. Rather, unwanted babies would be adopted and discipled instead of aborted or discarded." Tony Perkins, *Personal Faith, Public Policy*, 2008.

Yes, unwanted babies would be adopted out and discipled. That means that more and more children would be raised to believe that the Religious Right way and dominionism are imperative. There are Wait No More Adoption Conferences, and Focus on the Family encourages adoptions and provides support and resources. This paints abortion as limiting the amount of Religious Right adherents, on top of its other faults.

Over the last several chapters we have looked at the *traditional family values* and the Family Mountain agenda from a few perspectives. We have established that women's role is have babies and work in the house, with the husband providing headship over this family unit. The ideal template for a good and proper family is epitomized in the Quiverfull movement and what that really looks like. We have examined how the family is important in the scheme of things, so that it is warranted being one of the targeted Seven Mountains. And, we unveiled the war on not just abortion but birth control in general. There is much at stake here. Children and how they are part of the orchestrated plan is next, and you may be further surprised.

We leave this chapter with a quote from history that is shocking, but perhaps the American people need to be shocked?

> *"The preservation of the family with many children is a matter of biological concept and national feeling. The family with many children must be preserved ... because it is a highly valuable, indispensable part of the ... nation. Valuable and indispensable not only because it alone guarantees the maintenance of the population in the future but because it is the strongest basis of national morality and national culture ... The preservation of this family form is a necessity of national and cultural politics ... This concept is strictly at variance with the demands for an abolition of paragraph 218; it considers unborn life as sacrosanct. For the legalization of abortion is at variance with the function of the family, which is to produce children and would lead to the definite destruction of the family with many children"* Völkischer Beobachter [the newspaper of the Nazi Party], October 14, 1931.

Take With You From This Chapter

➢ Abortion was initially a non-issue or even supported by many ministers. It was not the catalyst for the Religious Right as many believe.

➢ Birth control has been illegal or access limited for much longer than it has been legal in this nation. It was long considered immoral, and that sentiment is making a strong comeback.

➤ Abortion is the marketing bonanza for the Religious Right, but it is being used to turn the tide against common birth control methods now.

➤ The faith or conscience of medical or pharmacy staff legally allows them to deny access to birth control in many states now.

Chapter 24
Children are the Prize to the Winners

<u>What to Expect From this Chapter</u>

➤ How the nation's youth are specifically targeted by Religious Right organizations for recruiting.

➤ Evidence that this is a growing tactic that utilizes modern devices such as concerts to reach youth and sway their emotions.

> *"Children are the prize to the winners in the second great civil war. Those who control what young people are taught and what they experience – what they see, hear, think, and believe – will determine the future course for the nation."* James Dobson, *Children At Risk: The Battle for the Hearts and Minds of Our Kids*, 1990, page 35.

In this atmosphere of a cultural war being fought, a civil war, to use James Dobson's words, and children are the battleground. The proper family is an institution that the Religious Right believes has been deliberately compromised by feminists and gay rights groups. A critical part of the proper family is the children. Children represent a linchpin critical to the Dominion plan and a tactical necessity. Children, like the island of Iwo Jima in WWII, are so vital in this war that schools are not the only weapon to ensure their usability.

We have many efforts outside schools to reach and capture the children of the nation. If you are a parent you might want to pay particular attention.

<u>BattleCry.com</u>

Battlecry.com is geared towards rising up the youth of America and Canada to be zealots for Christ. Music and video are the utilized to capture this generation's attention by bringing several media partners on board with the Battle Cry Campaign to succcessfully invade the lives of our youth and challenge, or indoctrinate, them to live passionately for Christ. On their website they place particular emphasis on reaching *unchurched* youth. They hold large rallies that are more like those *evil* rock concerts – because of course, group dynimics work.

Interestingly back in 1990, James Dobson wrote in *Chidren at Risk*: "*Anyone who has worked with teenagers has surely witnessed this mind-bending process at work... Rock concerts subject masses of emotionally needy kids to deafening noises, eerie lights, wild behavior...an adolescent begins to lose his grip on reality. His fight to preserve individuality slowly ebbs away. A passion for conformity rises from deep within. His peer group becomes lord and master until finally, the wonderful freedom of youth is traded for slavery and domination.*" Thus you have everything you need to know in a nutshell about how the Religious Right take that and use it for their own ends, such as in the work of Battlecry.org.

BattleCry holds its *Acquire the Fire* concerts throughout America in stadiums or other such large venues, with the same lights and loud music high-energy pump-them-up staging as the most aggressive rock band. Navy SEALs are paraded on stage screaming about being Christian Warriors. When George W. Bush was president, there was a letter reportedly read from him endorsing the movement; that only increased the emotional high of the moment for the thousands of teens attending. Yes, the Religious Right knows how to fight a war using everything at its disposal, particularly the youth of the nation. The biggest push of BattleCry is for each member to drag an *unchurched* friend to these mind-bending concerts, for the glory of Christ. That means your child too. Dr. C.J. Pascoe discusses BattleCry with me:

"*Evangelicals have known for a long time that teens are a receptive and easily manipulated audience. Teens are at a moment in their lives when they are supposed to be figuring out who they are and are trying to navigate the intense social world that is high school. Evangelicals bring them into these rock-concert – like rallies and offer an easy solution to all of their problems. Churches create social events (like Hell Houses or BattleCry rallies) that deliberately whip up teens' emotions and appeal to their sense of drama. Then, at a point in the program (usually after enduring tales of drug use, suicide attempts or other social problems) when the teens are emotionally vulnerable, they reel them in with the promise of eternal life. It's always smacked, to me at least, of emotional manipulation."* Dr. C.J. Pascoe, email interview with author, 2008.

Hell House for Halloween

Hell House is the alternative to the Halloween haunted house experience, with the sole mission of scaring children, not of things that go bump in the night, but of sin and hell. It is a great way to ask *un-churched* friends to go to a scary haunted house that is intent on getting them to convert. The horror scenes in a typical Hell House that spring up all over the nation each year are of graphic and bloody late-term abortions, the evils of gay people, a supposed human sacrifice by Satanists, hell, and the final scene of an idealistic utopia of Heaven. Many of these Hell Houses are cloaked to seem like your average Halloween haunted houses. Hell House outreach kits are sold so that any church or religious organization can effectively create these scared-straight-to-conversion Hell House experiences.

"Each Halloween, members of the Trinity Church in Cedar Hill, Texas, put on a haunted house. But instead of ghostly howls and skeletons in coffins, 'Hell House' depicts what the Pentecostal church considers to be sins: a girl having an abortion... another taking drugs at a rave, getting raped, then killing herself... a boy committing suicide in a classroom. In each elaborately staged scene, Satan taunts the sinner, and then drags him or her off to hell. The aim is to save souls through fear.

About 40 people at a time are shepherded through a dozen such scenes. At the end, the sinners are shown suffering their eternal damnation. Then visitors are asked if they want to accept Jesus and join the church. About one in five do." "Hell House", *NPR website*, Aug. 17, 2002.

Jerry Falwell helped to popularize Hell Houses, but Kennan Roberts is the true force behind them by developing and marketing the do-it-yourself kits around the nation. That is yet something else to consider when your kids are asked by a friend to go to a haunted house – will it have a gory abortion scene or human sacrifice in it and try to convert children on the spot?

Jesus Camp

Another example of children being the spoils in this war is found in the 2006 documentary *Jesus Camp*, directed by Rachel Grady and Heidi Ewing, about a highly successful summer camp to indoctrinate youth into a Religious Right world view. Only four minutes into the documentary we see children ranging from 6 years to perhaps 13 who are wearing face paint, even camouflage, at a church assembly for a musical number. After 5:45 minutes, we have Becky Fischer, the founder of Jesus Camp, marketing *The School of Evangelism* to an auditorium of people. *"There's a hands-on manual in the back that teaches children how to actually start a conversation with their friends and how to win the lost,"* Ms. Fischer proudly proclaims to the young children and their parents in attendance. She proceeds to instill in these young children how badly the world needs fixing, and that they have to fix it.

7:14 minutes – Becky Fisher: *"Do you know Muslims train their children from the time they are five years old to fast during the month of Ramadan on? We hold the keys, we can change the world! Boys and girls can change the world? Absolutely! Absolutely! I need you to get serious, serious with God. Say 'God, I'm here to be trained. I'm here for an education. I'm willing God. I'll do what you want me to do. I'll say what you want me to say.'"*

9:49 – Ms. Fisher says *"I can go into a playground of kids that don't know anything about Christianity and lead them to the Lord in just a matter of no time at all. And just moments later they can be seeing visions and hearing the voice of God because they are so open. They are so usable in Christianity."*

In an interview section, Ms Fischer adamantly proclaims, *"If you look at the world's population, one-third of that 6.7 billion people are children under the age of fifteen. One third. Where should we be putting our efforts? Where should we be putting our focus?*

I'll tell you where our enemies are putting it. They're putting it on the kids. They are going into the schools. You go into Palestine – and I can take you to some websites that will absolutely shake you to your foundations and show you photographs of where they are taking their kids to camps like we take our kids to Bible camps and they're putting hand grenades in their hands. They're teaching them how to put on bomb-belts. They're teaching them how to use rifles. They're teaching them how to use machine guns. It's no wonder with that kind of intense training and disciplining that those young people are ready to kill themselves for the cause of Islam.

I want to see young people who are as committed to the cause of Jesus Christ as the young people are to the cause of Islam. I want to see them as radically laying down their lives for the Gospel as they are over in Pakistan and Israel and Palestine and all those different places because, excuse me, we have the truth!' ”
Heidi Ewing director, *Jesus Camp*, Magnolia, 2007.

Children are the prize, remember. They are the tactical advantage to whichever side influences them, so it is a battle waging as to who gets the youth of this nation under their control.

Children are usable

Many view this as indoctrination of youth to serve in this war, because they are so very *usable* to the Religious Right. The parents who wanted their children to attend Jesus Camp did not go away, and the idea of children as easy converts has not gone away, either, just because Jesus Camp was closed down as a result of the documentary.

If you have children, please notice that now Suzy and Bobbi are being trained in how to convert unsuspecting playmates – maybe your children? That puts a different spin on the next slumber party, thanks to this war using children. Is your child being converted on the playground or in a haunted house because of his/her vulnerability? Jesus Camp was discontinued because of the fall-out from the documentary. But do you honestly think that the indoctrination of children stopped there?

> *"I was taught that children must be trained up in the way they should go every minute of every day ... By homeschooling, these parents can control every interaction their children have and every piece of information their children come upon."* Libby Anne, "My Life as a Daughter of Christian Patriarchy," *Butterflies and Wheels Blog Article*, September 3, 2011.

The intention is that every moment, children should be surrounded with what they should think, what lens they should experience the world through so they will propagate the same for future generations. The focus of Religious Righters to adopt, the view that all contraceptives are against God's express command to couples to *be fruitful and multiply*, creating large families or adopting children out to the right family and so forth, is specifically designed to raise-up a Religious Right army that thinks in the *proper* way. It is beyond just the schools, but anything that a child, any child, comes into contact with, should reinforce the desired message.

For the Religious Right family, raising children is to raise an army. This was touched on in the Quiverfull chapter, but lets see another insider speak on this in glowing tones.

> *"You're sipping lemonade and the conversation turns to what 'the children' are doing. Mrs X says, 'Oh, my John is a pastor!' Mrs. Y chimes in with, 'My Archibald teaches in a Bible College.' Others list things their children are currently involved in. Now it's your turn. Sit up straight and smile as you begin, 'Well, Jack is a missionary in Yugoslavia; Jill works with her husband as a Bible translator in Antarctica; Bill, his wife, and their seven children are church planters in the Hudson Bay area; Janice is discipling young women in Vladivostok; Abigail works at a Christian radio station in the Middle East with her husband and their five children; Mezuzah (you and your Bible names!) and his wife head an indigenous work on one of the Martian mining colonies. It's quite a story how God provided space suits for their eleven little ones! And*

Joseph is a car mechanic on 14th street. He has two Bible studies going for the men he works with and brings one of his six boys to work with him on Fridays. I don't remember what all his girls do.' Go ahead – have another sip of lemonade – you've earned it! And now finish, 'Paul, Timothy, and Titus are still shepherding churches and helping their wives educate their children at home. All sixteen of them.'

...The political blessings of Christian fruitfulness are invigorating to ponder and plan, but the missionary blessings are overwhelming. What a missionary force we could send! And the financial blessings possible from a vast number of giving Christians are enormous. Imagine if corporations, then headed by Christians, switched their tax-deductible contributions from funding the Mesopotamian Coastal Drum and Bugle Corps to funding missions organizations.

Let us pray and ask the Lord of the harvest to use our own families to raise up a host of dedicated young men and women who will serve Him anywhere." Rick and Jan Hess, *A Full Quiver: Family Planning and the Lordship of Christ*, Hess Publishing, 1989.

A picture speaks a thousand words! Those children are needed, not to realize their own dreams of a ballerina or firefighter, but to ensure the continuance of this religious expression. Not one child in that scenario was a doctor or a scientist finding the cure for cancer, a lowly public employee such as a firefighter, saving lives. Their lives were defined by how they were spreading the Religious Right worldview, converting people to their way of thinking. This is how they measure being a good parent – you raised them right and they have done their duty.

...If there are, say, 8 million Christian couples of childbearing age in the United States and they each have six children, that means that in twenty to thirty years those 16 million folks will have around 48 million children Add that to the parents and we have 64 million people. If 90 percent of those 48 million children

get married…and the resulting 22 million couples each have six children, we arrive at a staggering 132 million children, which, when added to the previous generation (our kids), us, and some before equals around 200 million in 40-80 years…

…a half-billion person boycott of a company which violated God's standards could be very effective. And what a majority in elections the elect would enjoy. Whew – it's exciting! Through God's blessing we would be part of a replay of Exodus 1:7, 'But the sons of Israel were fruitful and increased greatly, and multiplied, and became exceedingly mighty, so that the land was filled with them.'

And we have quite an advantage which the Israelites did not: we can vote.

If the Body of Christ had been reproducing as we were designed and told to, we would not be in the mess we are today." Rick and Jan Hess, *A Full Quiver: Family Planning and the Lordship of Christ*, Hess Publishing, 1990.

The "no contraceptives" bandwagon will increase the numbers of unwanted children, and adoption fairs to snatch up unclaimed children by Religious Right families are encouraged, combined with the movement to convert *un-churched* children. The pieces are coming together. Assemblies such BattleCry specifically want those *un-churched* children to attend, reaching the children who are not already in a church and getting the message delivered to them weekly.

"May the future testimony of our children's generation of young Christians be Psalm 105:24:

And He caused His people to be very fruitful,

And made them stronger than their adversaries." Rick and Jan Hess, *A Full Quiver: Family Planning And the Lordship of Christ*, 1989. (Emphasis added)

Insider's view

It is important to understand why children are so critical to the Religious Right.

Not only will they continue this specific worldview and pass it along and increase the ranks, but this also ensures the survival of their particular views and attitudes and perpetuates the Family Mountain of influence. Let's take a look at what a person raised in this atmosphere has to say about it.

"A surge of political fervor marked my soul's revival, and the vision of a godly America was my promised land. My faith was so intertwined with conservative politics that I viewed them as one and the same. In my ironclad worldview, faith and politics were inseparable. ...

I had been picketing since before I could walk. Before my parents moved to Oregon from New Mexico, they had bundled me into a carrier twice a week and hauled me and their signs to the local abortion clinic, where they paced the road across the street, praying as pregnant women walked in and empty women came out. ...

The music video on the screen at the front of our church reminded me that we were fighting a war. Carman, the Christian pop music artist turned cowboy, reminded me. Our youth group reminded me when they reenacted Carman's song to great acclaim, carousing on the church stage with bottles of apple juice while the pastor's son strode between the church pews wearing a black hat and boots and chanting, 'Satan: bite the dust.'

I'd been reminded regularly since my preschool days in children's church, where I marched in place and bobbed up and down, spreading my arms into plane wings while I sang,

I may never march with the infantry,

Ride in the cavalry,

Shoot the artillery,

I may never fly o'er the enemy.

But I'm in the Lord's Army." Alisa Harris, *Raised Right: How I Untangled My Faith from Politics*, Waterbrook Press, 2011.

Children are under assault. First they have their schools compromised by Religious Right to bring in revisionist history and stealthy evangelizing assemblies, if not blatant creationism taught as science. Secondly they have outside influences trying to capture their attention and allegiance to a religious construct. They are targets, and vital to propagating the Religious Right agenda.

Take With You From This Chapter

➢ Outside of school children, particularly *un-churched* children, are being targeted by groups such as BattleCry, Hell Houses, and Acquire the Fire concerts.

➢ Children are seen as usable in this war and are highly prized and viewed as spoils in the war being waged.

Chapter 25
Gay's and the Traditional Family

What to Expect From this Chapter

➤ Behind the *gays converting children* hysteria, and how gay people really are destroying the family.

➤ Sodom and Gomorrah were not about gays.

➤ What the Bible text says is really wrong with gays goes back to a woman's proper role.

We have looked at the role women are to have in the traditional family values arena, as having babies and working in the home. We briefly mentioned how single motherhood is looked down upon, and that the Quiverfull template is the model for the ideal family and home structure. In all the talk of traditional family values, you inevitably hear about how not just feminists or abortion and the birth control pill are the undoing of the family, but that gay people, by their very existence are detrimental to the family. How does being gay affect the ideal of the family? Honestly, explain how the one affects the other? This is not an easy jump to make, but actually goes back to the woman's role again.

> Romans 1:26-27
>
> *"For this reason God gave them over to degrading passions; for their women exchanged the <u>natural function</u> for that which is unnatural. And in the same way also the <u>men abandoned the natural function of the woman</u> and burned in their desire toward one another..." (Underline added.)*

Woman's role, gays and the family

From the preceding Bible passage, please notice how the offense all rests on the *natural function* of the woman, which is to bear children and *"men abandoned the natural function of the woman."* Combine the Romans quote with the Genesis account of the judgment of Eve, which is three fold. Genesis 3:16 *"To the woman He said, 'I will*

328

greatly multiply your pain in childbirth, in pain you shall bring forth children; Yet your desire shall be for your husband, and he shall rule over you." The judgment on Eve for eating the forbidden fruit was: 1) Eve, and thus all women, will have multiplied pain in childbirth; 2) women cannot avoid this judgment because they will desire men sexually; and 3) men, whom women cannot avoid desiring and making them have painful childbirth, will rule over them.

If a woman is attracted to another woman, it means she isn't desiring the man nor fulfilling her function, and a man isn't ruling over her, which is counter to the judgment on women in the Garden. The woman was not supposed to be able to avoid the penalty of painful childbirth by avoiding pregnancy, because her *"desire shall be for your husband."* The judgment was that women could not refrain from desiring a man sexually, thus resulting in painful childbirth ,which is the unavoidable judgment that a lesbian defies. In the Romans 1:26-27 quote, lesbians aren't fulfilling their child-bearing function, and the gay man isn't using the woman for her natural function of having babies either, nor is the gay man fulfilling his part in the woman's judgment by ruling over the woman.

It is a contradiction to have the order of male / female relationships established in the judgment in the Garden of Eden, and then say gay people are born gay. The existence of gays and lesbians is contrary to the beginning of the Bible if you interpret it literally, as the Religious Right does, and not as allegory or symbolic. Yet many Christians have reconciled women's changed status so that women working outside the home becomes the same issue as the issue of gay men and women.

Gay people's status comes down to women's role. If you can accept women are not mandated to stay at home having babies, then making an issue of gay rights is moot. It doesn't mean one is gay, but that one recognizes that the role of women has changed, and an entire section of the population is not destined for only having babies and being submissive. Thus if a person is gay, the same applies, because being gay was only an abomination in that the woman wasn't submissive to a man and having babies. This is the very same issue, and they are inseparable. That is why everything concerning gay rights and issues falls under the Family Mountain of influence in the Seven Mountains blueprint for dominion.

When David Bahati, the man who introduced the "kill-the-gays" bill in the Uganda legislature, appeared on a U.S. news program for an interview, he was not as concerned about public relations and image as his U.S. counterparts and reinforced the concept that having babies was the heart of the issue hurting the family.

> "*David Bahati: '...That's the bottom line we are looking at, to defend the traditional family in Uganda.'*
>
> *Rachel Maddow: 'How do gay people hurt the traditional family in Uganda? The existence of gay people living in Uganda, having relationships with one another – how does that hurt your family for example?'*
>
> *David Bahati: '... It distorts the cause of family. It hurts my family – it hurts the family of Uganda when <u>the purpose of procreation</u> is undermined.'"*

David Bahati Interview, "Rachel Maddow Show", <u>MSNBC</u>, December 8, 2010. (Emphasis added.)

It undermines the purpose of procreation because a gay woman isn't under a man's headship having babies, and a gay man isn't enforcing his headship over a woman and making those babies. That is the essence of how being gay impacts the traditional family, because it breaks down the strict role that women are destined for within the Religious Right mindset.

On CNN's Larry King Live (November 22, 2007) James Dobson said heterosexual marriage had to be protected because it "came from the creator Himself" and "*that people are just determined to mess with this wonderful institution called the family. And, again, when you're talking about children, it's very important that you preserve it... you don't establish national policy on the basis of an individual. You look at what the impact is, what the greater good is for the culture, and the best thing for a culture is to have a rock-solid foundation on which everything else is dependent. <u>Everything rests</u>*

on the institution of the family. When you start to mess with it, things happen." Remember that Dobson is the Founder of Focus on the Family and the Family Research Council and is the man Time magazine once called "the nation's most influential evangelical leader, and has served on government advisory panels by invitation of presidents and attorney generals. It is all about a man having dominion over a wife and raising children to be proper Christians and propagate the same over-and-over-and-over again. Remember, Christian Reconstruction and Dominionism view the family as one of the God ordained institutions to govern, thus the proper family makeup is imperative.

It is amazing how time-and-again the Religious Right states that this country is to be grounded in the family institution, not in the institution of democracy that is to represent the people. During the Cold War, the phrase "One nation under God" was added to the pledge of allegiance claiming that a particular faith was the greatest strength of the nation, and not democracy. The Religious Right has also used the traditional family as their flag to wave as a core value that glues America together. Anything short of that, or that is viewed as challenging that premise, is the height of evil.

They must be converting the children

As was mentioned previously, in the Religious Right the prevalent mindset is that children are spoils in the war, and that they must be won to carry the Religious Right culture and mindset forward in the future. Since a gay couple can't have kids through procreation in usual ways, and since they believe a gay person is not born gay, they must focus on converting people – particularly children. Children are the spoils and the Religious Right and gays must be fighting over the same commodity.

> *"I say this is a myth because the people whose job it is to know these things say it is a myth – they've proved it. The American Psychological Association says 'homosexual men are not more likely to sexually abuse children than heterosexual men are.' Quote 'no specific psychosocial or family dynamic cause for*

homosexuality has been identified, including histories of childhood sexual abuse.'

That, of course, does not stop anti-gay activists from making that assertion – that gay people are out to recruit kids, making that assertion over-and-over again. Jerry Falwell telling supporters of his Old Time Gospel Hour by direct mail in 1981 that, quote, 'Please remember homosexuals do not reproduce, they recruit! And, many of them are after my children and your children.' Senator Jessie Helms of North Carolina pushing for years for anti-gay restrictions in federal education law because the homosexuals are out to recruit in the schools."

The David Bahati Interview, *The Rachel Maddow Show*, <u>MSNBC</u>, December 8 2010.

The myth of converting children to be gay completely rests on the idea that people are not born gay, so how else do gay people keep springing up? They must be *converting people* to a gay lifestyle, of course. But if you should believe that people are born gay, then you have no need whatsoever to recruit, because there will always be gay people. The Religious Right worries about growth in numbers, spreading and ensuring that more and more children are raised with extremist Religious Right views. Using that logic as a model, gay people must be equally obsessed with children also, and contending for the same children. The Religious Right goes even further, to legislatively ensure that gay couples don't have kids; they sponsor legislation to ban them from adopting, while the Religious Right has "Wait No More" Adoption Conferences to spur proper Religious Right families to adopt.

<u>Same sex marriage debate</u>

As for same sex marriage, the Religious Right fights incredibly hard to say this isn't about civil rights but a moral institution being sullied; the same thing was said about inter-racial marriage not very long ago. The Religious Right holds that they have to protect a holy sacrament from being forever desecrated. Did you know that going down to Town Hall to get that marriage license was such a holy act? Which brings up the idea that a civil licensing process is being regulated by religion. What about separation of church and state? If a particular church doesn't agree with same sex marriage, then they are free to not perform any same sex marriage ceremonies, but rather, they are dictating to everyone else what is legitimate in a civil issue.

So long as gay or lesbian couples aren't allowed "marriage" then they are second (even third or fourth) class citizens. The Religious Right is protecting that ideal template of the family we saw with Quiverfull.

Even the bone thrown out of civil unions is still creating an inferior class. Civil unions are being publicized as being "equal" to marriage in the rights they secure for couples, yet *separate* in order to protect the institution of marriage. This sounds exactly like the "separate but equal" segregation of blacks until 1954 when the Supreme Court struck down that law in the Brown vs. Board of Education.

> *"Making your marriage sacred should be between you and your goddy thing. Making your union legal, on the other hand, should be between you and state-guaranteed legal and human rights."* Terry J Allen, "Forget Marriage – Civil Unions for All", *In These Times*, February 12, 2009.

This is why the fight against same sex marriage is really a forced lesser-class citizenry, because the Quiverfull template of a family is not followed. How long will it be before common law couples are similarly treated?

Reflect on David, who was known as the "man after God's own heart," and consider what sort of traditional family values and marriage he presented? David had multiple wives; he sent a man to his death to take his wife; one of David's sons raped his own sister, and another son avenged her rape. Then there is Solomon, one of David's sons who somehow avoided the family drama. Solomon was allowed the honor of building the Temple in Jerusalem, that David never did, and he had about seven hundred wives and a reported three hundred concubines.

Excuses are made for Solomon's bad family example by saying these thousand relationships were just political liaisons with surrounding nations to keep peace. Intermarriage with other cultures was strictly forbidden, even for international relationships, because other cultures had different religions and might tempt the Hebrews to worship other Gods. Solomon is violating that directive, and yet he is awarded the title of wisest man, essentially rewarding this horrifying example of traditional family values. Thus, how important are those traditional family values, when David and Solomon were such bad examples? This seems obvious.

Even Abraham fathered another nation with his female servant, because having a baby was more important than being monogamous in his marriage. But, Abraham had already passed his wife off as his sister when they were in Egypt to keep the Pharaoh from killing him to have Sarah. Are those traditional family values which are the foundation and bedrock the modern family must build upon?

When did the church become involved in marriage, anyway? It wasn't until the Council of Trent in the year 1563, that the Catholic Church declared marriage a spiritual sacrament. Marriage existed in non-Judaic cultures long before Christianity. It is the Religious Right claiming that the Judeo-Christian God somehow created this perfect idea, and it is the church's construct and that they must preserve intact.

We do know that when the church started interjecting itself into marriage customs, the more powerful the church became in Europe. But now we see the Religious Right dictating to everyone what a marriage is and is not, and what is acceptable and what is not. We are so close to Calvin's Geneva in 1500s, where home-visits determine how moral our personal lives are. Can your personal life pass the test?

> *"'Traditional' marriage used to be a business contract between families. It legitimized procreative sex and formalized property and inheritance. It was often polygamous* [multiple spouses] *and included child spouses. Men's conjugal rights included rape and the rule of thumb – the right to beat a wife with a stick no thicker than his thumb."* Terry J Allen, "Forget Marriage – Civil Unions for All", *In These Times*, February 12, 2009.

Which version of *traditional family* are we talking about here? The Right likes to use catch phrases and terms that can mean different things to different people that make it easy to obscure what they actually intend.

Colorado State Senator Scott Renfroe quoted Leviticus on the State floor on February 24, 2009, in a debate over a bill to provide health insurance to state employee's domestic partners. *"He called such relationships a sin, equal in some sense to murder and adultery, and noted one Bible passage says homosexuality is punishable by death. 'Homosexuality is seen as a violation of this **natural creative order**, and it is an offense to God,' Renfroe said. '... When we create laws that go against what biblically we are supposed to stand for, I think we are allowing to go forward a sin that should not be treated by government as something that is legal. We are taking sins and making them legally OK.'"* John Ingold, "State Senate Backs Partner Benefits", *Denver Post*, February 24, 2009. There is absolutely no concept of separation of church and state in that statement, nor of a segment of tax-paying citizens being persecuted.

We have Bible passages as the basis for who gets health insurance coverage and who does not, as evidenced by a state senate debate. Where is the separation of church and state? Mr. Renfroe brings us back to Genesis, with women multiplying and staying in their places, with his reference to the "creative order." Mr. Renfroe further stated that women were created to be *helpers* of men and had the audacity to refer to the Leviticus quote that most Religious Right won't say publicly because it doesn't strike the proper marketing tone, even if they personally accept that quote. The Bible quote referenced is Leviticus 20:13 *"If a man lies with a man as one lies with a woman, both of them have done what is detestable. They must be put to death; their blood will be on their own heads."*

That murderous directive doesn't bring visions of *Leave It To Beaver* at all, so it isn't often used. Which brings up the question, does the Religious Right feel they are gaining enough support so that they can begin to be more bold? The boiling a frog, or the creeping normalcy example is apropos here. Are the American people getting so used to politics and religious extremism cohabiting that they don't blink an eye when a politician makes reference to a Bible passage commanding murder of a segment of society? Just how close is the U.S. to introducing a kill-the-gays legislation like the one the Religious Right helped David Bahati introduce in Uganda?

Demonizing of gays

True to the propaganda techniques of the Religious Right – and their own us-versus-them mentality, gay people become the epitome of evil personified, and evil is ascribed to them without the Religious Right admitting that the heart of the problem is women's role. They paint gay people as a vile enemy to the nation, just like feminists, because of a perception of challenges to the family template they insist upon.

The Religious Right consider gays and lesbians not as human beings who love their parents and brothers and sisters, not as valiant service men and women who fight for their country (thus the repealing of don't ask, don't tell controversy), not as brave police-men and women, nor as self sacrificing firefighters, or hardworking medical professionals, etc. The Religious Right continues to portray gays and lesbians as subhuman and evil personified, who plot to convert youth to their way of life.

Recently Oklahoma Representative Sally Kern (wife of a Baptist Pastor) stated in a speech, *"homosexuality is a bigger threat to this country than terrorism."* Of course her Religious Right point of view being expressed in a political speech, at tax payer expense, was that gay and lesbian people are destroying the fabric of everything good and pure in the U.S. This attitude is evidence of how all gay or lesbian people must be viewed as against everything good and American, rather than tax-paying equal citizens, or victims of prejudice, rather than responsible citizens fighting in the military, working as doctors, or emergency professionals, and responsibly contributing to our nation and society.

If a state representative can give a speech claiming gay and lesbian citizens are a worse threat to this nation than terrorists, how long before they are sent to jail and it is somehow justified by the increasingly Religious Right controlled government as preserving America from its enemies?

"It's much easier to point a finger at a group or several groups of people than it is to look at the complex reasons a society might fail. It's the same reason Americans blame undocumented immigrants for a (perceived) lack of jobs. Scapegoating happens when those with a bit of power can blame systemic social problems on groups that are already socially disenfranchised in order to whip up nationalist sentiment." Dr. C.J. Pascoe, email interview with author, 2008.

This is classic Religious Right rhetoric. First, they proceed on the assumption that they have the monopoly on virtue and all that is wholesome and good, then they pass judgment on a group of people and demonize them, and put words in their mouths for a scare tactic.

"The Religious Right's constant need for money all but guarantees a steady stream of anti-gay rhetoric. Thus, Kennedy, Dobson and other Religious Right leaders, who refrain from using words like 'pervert' and often speak of loving homosexuals while hating their sin, may claim to have a kinder and gentler attitude toward gays – all while continuing to incite their members' fears to raise funds.

Many gay activists are not impressed by some Religious Right leaders' claims of 'love the sinner, hate the sin.'

'These letters create a vicious atmosphere,' says Wayne Besen, associate director of communications for the Human Rights Campaign (HRC), a leading gay rights group in Washington. 'We all know about Matthew Shepard [a young gay man who was beaten to death in Wyoming last year]. The Religious Right has created a climate of fear, and one of the ways they do that is through their direct-mail campaigns. They keep ratcheting up the rhetoric. They will do what it takes to fill their coffers. Unfortunately, it's also filling coffins.'" Rob Boston, "How Jerry Falwell, Pat Robertson And Other Religious Right Leaders Use Gay-Bashing To Fill Their Coffers And Rally Their Troops", *Church & State*, October 1999.

Utah State Senator Chris Buttars is spreading the same derisive and fear-promoting opinions in his taxpayer-supported role. He has already been surrounded by accusations of racism and, not surprisingly, has attacked gay and lesbian citizens as well. Those two stances seem to go together quite often. The Salt Lake Tribune on February 18, 2009, reported that Buttars called the gay rights movement "probably the greatest threat to America," and likened gay rights activists to Muslim radicals in attempts to further demonize a segment of tax paying society. The Salt Lake Tribune further reported: *"Buttars' latest remarks come from an interview with documentary filmmaker Reed Cowan that aired on ABC 4 this week. Buttars told Cowan the lesbian, gay, bisexual and transgender (LGBT) community doesn't want 'equality, they want superiority.' 'It's the beginning of the end,' the West Jordan Republican said. 'Oh, it's worse than that. Sure. Sodom and Gomorrah was localized. This is worldwide.'"*

The September 22, 2011, Republican candidate debate witnessed the audience booing at a military member currently serving in Iraq, his life on the line defending the country that is booing him, because he is gay. None of the candidates showed leadership in the situation nor thanked the brave soldier for his service. Respect for our armed forces only goes so far, as well.

Gay rights, human rights

Martin Luther King Jr.'s widow, Corretta Scott King, has bravely fought for gay rights because she clearly saw it as a civil rights issue, just as her husband fought for civil rights for black Americans. Prejudice is prejudice, no matter how ancient it is, and this one is ancient. This prejudice goes way back to the Bible's Middle Eastern roots. The Religious Right mouthpieces in the wake of California's Proposition 8 claimed that civil rights leaders do not see gay rights as civil rights – they conveniently ignore that Corretta Scott King repeatedly spoke out in support of gay rights. The same people ignore that Julian Bond (NAACP Director and Sr Vice President) and Roger Vann (NAACP Vice President of Field and Membership) both spoke in support of gay rights as a civil rights issue at the October 11, 2009, National Equality March in Washington

D.C.

In December 2008, the United Nations presented a gay rights declaration (based on the Universal Declaration of Human Rights) attempting: "to ensure that sexual orientation or gender identity may under no circumstances be the basis for criminal penalties, in particular executions, arrests or detention" to its member nations. *"The signatories 'condemn the human rights violations based on sexual orientation or gender identity wherever they occur,' especially 'the use of the death penalty on this ground,' as well as their 'arbitrary arrest or detention and deprivation of economic, social and cultural rights, including the right to health."* "Gay rights declaration is presented to the U.N". *France 24 International News,* December 19, 2008. In an interesting twist, Israel signed the declaration but Arab nations, the U.S., and the Vatican, all came out against it.

So the US is standing tall with its perceived enemies in the war against basic human rights for all citizens. Notice how the U.S. won't stand up for its own tax paying citizen's rights against executions, arbitrary arrests, or even the simple right to health when Israel and 66 other countries did. This is the ugly truth of the Religious Right's agenda towards gays that they attempt to hide, the goal of lower class citizenship for a sector of Americans. Incidentally, that same Old Testament passage that is often used by the Right in Leviticus 20:13 specifically states that any gay man shall be put to death and his blood is on his own hands. So if the Religious Right gets their agenda with the Supreme Court (and the entire court system) pushed through that the Bible is the rule-book, then we really will see executions of citizens because of who they love. Does that shock you? I hope so. Does that remind you of radical fascist regimes? It does to many people, and it most certainly should shock every reader.

Religious Right proponents applaud the Sally Kerns, Falwells, and Dobsons of the world for *speaking the truth,* and they encourage those who would hurt, maim, and even kill people who are different from themselves and their view of how all people should be. Is this Christianity at its best and finest, or is it an extremist distortion? I would like to believe that there are Christians out there who would rather express the love of God, and leave judgment to God.

New look at Sodom and Gomorrah

Why were Sodom and Gomorrah really annihilated, according to the biblical story? That example is quite often used in arguments against gays, but what is the real story?

> Ezekiel 16:49-50
>
> *"Now this was the sin of your sister Sodom: She and her daughters were arrogant, overfed and unconcerned; they did not help the poor and needy. They were haughty and did detestable things before me. Therefore I did away with them as you have seen."*

In the Ezekial quote, many claim that the "detestable things" (other versions translate it "abominations") being done were gay and lesbian acts. The term detestable or abomination is open to interpretation and very subjective. To me detestable things would be animal sacrifices, but that includes the entire Old Testament priesthood of Israel, and is the basis for Jesus' sacrifice on the cross by offering a blood sacrifice to atone for sin. Thus you can interpret that Ezekiel verse as saying anything you want it to say under that sweeping term "detestable". But what is not blatantly said, is what shouts the loudest. There is a list of very specific sins here, but gay or lesbian acts are conspicuously absent. That omission is significant. If gays were so responsible for Sodom and Gomorrah, wouldn't they have warranted a specific mention with the arrogant and haughty who are called out?

A theme of the modern Religious Right is a constant hammer that God will punish gay and lesbian behavior.

The next time you hear Sodom and Gomorrah mentioned as a response from God towards gay people, just remember, the Bible doesn't actually say that. That is strictly a matter of forcing what the Religious Right wants Ezekiel 16 passage to say, when it does not. Nowhere in the Bible does it say that Sodom and Gomorrah was annihilated because of gays.

<u>Take With You From This Chapter</u>

➤ The issue of gays is directly tied to the woman's biblical role. If you can reconcile modern women having careers and being more than just baby-maker and housewives, then you can find peace with gays.

➤ The war over children as a prize in the culture war creates the mindset that gays are battling for the same children as the church to convert them. If you believe gay people are born that way, you see how ludicrous the myth of gays converting innocent youth is.

➤ The same sex marriage debate is about the Quiverfull template as the only valid family structure.

➤ When you look at Sodom and Gomorrah, it is not about gays.

Section 6: The Past and the Future

In this section:

History is a great teacher. Examples from the past are discussed to show their lessons for us today in the struggle over separation of church and state. Then, we look to what each reader can do to ensure our democracy survives with a bright future.

Chapter 26
The Soap Opera of Church in History

<u>What to Expect From this Chapter</u>

➢ Highlights of key times in history that demonstrate damaging a mixing of religion and politics has been.

"Those who cannot remember the past are condemned to repeat it." George Santayana.

The Religious Right maneuvering to gain political and legal control of the United States is not a new idea. History will give an excellent basis to judge how sound the separation of church and state premise is. Most likely our Founding Fathers had many of the lessons of the past in mind when approaching how to form "a more perfect union" in terms of this country.

"A grim pattern is visible in history. When religion is the ruling force in a society, it produces horror. The stronger the supernatural beliefs, the worse the inhumanity. A culture dominated by intense faith invariably is cruel to people who don't share the faith – and sometimes to many who do.

When religion was all-powerful in Europe, it produced the epic bloodbath of the Crusades, the torture chambers of the Inquisition, mass extermination of 'heretics,' hundreds of massacres of Jews, and 300 years of witch burnings. The split of the Reformation loosed a torrent of hate that took millions of lives in a dozen religious wars. The 'Age of Faith' was an age of holy slaughter. When religion gradually ceased to control daily life, the concept of human rights and personal freedoms took root....

Paradoxically, in spite of its gory record, religion is almost universally deemed a power for good, a generator of compassion. Former President Ronald Reagan called it 'the bedrock of moral order.' President George Bush said it gives people 'the character they need to get through life.'

343

Obviously, religion has a Jekyll-and-Hyde nature – with Dr. Jekyll always in the spotlight, and Mr. Hyde little noticed....

Harvard theologian Krister Stendahl commented: 'Religion is a very dangerous thing. These are enormous powers we are dealing with.'" James A. Haught, *Holy Horrors*, Prometheus Books, 1990.

We must look at the lessons that the dark side of history has for us about uniting religion and politics. To ignore what has happened repeatedly in the past is to invite the same horrors to take place again, and invariably we will look back and wonder how it happened to us all over again.

At this point we should take a quick overview of how the church and politics have been a lethal combination in our past.

From persecution to Roman acceptance

The early church started political manipulations to advance from the underdog to the head of the big dog. They wanted to gain a foothold in the Roman Empire. They ultimately become the official religion of the Roman Empire, in the Fourth Century. These manipulations t may have begun as self-preservation in light of the persecutions of the early church and believers, but they became more than self defense once they entered the arena of politics.

"Christianity owes its large membership to the political maneuvering of orthodox Christians. They succeeded in turning Christianity from an abhorred minor cult into the official religion of the Roman Empire. Their goal was to create what Bishop Irenaeus called 'the catholic church dispersed throughout the whole world, even to the ends of the earth.' To that end, they used nearly any means. They revised Christian writings and adapted their principles to make Christianity more acceptable. They pandered to Roman authorities. They incorporated elements of paganism. Orthodox Christianity appealed to the government, not as a religion that would encourage enlightenment or spirituality, but rather as one that would bring order and conformity to the faltering empire.

The Roman government in turn granted orthodox Christians unprecedented privilege, enabling the Christian church to become the very sort of authoritarian power that Jesus had resisted...

By 435 a law threatened any heretic in the Roman Empire with death. Judaism remained the only other legally recognized religion. Yet, Jews were isolated as much as possible, with intermarriage between Jew and Christian carrying the same penalty as adultery; the woman would be executed. The Church had triumphed. The belief in but one face of God had led to the legal enforcement of but one religion...It was through political maneuvering that the Church won its standing as the official religion of the Roman Empire and the accompanying secular power and privilege." Helen Ellerbe, *The Dark Side of Christian History*, Morningstar Books, 1995.

Here we see Christianity's early entry into politics, that began centuries of political involvement. Whether it was a matter of survival in that ancient world or not, we see the same fight to gain political influence and become the one and only official religion of the United States. Déjà vu? No, just history repeating. There are many differences between then and now. In those days religions warred for equal footing or superiority in the political scene because of discrimination. In the U.S. we are all to have the same liberty to follow the spiritual path of our choosing and to be treated equally, thus removing such a need for political superiority.

The Dark Ages (476-1000 ACE)

This era is called the Dark Ages because the Roman Empire had fallen, but most scholars refer to it as the Early Middle Ages now. Some historians have blamed the Roman Empire's fall on the Church and its ever increasing influence. The Church, however, views this time-period as 600 years of degenerate and godless peoples.

"The Middle Ages have been known as the Age of Faith because Christianity did much to shape the hearts and minds of the people. In addition, the church as an institution dominated life in medieval times. At the top of its game under

Pope Innocent III, the church claimed its supremacy as the power on earth.

The church used several methods to hold this power. First, through its sacraments, it held the key to the people's spiritual salvation. Second, through its courts, it acted as a judicial power. It also gained spiritual and political power through the reform that swept across Europe. And finally, the church maintained political power with the people, as was evidenced in the launching of the Crusades...

Church courts tried both criminal and civil cases involving the clergy and even the people...The church courts made decisions about marriage, divorce, and wills. On other issues, church decisions were accepted as law by Christian lords and monarchs and thus enforced by public officials." Timothy C Hall, *The Complete Idiot's Guide to the Middle Ages*, Alpha, 2009.

Until recently, the Dark Ages were viewed as a cultural void and the church was blamed for its spiritual and political choke-hold, and prevalent superstition throughout Europe. Superstition was rampant; everything was of the Devil, and fear ruled. The only vestiges of any learning were reserved for men, typically in monasteries. Thus, this is known as the Monastic era where the only learning was primarily in Latin and only for men. But notice from the prior quote how the church acted as the judicial and political power, much like the Religious Right is currently gaining control of the courts and politics now. The control over a person's salvation was also what the Catholic Church exercised to control the people, and was similar to the manipulation of determining how a good, proper, or dedicated Christian should vote.

"The Church had a devastating impact upon society. As the Church assumed leadership, activity in the fields of medicine, technology, science, education, history, art and commerce all but collapsed. Europe entered the Dark Ages. Although the Church amassed immense wealth during these centuries, most of what defines civilization disappeared...[Likewise] the Church had devastating impact upon artistic expression. According to orthodox Christianity,

art should enhance and promote Christian values; it should not serve simply as an individual's creative exploration and expression." Helen Ellerbe, *The Dark Side of Christian History,* Morningstar Books, 1995.

For our purposes, this illustrates what happens when a church, any church, is also the law of the land. What happens when a religion, even Christian, makes the laws, is the jury, sets the political agendas and controls the culture? The mentality of that time-period that set back science and the arts until the Renaissance, was that everything in life must "enhance or promote Christian values." We see the same mentality at work today with the Seven Mountains Mandate.

That is what the Religious Right would like to go back to, biblical or approved ideals only, in all media, medicine, technology, science, education, history, and art. Thus the Religious Right attains the power of a dictatorship over every aspect of life and culture to control thoughts and ideals. The Dark Ages are also important because of the struggles between the kings and minor royals clashing with the church over issues of how to run the lands.

"But tension grew between secular rulers and the church in jurisdiction. One of the most disputed issues was whether secular or church court would try members of the clergy charged with criminal offenses. As in the case of Henry II and Thomas Becket, this issue created bitter struggles between church and state that still resonate into the twenty-first century." Timothy C Hall, *The Complete Idiot's Guide to the Middle Ages,* Alpha, 2009.

At this point in history, the Catholic Church was the power-broker and the only authorized expression of faith. As part of the Catholic Church's ritual structure, salvation and spiritual blessings were administered through sacraments such as baptism, communion, and last rites to the dying. These sacraments administered to the everyday people were used as political bargaining chips. What do you think simple rural people would do if they were denied spiritual blessings and risked damnation because their Duke had angered the Church? Uprisings were a convenient way to strong-arm the local ruling powers.

"Only through the sacraments were people able to obtain salvation in the next life. Generally, people could be denied the sacraments for doing evil acts or disobeying the church, and those denied the sacraments were shunned in this life by the people and in the next by God. The church used the threat of excommunication or being outside of the sacramental life to maintain social order and public morality. It also became a powerful weapon in the hands of church leadership in political struggles. Many powerful lords and kings were forced to yield to the church politically when threatened with the penalty of excommunication or, even worse, interdict, in which no one living in their territory could participate in the sacraments of the church." Timothy C Hall, *The Complete Idiot's Guide to the Middle Ages,* Alpha, 2009.

The Dark Ages is a pristine example of mixing church and state. Medicine, technology, science, education, history, art, and commerce nearly died under the iron grip of the church leadership interfering in the rule of the lands. Today we see threats of large numbers of hospitals being shut down if politicians don't vote and do as the Religious Right wants them to. We have the Religious Right going for federal money for social programs that can also be used as more bargaining chips to exercise power, similarly to the abuse of power in the past. We really have *been there and done that,* and we don't need to go there again.

The Burning Times

The atmosphere coming out of the Dark Ages was of witch-hunts. Reportedly eighty percent more women were accused of witchcraft, and eighty five percent more executed than men, although those statistics vary by country. Anne Llewellyn Barstow in her book *Witchcraze: A New History of the European Witch Hunts,* by Pandora, claims a great fear of women as inherently evil (women are susceptible to Satan since the Garden) created a prejudice against women, even when the charges against them were identical to those against men.

"The Reformation did not convert the people of Europe to orthodox Christianity through preaching and catechisms alone. It was the 300 year period of witch-hunting from the fifteenth to the eighteenth century ...that ensured the European abandonment of the belief in magic. The Church created the elaborate concept of devil worship and then, used the persecution of it to wipe out dissent, subordinate the individual to authoritarian control, and openly denigrate women." Helen Ellerbe, *The Dark Side of Christian History,* Morningstar Books, 1995

It may seem a bit extreme to attribute the horrific European witch-hunts with all those ulterior motives. But yet, this is an undeniable part of history, and the rampant superstition plus the headhunting paranoia or fear was prevalent in every town and family. This is very similar to the Religious Right's blaming every catastrophe, and even the economic collapse brought on by Wall Street greed, to sin, abortion, gays, feminism, humanism, etc. This is creating the same atmosphere, yet again, where neighbors could be your enemies and law-abiding citizens are called a greater threat than terrorists because their thoughts or deeds are not what the church sanctions.

"The number of victims is estimated widely from 100,000 to 2 million...

In 1484 Pope Innocent VIII issued a bull declaring the absolute reality of witches – thus it became heresy to doubt their existence...

Soon afterward, two Dominican inquisitors, Jakob Sprenger and Heinrich Kramer, published their infamous Malleus Maleficarum (Witches' Hammer) outlining a lurid litany of magical acts performed by witches and their imps, familiars, phantoms, demons, succubi, and incubi. It described how the evil women blighted crops, devoured children, caused disease, and wrought spells. The book was filled with witches' sexual acts and portrayed women as treacherous and contemptible. 'All witchcraft comes from carnal lust, which is in women insatiable,' they wrote. Modern psychology easily perceives the sexual neurosis of these priests – yet for centuries their book was the official manual used by inquisitors sending women to horrible deaths." James A. Haught, *Holy Horrors*, Prometheus Books, 1999.

We even see a resurgence of the Religious Right obsession with demons and witches. We see in our modern twenty-first century the burning of Harry Potter books by people such as Pastor Jack Brock of Christ Community Church in southern New Mexico claiming *"'Behind that innocent face is the power of satanic darkness,' he said. 'Harry Potter is the devil and he is destroying people.'"* (BBC News: Entertainment, "'Satanic' Harry Potter Books Burnt," December 31, 2001). Then we see Pope Benedict XVI ordering exorcist squads (Nick Pisa, 'Pope's exorcist squads will wage war on Satan," *Daily Mail,* December 29, 2007.) Before that it was the game Dungeons and Dragons that was evil, and back-masking (the recording of a message that is audible when a music track is played backwards, believed to be satanic messages) in rock music.

As recently as October, 2009, we saw Pat Robertson claiming on his CBN website that all Halloween candy purchased had time-released curses placed on the sugary treats by witches. When I was involved with the Religious Right, I can remember back as far as the 1980s the urban legends eagerly spread that witches prayed daily to Satan for all Christians to lose faith or to die. Such scare tactics were regularly circulated and fervently believed. Never mind that modern witches are aligned with Wicca, who don't include Satan anywhere in their theology. How about Sarah Palin being prayed over in her church to prevent the witches from stopping her success. Pastor Thomas Muthee, who prayed over her, once led a witch hunt in Kiambu Kenya, where he directed the deliberate persecution of a local woman, blaming her for accidents and any problems in town. It is interesting to note that this throwback to the middle ages is funded by America Religious Right money. The ancient superstitious and chauvinistic book *Malleus Maleficarum,* from the Dark Ages has returned. One can hear that title now being mentioned in Religious Right circles. Yes, it does sound like we are reverting back to dark and superstition-filled times, doesn't it?

But, the fact remains that persecutions took place of anything that didn't fall strictly in line with the Church teachings, and made one suspect. This illustrates how lethal the unification of a religion with the government can be, when a religion can be the law-maker, police, judge, and jury.

The Crusades

The Crusades took place during the time period known as the Middle Ages, when the struggle between the established church and kings for control was accelerating.

"During the period from 1050 to 1300 there took place a series of conflicts between kings and popes which merged into one another in such a fashion that we may regard them all as changing aspects of one long, continuing crisis...

We may be disconcerted by the pretensions of popes who tried to depose emperors or of emperors who expected to appoint bishops, but in fact, a theocratic ordering of society is a very common pattern of human government...The most common solution has been to endow the ruler who controls the physical apparatus of state coercion with a sacral role also as head and symbol of the people's religion." Brian Tierney, *The Crisis of Church and State 1050-1300,* Prentice Hall, 1980.

A few items from the preceding quote need to be highlighted. First, it was a time of Popes and the church struggling for power over the people, who were the pawns, against the worldly rulers. This struggle is seen as a continuation of the primitive systems in which the ruler was somehow special in the Divine's eyes. In the Middle Ages, this was seen in either the Pope or the kings/emperors' assertions that they were directed by God, and were better qualified to lead the people.

We see today that the Religious Right has as a primary goal to remove any separation from their controlling the government and the prevailing culture. But this history lesson says it would be perhaps the worst thing to happen to America. It was in this political tug-of-war that the Crusades took place. Most people have at least heard of the Crusades, but fewer have heard of the massacre of Jews in Germany by

Crusaders on their way to Jerusalem. One Crusader group decided to go through Mainz, Worms, and various additional German cities, killing Jews – including the women and children, whom they considered as bad as the Islamic infidels they were to kill in Jerusalem. The label given to Jews, as Christ-Killers, fueled that rampage, and that was all before Hitler and his extermination camps. We have the example of repeatedly labeling Dr. Tiller as a baby-killer, until somebody murdered him in cold blood, which parallels the massacres in Germany by Crusaders. This is what happens when religious extremism runs unchecked. The Crusaders were told that whatever vile, inhuman acts they carried out were forgiven beforehand by the church, and were not sins.

...Five horrible centuries of religious persecution – from 1100s through the 1500s – decimated the Jewish population of Western Europe. Vast numbers were killed. (Historian Dagobert Runes estimated that 3.5 million Jews died at the hands of Christians during the long epoch of religious persecution.)" James A Haught, *Holy Horrors*, Prometheus Books, 1990.

The medieval Crusade was essentially a Christian holy war. A Crusade would be sanctioned by the Pope or a church leader, and conducted against groups seen as enemies of Christendom. Historians have also recognized campaigns against heretics, Pagans and Muslims in Europe as Crusades.

Historians have numbered eight expeditions to the Holy Land, though some lump the 7th and 8th together for a total of seven crusades. However, there was a steady stream of armies from Europe to the Holy Land, so it is nearly impossible to distinguish separate campaigns.

Not content with just rooting out Christian heretics by launching a bloody crusade against the Cathars in southern France, Pope Innocent III (1160-1216) declared himself *ruler of the world*. He sacked Constantinople and massacred every Muslim he could who was encountered.

Today, we have a holy war with Dominionism fighting to take over every area of

American life and ideas. As we have covered in previous chapters, they feel they must win at all costs. This has bred the *higher law* excuse that has much in common with the Crusaders. The Crusades are a lesson in extremism and how that *higher law* becomes bloody and proliferates.

The Jesuit Order

The Jesuits have had mystery associated with them, and thus historians have had differing interpretations as to their intentions. But one thing we can learn from them is how education has been a long-standing religious strategy to convert and combat the populace.

According to Jonathan Wright's book *God's Soldiers: Adventure, Politics, Intrigue, and Power – A History of the Jesuits,* when Ignatius of Loyola founded the Jesuits (or the Society of Jesus) in 1534, his initial goal was only to lead a handful of like-minded students at the University of Paris on a pilgrimage to the Holy Land to convert the Muslims, a peaceful Crusade, if you will. Loyola also evolved the ministry to reclaim Europe from Protestants in the name of and for the Catholic Church. By the time of his death in 1556, approximately one thousand priests were Jesuits. As part of their determined efforts to reclaim Protestant Europe for the Catholic Church, they built schools and colleges in nearly every important city; by the mid-eighteenth century, they had established more than 650 educational institutions.

This corresponds with the Religious Right's adamant goal for schools to be indoctrination centers. Whereas Ignatius was combating the spread of Protestants throughout Europe by building Catholic schools, the Religious Right seeks to spread their worldview to combat every competing thought or law. Schools have been used before for these purposes, and it has proven time and again to be important to the church's agenda, in 1534.

King makers

In times past, a church official could even affect *who* was crowned. In the book, *A*

Short History of the Papacy in the Middle Ages, Walter Ullman details how Pope Innocent III worked hard to expand the power of the Pope to control even the kings. He took interest in Germany's successor, and felt he had a control over the matter. He felt that the Roman Catholic Church had sway over all matters of government and society, and thus who was crowned king also fell under his jurisdiction, essentially worldwide.

The Archbishop of Canterbury, who is the senior church official in England, still crowns the king or queen in Westminster Abbey, although today his participation is more ceremonial than a sign of approval. Whoever takes the throne of England is to oversee the Church of England, which has been the case since a national church was established.

This is the level of power that the Religious Right seeks, and the U.S. has never experienced anything like this, so it may be hard to comprehend just how oppressive such church control is.

Henry VIII (1491–1547)

Henry VIII. is probably the most infamous King of England. The King had no legitimate sons due to the death in infancy of all Catherine of Aragon's children, except for his daughter Mary. Henry VIII wanted a divorce, reportedly so he could remarry for the sake of providing a legitimate male heir to the throne. The Reformation had made its way to England and the king saw a chance to escape from the Pope and the church's hard-line against divorce.

Henry flexed his royal muscles and executed several monks who openly disagreed with his divorce of Catherine of Aragon. The most famous opponent of Henry's desire to divorce and remarry was Sir Thomas More, Henry's former Lord Chancellor, who was reportedly tried on false charges. Sir Thomas More vehemently opposed the Protestant church, Henry's desire was to divorce, remarry, and break from the one true Catholic faith.

For a large majority of King Henry's reign he had to deal with the Pope and devout church followers who made an extreme issue of his divorcing – yet didn't seem to have an issue with his beheading of two of his wives. It was a matter of doctrinal integrity, although murdering one's wife was not an issue. The Church of England was bolstered by these developments and began to spread widely throughout the nation. This is the same church of England from which the Pilgrims would later flee, in 1619.

Edward VI, Henry's only legitimate son, took the throne and continued to encourage the Church of England, that was a result of the Protestant Reformation in England. It became more a State church, with the language of public services specified.

Today, a key issue is abortion, and we see no end of political turmoil over it, just as divorce was the no-compromise issue of Henry VIII's day. Henry accomplished much during his reign, but few remember anything else except the controversy with the church over divorce. Two women's lives were sacrificed without much comparative notice because of the rigid stance of the church against the government of that day. We could learn much from this power struggle from the 1500s, and how destructive it was.

Lady Jane Grey (1553)

Jane's accession to the throne was because of the express wishes of Edward VI's will. Edward's will naming Lady Jane Grey to take the throne was purely to keep a Protestant ruling the nation, and to keep the rightful heir (Mary, a staunch Catholic) out. This breached the laws of England under the Third Success Act. Mary Tudor, Henry VIII's oldest daughter, was the legitimate and rightful heir to the Crown. Mary had been declared illegitimate by her father, soley to keep a Catholic from gaining the crown, which Henry strongly wanted to keep in Protestant hands. Henry had made the same claim about Mary's younger half-sister, Elizabeth, later Elizabeth I.

Jane, grandniece of Henry VIII of England, reigned as uncrowned Queen Regent of the Kingdom of England and Kingdom of Ireland for nine days, in July, 1553. This was the shortest rule of England in its history, and she was England's first female monarch. The rule of Jane, a Protestant, soon ended when the authorities abandoned their support for her as Queen when they realized Mary had won-the-day through political maneuvers. Mary subsequently had Jane executed for high treason.

355

Why is this account important? It highlights how a country's laws can be circumvented for the sake of religious posturing, and not for the good of the country. King Edward placed his niece's life in jeopardy for the sake of keeping a non-Catholic on the throne. These are the lengths and absurdity that take place when mixing political power and religious fervor. What followed was horrendous, in terms of a conflict between the Catholic and Protestant faiths.

Remember John F. Kennedy being scrutinized because he was Catholic, or Mitt Romney because he is Mormon? And there is all the controversy over whether Barrack Obama is Christian enough or not. As in the 1500s, there is attention on the wrong priorities and not what is best for the nation.

Bloody Mary

Mary Tudor, or Queen Mary I, took the throne from Lady Jane. As the oldest of two daughters of Henry VIII, she was the rightful heir. And she did exactly what Henry VIII and her half brother Edward VI feared, and returned England to Catholic rule.

As Queen, Mary was very concerned about returning her kingdom to the Catholic Church. She had England reconcile with Rome and Reginald Cardinal Pole. Edward's religious laws were abolished by Mary's first Parliament in the Statute of Repeal Act.

Mary also persuaded Parliament to repeal the Protestant religious laws passed by Henry VIII and The Revival of the Heresy Acts were passed in 1554. The persecution of Protestants earned Mary the infamous name "Bloody Mary," and Lady Jane was one of the first to be executed. There is disagreement as to the number of people put to death during Mary's five-year reign. The persecution lasted for almost four years. John Foxe estimates in his *Book of Martyrs* that 284 were executed because they were non-Catholic and refused to convert.

As we face the Religious Right's growing power and influence, the nation must focus on the policies that will ensure that the nation will flourish and prosper. But instead, we are continually dragged into abortion funding battles, marriage definition battles, and endlessly on and on they go. These social issues are the distractions that keep genuinely effective governmental policies from being enacted. Bloody Mary should be a reminder to us all about how mixing politics and religion can cause a government to degenerate.

Inquisition (1200 – 1834 ACE)

Religious leaders of the early 1200s created the Inquisition to eradicate heretics, those individuals who don't think and act the same as the ruling religious leaders. The concept was to remove anyone who was diverse, who might challenge established thinking. This is an excellent example of what happens when extremist religion rules a country, when church leaders are able to set laws and to be police, judge and jury, whether they are Christian or not.

"In the early 1200s, local bishops were empowered to identify, try, and punish heretics. When the bishops proved ineffective, traveling papal inquisitors, usually Dominican priests, were sent from Rome to conduct the purge.

Pope Innocent IV authorized torture in 1252, and the Inquisition chambers became places of terror. Accused heretics were seized and locked in cells, unable to see their families, unable to know the names of their accusers. If they didn't confess quickly, unspeakable cruelties began...

'So that the torturers would not be disturbed by the shrieking of the victim, his mouth was stuffed with cloth. Three-and-four-hour sessions of torture were nothing unusual. During the procedure the instruments were frequently sprinkled with holy water.'

...Historically, the Inquisition is divided into three phases: the medieval extermination of heretics; the Spanish Inquisition in the 1400s; and the Roman Inquisition, which began after the Reformation....

Lord Acton, himself a Catholic, wrote in the late 1800s: 'The principle of the Inquisition was murderous...The popes were not only murderers in the great style, but they also made murder a legal basis of the Christian Church and a condition of salvation.'" James Haught, *Holy Horrors*, Prometheus Books, 1990.

The Spanish Inquisition used religion to further the leaders' apparent prejudice, and became the epitome of atrocities and cruelty. *"Many Muslims and Jews had converted to Christianity and stayed in Spain, making a great contribution to its culture. But their success was resented. The king and queen decided that all non-Christians should leave Spain. They wanted to find those who had 'converted' but still followed the old religion secretly. Spain used religion as a political weapon. The pope gave permission for an Inquisition, a court that investigated heresy..."* The Kingfisher History Encyclopedia, 1999, Kingfisher Publications. pg 200.)

The Roman Inquisition during the 16th century acquired a new target: the newly non-Catholic Protestants. About 100 were burned as heretics. An index of prohibited books was drawn up that were alleged to contain heresy.

Now consider in our modern world that torture has reappeared with imprisoned suspected terrorists. Yes, we have the mentality here in America currently that is the foundation for a modern Inquisition, if the Religious Right should succeed in obtaining the full measure of political power they are striving for. Add to this already volitile mindset, the reported findings from the *Pew Forum on Religion & Public Life* are that regular church attenders are more likely not to oppose torture.

> *"The more often Americans go to church, the more likely they are to support the torture of suspected terrorists, according to a new survey.... More than half of people who attend services at least once a week -- 54 percent -- said the use of torture against suspected terrorists is 'often' or 'sometimes' justified."* "Church Going Americans More Likely to Support Torture", *Huffington Post*, May 1, 2009.

It would seem that the mindset of the old Inquisition days is seeing a revival. This is why the established laws of the land are so important, and why rights of the individual are critical. It makes the violations of individual rights the initial slide down the slippery slope to allowing such atrocities as the Inquisition. It is also why the separation of church and state is vital. Excuses for calling a group dangerous were invented, when they didn't comform to a relgious standard; that could in this nation, as well. Yet again we see why keeping the ruling of the nation and local state governments and religion separate is vital to any individiual rights.

John Calvin and Geneva (1536-1564)

Since the Dominionists hold up John Calvin and Geneva as some sort of Christian State model, it might be informative to highlight some of what took place there, so you can see what the Religious Right has in mind.

What is most relevant to our topic is how the church was integrated into the government (state) so that punishable crimes listed on the books (according to William Naphy in his book *Calvin and the Consolidation Of The Genevan Reformation*) included sexual immorality, blasphemy, holding Catholic views, religious violations in general, witchcraft, dancing, holding Anabaptist views, immorality in general, and missing church, were prescribed punishments ranging from death, jail, banishment, and fines, to a loss of rights. Schools were solely places to teach Bible theology. For the average American, Geneva doesn't seem like such a paragon of a perfect society after which to model the United States.

"In 1542 the Consistory was occupied with the establishement of good religious habits in Geneva. Thus cases involving sermon attendance, the correct recitation of the Creed and the Lord's Prayer, and, especially, the eradication of latent Catholic superstitious practices represent the majority of the cases... The majority of the cases in 1542 related to sermon attendance and irregularities in religious practices. These cases tended to involve women who often said they found it difficult to attend sermons because they had to care for the children." William G Naphy, *Calvin and the Consolidation Of The Genevan Reformation*, Westminster John Knox Press, 2003.

~ ~ ~ ~ ~ ~ ~

On the basis of charges preferred by Calvin, [Michael] Servetus was put on trial. The trial was carried on by the civil authorities, but the accusations were all based on Servetus's writings and theology. Much of the proceedings consisted of direct encounters between Servetus and Calvin himself, during which Calvin was not always fair or just. The same can be said of the civil authorities, who refused Servetus's request for counsel and kept him imprisoned under filthy and uncomfortable conditions. On October 26, he was condemned to death for decrying the doctrine of the Trinity and infant baptism, in other words, as a heretic." William Gilbert, *The Renaissance and The Reformation*, W. Gilbert, 1997.

This is what the Dominionist-influenced Religious Right is looking to as their shining example of a state controlled by the Bible and Christianity. This is not all Christians ideal, by any means, because there would be many, many Christians whose personal faith would not be good enough within an American version of Geneva. Geneva even had legal home inspections to scrutinize personal lives and ensure citizens stayed within those moral and spiritual laws. This was big, big government in everybody's business.

The Religious Right isn't openly advocating a mirror of Geneva; that isn't wise from a salesman's perspective. No, they keep insisting the U.S. is first and foremost a Christian nation built upon Christian ideals and the Bible (rewriting history), so it seems only natural to introduce more Bible-focused politicians, more laws based on biblical morality, and then a few more, until it is too late to turn back.

Pilgrims fleeing England

The pilgrims were fleeing from a country that had mixed the church and state. They were also known as Separatists because they wanted to be completely separate from the official Church of England. The Church of England felt no kindred spirit with the Separatists, claiming that they were too radical. The modern Religious Right political agenda is attempting to create a church-state bond that is exactly what the Pilgrims were escaping. So, in a sense, our country was founded not just on freedom of religion, but even more on not being regulated by a church-state.

Salem witch trials – America

In the midst of the long running Inquisition happening in Spain, America was experiencing witch-hunts.

The infamous Salem witch trials were a series of trial hearings before local magistrates and by county court trials, to prosecute people accused of witchcraft in Essex, Suffolk, and Middlesex Counties of colonial Massachusetts. These happenings have been attributed to mass hysteria.

It is estimated that approximately 150 people were arrested on witchcraft charges and imprisoned. More fell under suspicion or were reported that did not result in formal charges or jail time. Ultimately twenty-nine people were convicted of the crime of witchcraft. It is interesting to note that Dominionists and the Salem Village have something in common. Salem followed a strict Calvinist model, including their government and legal system, much like the Dominionists hold up as a shining example for a model of America. Yet again, history shows us what a bad idea it is to mix religion and government, let alone the legal system.

Ireland: advent of modern terrorism with Protestant versus Catholic.

I grew up with stories of violence in Ireland, and bombings of public places filled the news. Ireland's internal struggle began as far back as when England's King Henry VIII. created the Anglican Protestantism, in the late 1400s, and he also became the *King of Ireland*. He attempted to institute his new religion in Ireland, which sparked hundreds of years of religious fighting that saw modern terrorism born with the Catholic paramilitary Irish Republican Army (IRA) and Protestant extremists waging a war.

America saw some of this religious prejudice when John F Kennedy was scrutinized because he was Catholic. *"By 1990 the death toll from the latest two decades of Ulster's [Northern Ireland] hostilities was near 3,000."* James Haught, *Holy Horrors*, Prometheus Books, 1990.

<u>Take With You From This Chapter</u>

➤ History gives example after example of the disasters that resulted from mixing religion and politics. The examples mentioned are all of Christians intermingling with politics. America would be wise to realize they will fare no better.

Chapter 27:
Resources to get Involved

<u>What to Expect From this Chapter</u>

➤ Discussion of how you can get involved, in small and large ways, and protect the nation.

Here is the same advice for involvement that James Dobson has given Religious Right adherents. It is important to know just how involved they are, and consider how you might get involved.

"If you are among the body of concerned citizens, I urge you not to just sit there. Get out and work for what you believe. Democracy only succeeds when people get involved. Campaign for a position on the local school board. Write your representatives in Washington. Better yet, help elect congressmen and senators who ...

Serve on a hospital lay committee. Take a teacher to dinner....Warfare has always been exhausting, dangerous, and expensive. But how can we remain uninvolved when the welfare of our children and subsequent generations is on the line? That is the question of the hour." James Dobson, *Children at Risk*, Word Pub, 1990.

First you have to believe that you can make a difference. The initial step is to see how important it is for you and your family to get involved.

"A small group of thoughtful people could change the world. Indeed, it's the only thing that ever has." Margaret Mead

The second thing always to keep in mind is that you are *for* something rather than *against* something. You are for the full separation of church and state; you are for keeping recognized science taught in science classes; you are for religious liberty for all; you are for democracy and representative government. If you identify exactly what you are for rather than against, your mission remains clear and focused.

There are many small steps that you can take that will add up. Please look at the list below to start on your small steps.

"What we are seeing is when people do fight, they sometimes win, which is a really well kept secret. In all that sort of mocking of protests in glib post-modern times, sometimes they win. Especially if they are willing to do more than just go to a march once."' Naomi Klein, "Rachel Maddow Show," *MSNBC* March 8, 2011.

Organizations to get involved with

This step is small, it could be just signing up for a free newsletter and staying informed. You could volunteer if there is a local branch, or donate whatever you can afford.

Americans United for Separation of Church and State

http://www.au.org | email: americansunited@au.org

518 C Street NE, Washington, DC 20002

Phone: (202) 466-3234 | fax: (202) 466-2587

Military Religious Freedom Foundation

13170-B Central Avenue, SE, Suite 255, Albuquerque, NM 87123

http://www.militaryreligiousfreedom.org | email: info@militaryreligiousfreedom.org

800-736-5109

Interfaith Alliance

1212 New York Ave, NW, Suite 1250, Washington, DC 20005

Tel: (202) 238-3300 | Toll-Free: (800) 510-0969 | Fax: (202) 238-3301

** There are many branches of the Interfaith Alliance in states across the U.S. Check to see if there is one near you and sign up for their newsletter.

Religious Coalition for Reproductive Choice

http://rcrc.org | E-mail: info@rcrc.org

Phone: (202)628-7700 | Fax: (202)628.7716

Jews On First

Defending the First Amendment against the Christian Right

http://www.jewsonfirst.org

P.O.Box 33821, Washington, DC 20033

310-910-9153 or 240-293-2063

Freedom to Marry Organization

116 West 23rd St, Ste 500, New York, NY 10011

ph: 212.851.8418

fax: 646.375.2069

Progressive Christianity

http://www.tcpc.org | email: center@tcpc.org

4916 Pt. Fosdick Dr. NW #148, Gig Harbor, WA, 98335

253-303-0352

Catholics for Choice

http://www.catholicsforchoice.org

1436 U Street NW, Suite 301, Washington, DC 20009-3997

Office: +1 (202) 986-6093 | Fax: +1 (202) 332-7995

National Women's Law Center

http://www.nwlc.org | email: info@nwlc.org

11 Dupont Circle, NW, #800, Washington, DC 20036

(202) 588-5180

GLAAD

Gay & Lesbian Alliance Against Defamation, media watchdog non-profit

http://www.glaad.org

Los Angeles

5455 Wilshire Blvd, #1500, Los Angeles, CA 90036

Phone: (323) 933-2240 | Fax: (323) 933-2241

New York

104 West 29th Street, 4th Floor, New York, NY 10001

Phone: (212) 629-3322 | Fax: (212) 629-3225

Feminist Majority

feminist.org

1600 Wilson Boulevard, Suite 801 Arlington, VA 22209

phone: 703-522-2214 | Fax: 703-522-2219

NARAL

www.naral.org

1156 15th Street, NW Suite 700, Washington, DC 20005

Phone: 202-973-3000 | Fax: 202-973-3096

NOW

www.now.org

PO Box 1848, Merrifield, VA 22116-9899

Phone: (202) 628-8669 | Fax: (202) 785-8576

Jewish Orthodox Feminist Alliance

www.jofa.org, email: jofa@jofa.org

520 8th Avenue, Fourth Floor, New York, NY 10018

Phone: 212-679-8500, or 888-550-JOFA | Fax: 212-679-7428

Republican Pro-Choice Coalition

www.gopchoice.org

1900 L Street NW, Suite 320, Washington, DC 20036

Tel: 202.629.1300 | Fax: 202.629.1313

Union of Concerned Scientists

www.ucsusa.org

National Headquarters

2 Brattle Square, Cambridge, MA 02138-3780

<u>Other easy ways to get involved:</u>

1. Pray or put forth the intention (however your belief system engages) for the separation of church and state to be vigilantly protected in the United States.

2. Support independent press – really!

3. Start a city-specific social networking movement for your community around separation of church and state issues by creating an action alert network using Google groups or Yahoo groups to keep up on State legislation, school board actions, county board meetings, and issues. Sharing the load is a great way to stay on top of issues even though you may be busy. Also buy the business cards you can printout on your computer and make your network business cards to hand out to people you come across who are interested. Post the business card file on the group site so others can do the same.

4. Coordinate a regular meeting of like-minded individuals, perhaps through the above-mentioned networking group, that can write letters to the editor of your local newspaper and conduct letter-writing campaigns to your state and federal representatives. Templates are included at the end of this section to guide you in your letters.

5. Again, utilizing such a networking group, you may feel a petition is in order. You can do physical petitions to print out and take to events. Alternatively, there are several online petition sites that make it very easy, and you print out the results and deliver them. You will need to publicize your petition for the greatest impact. Here are a few of the petition sites available:

> www.change.org/online-petitions
>
> http://www.ipetitions.com
>
> www.thepetitionsite.com/
>
> Here is a tool specifically to petition Capital Hill at www.petition2congress.com.
>
> a. Writing a petition is like a letter; address it to who will receive the petition and

the signatures (School board of _____,). State in a sentence or two what the petition is asking (i.e. keep Intelligent Design from being taught in science class), then state why you and all those who will sign are asking this (separation of church and state – parents can teach spiritual issues at home). Stick to facts; use bullet lists if you have to. Find statistics to back up your position that would help drive your points home. You can ask the research/reference desk at your local library to help you with the finding of facts and statistics to include. Some of the books listed in the Bibliography of this book may help you as well. Be sure to have others proof-read for errors before you publish it online or start distributing printouts to your network. Either way, send emails, put it on your Facebook, twitter about it, get your kids to spread the word, finally send a press release to your local radio and TV news etc.

6. Also utilizing such a networking group, coordinate a demonstration when attention needs to be brought to an issue in your community such as Intelligent Design being taught in science or actions that violate the First Amendment. If you do plan a demonstration, keep these items in mind;

a. Pick a location that is related to what you are demonstrating about, outside the school board meeting or city hall steps.

b. Contact your city officials to get any license for public gatherings that you may need.

c. Contact your local newspaper and television news to get coverage. Include when and where the event will occur.

d. Keep focused on your message.

e. Do not obstruct traffic and keep it civil.

f. Plan for: signage to carry, a microphone, sound system (depending upon city ordinances), plus the electricity needed.

g. Get speakers to give speeches to inspire enthusiasm about the mission.

h. If you have a petition drive for signatures, have people circulate them during the rally – or even at other events that have a similar topic or audience.

i.Provide a sign-up sheet for people who stop by, to join your network. Make it clear on the sign-up sheet that this is to receive emails from your network, and what your network's mission is.

7. If you are a professional, such as a lawyer, consider pledging your services for free up to a certain amount of hours per month or year to Americans United for the Separation of Church and State.

8. If you are a Christian Church attendee, then help to take back your church.

a. Network with others who don't agree with the goals of the Religious Right

b. Host a book discussion group out of your home on *this* book and these as well: *Thy Kingdom Come, An Evangelical's Lament: How the Religious Right Distorts the Faith and Threatens America* by Randall Balmer, *Steeplejacking: How the Christian Right is Hijacking Mainstream Religion* by Sheldon Culver and John Dorhauer.

c. Look into the more Christian Left organizations such as The Center for Progressive Christianity or The Christian Alliance for Progress. There is always the Interfaith Alliance, as well.

d. Park with your more inclusive bumper sticker showing. How about the "Freedom of Religion Means Any Religion," or even a bumper sticker in support of the separation of church and state. There are stickers that declare Proud Member of the Religious Left that might appeal to some.

e. Consider giving a gift subscription of *Church and State* magazine (via American United for the Separation of Church and State) to your church or public library.

9. Personally subscribe to the *Church and State* magazine from Americans United for the Separation of Church and State.

10. Take back your school boards and be active in your Parent/Teacher organization. Stand for the scientific method in science class, and no altered history textbooks to enforce a Christian nation myth in your schools. Regularly attend your school board

meetings and stay informed.

11. Write your state and national representatives in support of the separation of church and state, in support of public schools, preserving our nation's history in textbooks, keeping the scientific method in science class, etc. Find out how to contact your state representatives here:

 http://www.usa.gov/Agencies/State_and_Territories.shtml.   See the template at the end of this chapter that you can use for your convenience.

12. Write your newspaper in support of the separation of church and state, public schools (opposed to vouchers), accurate history in textbooks, and keeping the scientific method in science class etc.

13. Get a copy of your State Constitution, print it, highlight and know it fully so that you understand any ballot initiatives that amend your state constitution and those areas that break down the separation of church and state.

14. Sign up for any email notices from your State Agency on Rulemaking Hearings, and for any state newsletter.

15. Some state web pages may have the legislative calendar, and even legislative bills that you can access. Educate yourself with a visit every few weeks or once a month on what is happening so you can have your voice heard.

16. Join the local branch of Americans United for the Separation of Church and State (http://www.au.org/take-action/get-local/chapters/). If there is no local branch, AU will help you start one in your area. There are several states without any branch. Every state needs at least one chapter. To become a chapter of Americans United for Separation of Church and State, a group of individuals (no less than five) must file with the national office the following:

- A Statement of Intent
- A Community Issues Survey
- An Action Plan
- A signed copy of the "Chapter Bylaws"

Once that has been accomplished, the chapter will be officially recognized by the national office. Their website at www.au.org/take-action/get-local/chapters/start-a-chapter.html has more information.

<u>Template for writing a city, state or federal representative follows</u>.

This template is just to give you a framework to begin with.

Date

President / Senator / Representative/ Governor/ Mayor name

Street address

City, State, Zip

Dear (President / Senator / Representative/ Governor/ Mayor name),

Clearly state what you are writing about. Is it a particular piece of legislation up for a vote, or are you encouraging this official to support separation of church and state in a specific case? Be specific and relate it to something currently of importance.

Next, you will specify what it is you wish this official to do, what action they should take. This should be reasonable, within their duties and jurisdiction, and clearly stated.

Support why you believe they should take the action you are requesting. Try to back up your arguments, and remain civil and respectful.

Thank you for your time,

Your Name,

Your address

Your email &/or phone

<u>Writing to your newspaper / letters to the Editor</u>

Do not respond to hearsay, but a verified event such as a proposed legislation in your state or city, a specific School Board decision, response to a published article in the newspaper, etc. You should respond in a timely fashion while the topic is still fresh in people's minds.

Don't rush this; take some time to write your piece of persuasion when you won't be rushed. Think it though.

Keep the focus of the letter to one main point, even though you may have a few points elaborating your stand.

Get to your concern or issue in the first paragraph, and use the body of the letter to layer points that support the thesis. Don't misspell words or allow common grammatical mistakes. They detract from the writer's credibility. Close the letter with a summation or challenge for the newspaper or the readers.

Keep the tone civil and respectful, which will increase your chances of it getting published, even if it is an opposing point of view. Do not send letters to editor too frequently. Some newspapers have restrictions of one letter per reader per month in order encourage a variety of readers to write in.

Find out from your paper if they have a limit to the length of letters. For instance, many papers limit what they will publish from 150 to 250 words, maximum. This will greatly impact how many counter points or how many facts you can use, so keep that in mind. Even though my local paper has a limit, if the opinion is well written they will allow more words, but you can't count on that. Examine what has been published and use that as a gauge as well.

Check all your facts before submitting your letter. Be clear and succinct. Eliminate unnecessary or extra words. Have one, preferably two, supportive people read the letter for any errors, spelling, and clarity.

Encourage others who feel strongly about this issue to also write letters to the editor. More letters means more awareness for the populace and like-minded people. They may not all get printed, but it may get the paper's attention and a published story or two that are focused on the situation.

Do not be discouraged if your first few letters don't get published. Newspapers receive more letters than they can print. Letters most commonly published are those that have bearing to current issues and are within the word limit. Another reason to encourage others who feel strongly about the issue is because there is a better chance that one of them may get published.

Letters to the Editor Template

Date

Dear (name of the editor) or "Editor":

In the first paragraph, briefly introduce the topic and state your position. If you are referring to an article that was printed in the newspaper, remember to state the date and title of that article. If it is about a piece of legislation, be sure to reference the correct title and number. If you have official credentials or relevant job title, or unique experience that makes you an expert in some aspect of the situation, then you would provide that here, briefly (I am a teacher etc.)

As for the next paragraph or paragraphs, this section should be dedicated to one or two key points related to the topic. You might wish to include how the issue affects you, your family, or your community. Try to use facts to bolster your viewpoint when possible. Remember your word limit.

Finally, the conclusion should be a paragraph that sums up your argument and expresses what you think should be done concerning the topic under consideration. This section should be brief and should *not* reiterate the points elaborated on in the body of the letter. After this, you will simply conclude your letter and give the necessary contact information.

(Sign Your Name)

Type Your Name

Address

Phone Number

Take With You From This Chapter

➤ There are many ways to get involved, from a simple bumper sticker or joining an organization's email list, to writing letters and watching your local government and school board politics.

➤ If you are a professional, consider volunteering your services to an organization.

➢ Network to keep track of your local government and school boards. You can utilize Yahoo or Google groups to keep from burning out.

➢ Sometimes a demonstration is needed, and that networking group you set up can help get the word out for attendance.

➢ Write letters to your elected government officials or to the editor of your paper. Again, a letter writing campaign with your network group can make the task easier.

Chapter 28
Sum It Up

<u>What to Expect From this Chapter</u>

➢ Where an attempt is made to summarize the whole of the book and provide encouragement.

Since Ronald Reagan began ushering them into the White House, Supreme Court judges succumbing to Religious Right influence, State legislatures are being filled with them, city administrations' taken over, and corporations of every kind are now mission fields. They have been diligently advancing their worldview politically and culturally. They have learned how to use marketing and propaganda techniques; they have waged a culture war and are making astounding gains every day. Your children or grandchildren are being targeted via school and the culture. Women's advances and rights are being rolled back with the specific goal of having no options but raising families. This is not a science fiction movie; this is taking place all around the country each minute.

"In a recent non-fiction book titled Mind Siege (coauthored with David Noebel), LaHaye outlines his model society, a Religious Right utopia where there is no separation of church and state. Abortion is outlawed and homosexuality is lumped in with pedophilia and prostitution as 'perverse sexual practices' that are 'universally viewed as immoral and would be shunned.' Censorship is rampant as the 'Christian and pro-moral community' use the federal government to promulgate 'decency' codes.

In LaHaye's perfect world, voucher subsidies for private religious education are freely available. Public schools are turned into centers for fundamentalist indoctrination with daily prayer, promotion of the Ten Commandments and creationism firmly ensconced. The Department of Education has been abolished, and teenagers are given no sex education at school. Instead, children are taught revisionist history about how the United States was founded to be a 'Christian nation.'

Women, in LaHaye's dream, would 'stay at home to raise their babies,' eschew feminism and submit to their husbands who would assume their God-given role as 'the spiritual head of the family.'" Rob Boston, "If Best-selling End-times Author Tim Lahaye Has His Way, Church-state Separation Will Be... Left Behind," *Church and State*, February 2002.

This is not just Tim LaHaye's vision; this is the Religious Right's ultimate goal. This book has presented the case that they have made progress towards these ends – more progress than the average person probably realizes.

It is inevitability that if the current path continues to be followed, the United States will no longer be a democracy, but a theocracy at best, and some fear even a fascist regime as the worst case. This book is not the only one sounding the warning bells and alarms; there are others proclaiming the danger.

"What the disparate sects of this movement, known as Dominionism, share is an obsession with political power.... Dominionists preach that Jesus has called them to build the kingdom of God in the here and now, whereas previously it was thought that we would have to wait for it. America becomes, in this militant Biblicism, an agent of God, and all political and intellectual opponents of America's Christian leaders are viewed, quite simply, as agents of Satan. Under Christian dominion America will no longer be a sinful and fallen nation but one in which the Ten Commandments form the basis of our legal system, Creationism and 'Christian values' form the basis of our educational system, and the media and the government proclaim the Good News to one and all. Aside from its proselytizing mandate, the federal government will be reduced to the protection of property rights and 'homeland' security. Some Dominionists (not all of whom accept the label, at least not publicly) would further require all citizens to pay 'tithes' to church organizations empowered by the government to run our social

welfare agencies, and a number of influential figures advocate the death penalty for a host of 'moral crimes,' including apostasy, blasphemy, sodomy, and witchcraft. The only legitimate voices in this state will be Christian. All others will be silenced." Chris Hedges, "Feeling the Hate with the National Religious Broadcasters," *Harper's Magazine*, May, 2005.

Steeplejacking: How the Christian Right is Highjacking Mainstream Religion, by Rev. Dr. John Dorhauer of United Church of Christ's Missouri Mid-South Conference, *Hard Ball on Holy Ground,* by Stephen Swecker, and *United Methodist @ Risk: A wake-up Call* (2003), by Leon Howell all expose how the Religious Right is working to take over moderate or progressive churches. Several individuals who were once Religious Right adherents have left the fold and are warning the country. Frank Schaeffer has written books and shared the dark secrets he witnessed in the privacy of back rooms as the Religious Right formed. Vyckie Garrison was deeply enmeshed in Quiverfull; Randall Balmer was prominent in evangelicalism, and Jason Childs was a Liberty University graduate and Evangelical pastor who is now proclaiming warnings to the nation, in addition to this book itself. We are raising our voices in unison to proclaim that there is a clearly defined threat to the core of this nation, and to democracy.

You feel frustrated, even angry, at the impotence of our political system today. It seems broken, but the truth is that the Religious Right has infiltrated the political system and are creating this stalemate with very little regard for anything outside their agenda. They have a specific plan for this nation, and political compromise is not part of that plan.

"I want you to know that the fundamentalist political movement is the beginning of a cultural revolution that will take our nation to a very dark place. You have to understand that this has been methodically planned and is being carried out with the utmost vigilance. In accordance with their worldview, my old friends do not in the least care about what you think. They are against democracy, and they are seeking to end the rule of the majority in our great

country.

You might be thinking that a minority fundamentalist group of zealots can't really take over the direction of a society. Just look at Iran, or the countless other places where people have allowed this to happen. Are you all really going to sit back and watch this happen? They will begin to attack all sources of accurate information. Public radio was first, next will be museums and then science books. Just listen to them argue against the scientific facts about the peril our planet is facing, because it does not fit in with their ideas. They represent a clear and present danger to our union.

If I told you that the Amish in Pennsylvania were running for public office in record numbers with the intention of outlawing electricity and forcing others to act, dress and think like them, you would not believe it. Well, that is exactly what is happening in America, only it is not the Amish, it is the fundamentalists. It is not outlawing electricity, it's placing limits on being a human with free will. Enjoying art and music, loving the person of your choice, dancing – the things that fundamentalists call 'sins' – are a big part of what it means to be a human.

The consequences of not acting are dire. We are not just fighting for ourselves. We are struggling to protect the future generations of Americans who will suffer from these ruthless actions of the far right. We are speaking out against the measures being taken against those in our community who can least afford to be marginalized." Jason Childs, "A Former Jerry Falwell Follower Reflects On How The Religious Right Gets It Wrong," *Church and State*, May, 2011.

The warnings have been sounded, but few hear or realize how successful the agenda has already been, how pervasive it is in our entire culture. The messy experiment of Democracy is at risk. Will Democracy last a little over two hundred years before being brought down? Or will you hear the warnings and act?

The Religious Right is an extremist faction. Christianity has done considerable good, so why in America have some turned it so ugly and anti-democratic? Charles Kimbal, author of the books *When Religion Becomes Evil* and *When Religion Becomes Lethal*, is Presidential Professor and Director of Religious Studies at the University of Oklahoma, and is qualified to speak on this. He puts forth in his book *When Religion Becomes Evil: Five Warning Signs,* that there are five distinct warning signs of when a religion is turning the corner from a conveyor of good to a perpetrator of evil.

The Five Signs are whenever a religion emphasizes that:

1) It alone holds the absolute truth – the one path to God or the only correct way of reading a sacred text – to the exclusion of others. The Religious Right's worldview is being pushed to moderate churches as well.

2) An obedience to religious leaders, this we see through the propaganda they utilize and their own version of everything from science to entertainment, is meant to insulate and isolate from opposing viewpoints.

3) An apocalyptic belief that the End Times will occur through a particular religion, and the apocalypse is imminent. In our case, this is what they want.

4) Religious goals are to be met at whatever means, even malevolent ends [the Crusades of old are replaced with Religious Right's dominion over all aspects of human life with the stealthy Seven Mountains.]

5) The declaration of holy war, which we witness in their striving for Dominion, but especially in their focus on the nation's children and school system.

Christian Reconstructionists and Dominionists have a blueprint, a vision of how to win this culture war and create a bible-based nation. But the Religious Right has left behind the best of the gospel, and their agenda is not in our nation's best interests. but is solely in preparation for Christ's Second Coming.

It is up to you to protect your rights, your children's rights, and possibly even your grand children's rights. This does not mean taking a position counter to Christianity, but in terms of religious liberty for all, and for democracy to endure – a democracy that states that your personal faith is not a government concern, but a private matter. By having read this book, you are better informed of what is occurring around you. It is up to you what you do with that knowledge. You can put this book away or trade it in, or you can get involved and start turning the tide. You can use the resources chapter for ideas on how to begin. You can begin to change the direction of this war, or you can be surprised when the day dawns that democracy has been replaced by a theocracy, or worse.

Is this the only threat to the nation? Probably not, but it is one that you can stand up against and make a real difference. It is the threat facing this nation that is structured to seem harmless and unsuccessful, but it is not harmless nor unsuccessful. This issue is one where you can really make a difference for democracy, as individuals, or in groups.

BIBLIOGRAPHY

8: The Mormon Proposition. Dir. Reed Cowan. Perf. Dustin Lance Black. Wolfe Video, 2010. DVD.

Alley, Robert S.. *Without a prayer: religious expression in public schools.* Amherst, N.Y.: Prometheus Books, 1996. Print.

Arnheim, M. T. W., and Andrew Jacobs. U.S. Constitution for Dummies. Hoboken, NJ: Wiley, 2009. Print.

Balmer, Randall Herbert. Thy kingdom come, an Evangelical's lament: how the religious right distorts the faith and threatens America,. New York, N.Y.: Basic Books, 2006. Print.

Berman, Ari. Herding donkeys: the fight to rebuild the Democratic Party and reshape American politics. New York: Farrar, Straus, and Giroux, 2010. Print.

Bernays, Edward L., and Mark Crispin Miller. Propaganda. Brooklyn, N.Y.: Ig Publishing, 2005. Print.

Boston, Rob. Why the religious right is wrong about separation of church & state. Buffalo, N.Y.: Prometheus Books, 1993. Print.

Brown, Ruth Murray. For a "Christian America": a history of the religious right. Amherst, N.Y.: Prometheus Books, 2002. Print.

Butler, Jennifer S.. Born again the Christian Right globalized. Ann Arbor, MI: Pluto Press, 2006. Print.

Chemerinsky, Erwin. The conservative assault on the Constitution. New York: Simon & Schuster, 2010. Print.

Coogan, Michael David. God and sex: what the Bible really says. New York: Twelve, 2010. Print.

Culver, Sheldon, and John Dorhauer. Steeplejacking: how the Christian right is hijacking mainstream religion. Brooklyn, N.Y.: Ig Pub., 2007. Print.

Detwiler, Fritz. Standing on the premises of God the Christian Right's fight to redefine America's public schools. New York: New York University Press, 1999. Print.

Dobson, James C., and Gary Lee Bauer. Children at risk: the battle for the hearts and minds of our kids. Dallas: Word Pub. 1990. Print.

Domke, David Scott, and Kevin M. Coe. The God strategy: how religion became a political weapon in America. Oxford: Oxford University Press, 2008. Print.

Ellerbe, Helen. The dark side of Christian history. San Rafael, CA.: Morningstar Books (P.O. Box 4032, San Rafael, CA. 94913-4032), 1995. Print.

Enlow, Johnny. The seven mountains prophecy. Lake Mary, Fla.: Creation House, 2008. Print.

Falwell, Jerry. America can be saved!: (Jerry Falwell preaches on revival). Murfreesboro, Tenn.: Sword of the Lord Publishers, 1979. Print.

Farber, Seth. Unholy madness: the church's surrender to psychiatry. Downers Grove, Ill.: InterVarsity Press, 1999. Print.

Folger, Janet L. The criminalization of Christianity. Sisters, Or.: Multnomah Publishers, 2005. Print.

Gilgoff, Dan. The Jesus machine: how James Dobson, Focus on the Family, and evangelical America are winning the culture war. New York: St. Martin's Press, 2007. Print.

Goldberg, Michelle. Kingdom coming: the rise of Christian nationalism. New York: W.W. Norton & Co., 2006. Print.

Gordon, Linda. The moral property of women: a history of birth control politics in America. 3rd ed. Urbana and Chicago: University of Illinois Press, 2002. Print.

Hall, Timothy C. The complete idiot's guide to the Middle Ages. New York, N.Y.: Alpha Books, 2009. Print.

Harris, Alisa. Raised right: how I untangled my faith from politics. Colorado Springs, Colo.: WaterBrook Press, 2011. Print.

Haught, James A.. Holy horrors: an illustrated history of religious murder and madness. Buffalo, N.Y.: Prometheus Books, 1990. Print.

Hedges, Chris. American fascists: the Christian Right and the war on America. New York: Free Press, 2006. Print.

Hess, Rick, and Jan Hess. A full quiver: family planning and the lordship of Christ. Brentwood, Tenn.: Wolgemuth & Hyatt, 1989. Print.

Hitchcock, Mark. The complete book of Bible prophecy. Wheaton, Ill.: Tyndale House Publishers, 1999. Print.

Holmes, David L., and David Lynn Holmes. The faiths of the founding fathers. Oxford: Oxford University Press, 2006. Print.

Howell, Leon, C. Dale White, and Scott Campbell. United Methodism @ risk: a wake-up call. Kingston, N.Y.: Information Project for United Methodists, 2003. Print.

Hunt, Dave. A woman rides the beast . Eugene, Or.: Harvest House Publishers, 1994. Print.

Jackson, Harry R., and Tony Perkins. Personal faith, public policy . Lake Mary, Fla.: FrontLine, 2008. Print.

Jenkins, Philip. The next Christendom: the coming of global Christianity. Oxford: Oxford University Press, 2002. Print.

Jesus Camp. Dir. Heidi Ewing. Perf. Mike Papantonio, Lou Engle, Becky Fischer. Magnolia, 2007.

DVD.

Johnson, Chalmers. Nemesis: the last days of the American Republic. New York: Metropolitan Books, 2006. Print.

Kennedy, D. James, and Jim Nelson Black. Character & Destiny: A Nation in Search of Its Soul. Grand Rapids: Zondervan , 1994. Print.

Kimball, Charles. When religion becomes evil . San Francisco, Calif.: HarperSanFrancisco, 2002. Print.

Lane, Frederick S.. The court and the cross: the religious right's crusade to reshape the Supreme Court. Boston: Beacon Press, 2008. Print.

Lindsay, D. Michael. Faith in the halls of power: how evangelicals joined the American elite. Oxford: Oxford University Press, 2007. Print.

Lindsey, Hal, and Carole C. Carlson. The late great planet earth . Grand Rapids: Zondervan, 1970. Print.

Loveland, Anne C.. American Evangelicals and the U.S. military, 1942-1993 . Baton Rouge: Louisiana State University Press, 1996. Print.

May, Elaine Tyler. America and the pill: a history of promise, peril, and liberation. New York: Basic Books, 2010. Print.

Meyers, Robin R.. Why the Christian right is wrong: a minister's manifesto for taking back your faith, your flag, your future. San Francisco: Jossey-Bass, 2006. Print.

Mooney, Chris, and Sheril Kirshenbaum. Unscientific America: how scientific illiteracy threatens our future. New York: Basic Books, 2009. Print.

Naphy, William G.. Calvin and the consolidation of the Genevan Reformation: with a new preface. Louisville: Westminster John Knox Press, 2003. Print.

North, Gary , and George Grant. The Changing of the Guard: Biblical Principals for Political Action. Waterbury Center: Dominion Press, 1987. Print.

Otto, Shawn. Fool me twice: fighting the assault on science in America. New York: Rodale :, 2011. Print.

Paterson, Frances R. A.. Democracy and intolerance: Christian school curricula, school choice, and public policy. Bloomington, Ind.: Phi Delta Kappa Educational Foundation, 2003. Print.

Perkins, Bill. Steeling the mind of America II. Green Forest, AR: New Leaf Press, 19971996. Print.

Pride, Mary. The way home: beyond feminism, back to reality. Westchester, Ill.: Crossway Books, 1985. Print.

Provan, Charles. The Bible and birth control . Monongahela, PA.: Zimmer, 1989. Print.

Rodda, Chris. Liars for Jesus: the religious right's alternate version of American history.. New Jersey: Chris Rodda, 2006. Print.

Schaeffer, Frank. Crazy for God: how I grew up as one of the elect, helped found the Religious Right, and lived to take all (or almost all) of it back. New York: Carroll & Graf, 2007. Print.

Shabo, Magedah. Techniques of propaganda & persuasion. Clayton, DE.: Prestwick House, Inc., 2008. Print.

Sharlet, Jeff. The family: The Secret: fundamentalism at the heart of American power. New York, NY: HarperCollins, 2008. Print.

Stewart, Katherine. The Good News Club: the Christian right's stealth assault on America's children. New York: PublicAffairs, 2012. Print.

Swecker, Stephen. Hard ball on holy ground: the religious right v. the mainline for the church's soul. North Berwick, Maine: Boston Wesleyan Press, 2005. Print.

Terry, Randall A.. Operation rescue. Springdale, PA: Whitaker House, 1988. Print.

Twitchell, James B.. Shopping for God: how Christianity went from in your heart to in your face. New York: Simon & Schuster, 2007. Print.

Viola, Frank, and George Barna. Pagan Christianity?: exploring the roots of our church practices. Carol Stream, Ill.: BarnaBooks, 2008. Print.

Whitten, Mark Weldon. The myth of Christian America: what you need to know about the separation of church and state. Macon, Ga.: Smyth & Helwys, 1999. Print.

Wilcox, Clyde, and Carin Robinson. Onward Christian soldiers?: the religious right in American politics. 3rd ed. Boulder, Colo.: Westview Press, 2006. Print.

Woodward, Bob. Plan of attack. New York: Simon & Schuster, 2004. Print.

Wright, Jonathan. God's soldiers: adventure, politics, intrigue, and power : a history of the Jesuits. New York: Doubleday, 2004. Print.

Religious Right: The Greatest Threat to Democracy

CPSIA information can be obtained at www.ICGtesting.com
Printed in the USA
BVOW020108280612

293639BV00002B/1/P